Dunster and its Lords, 1066-1881 ... With a descriptive sketch of Dunster Castle, by G. T. Clark ... and a chapter on the siege and surrender of Dunster Castle, by E. Green.

H. C. Maxwell Lyte

The BiblioLife Network

This project was made possible in part by the BiblioLife Network (BLN), a project aimed at addressing some of the huge challenges facing book preservationists around the world. The BLN includes libraries, library networks, archives, subject matter experts, online communities and library service providers. We believe every book ever published should be available as a high-quality print reproduction; printed on- demand anywhere in the world. This insures the ongoing accessibility of the content and helps generate sustainable revenue for the libraries and organizations that work to preserve these important materials.

The following book is in the "public domain" and represents an authentic reproduction of the text as printed by the original publisher. While we have attempted to accurately maintain the integrity of the original work, there are sometimes problems with the original book or micro-film from which the books were digitized. This can result in minor errors in reproduction. Possible imperfections include missing and blurred pages, poor pictures, markings and other reproduction issues beyond our control. Because this work is culturally important, we have made it available as part of our commitment to protecting, preserving, and promoting the world's literature.

GUIDE TO FOLD-OUTS, MAPS and OVERSIZED IMAGES

In an online database, page images do not need to conform to the size restrictions found in a printed book. When converting these images back into a printed bound book, the page sizes are standardized in ways that maintain the detail of the original. For large images, such as fold-out maps, the original page image is split into two or more pages.

Guidelines used to determine the split of oversize pages:

• Some images are split vertically; large images require vertical and horizontal splits.
• For horizontal splits, the content is split left to right.
• For vertical splits, the content is split from top to bottom.
• For both vertical and horizontal splits, the image is processed from top left to bottom right.

DUNSTER AND ITS LORDS.

DUNSTER

AND ITS LORDS

1066—1881.

BY

H. C. MAXWELL LYTE, M.A., F.S.A.

WITH

A DESCRIPTIVE SKETCH OF DUNSTER CASTLE

BY

G. T. CLARK, F.S.A.

AND

A CHAPTER ON

THE SIEGE AND SURRENDER OF DUNSTER CASTLE

BY

E. GREEN.

Printed for Private Circulation.

1882.

PRINTED BY WILLIAM POLLARD
NORTH STREET, EXETER.

Two hundred copies.

PREFACE.

M OST of the following pages have already appeared in different numbers of the *Archæological Journal*, for the years 1880 and 1881, having had their origin in a paper read before the Royal Archæological Institute at Dunster, in August, 1879. They are now reprinted in consecutive order as a slight contribution towards the much neglected history of the County of Somerset. I venture to hope that they may have some interest for persons who have visited "the Alnwick of the West." Mr. Clark, whose knowledge of English castles is probably unrivalled, has very kindly allowed me to reprint, in an abridged and revised form, the descriptive sketch of Dunster Castle which he made for the *Archæological Journal*, of December, 1879, and Mr. E. Green has likewise allowed me to incorporate with my own work a valuable chapter on "The Siege and Surrender of Dunster Castle" during the civil war of the seventeenth century. For assistance received in the course of my researches my thanks are due to the Rev. Frederick Brown, to Mr. J. Batten, to Mr. G. P. Boyce, to Dr. Drake, to Mr. Ponsford, and more especially to the present owner of Dunster Castle, who takes a just pride in all that concerns the ancient inheritance of his family.

Several of the plates contained in this volume have appeared as illustrations of the text in the *Archæological Journal,* several have been prepared expressly for it by my wife and by other persons. I am indebted to Mr. James Parker for the loan of the woodcut of the exterior of the North Wing of the Luttrell Arms Hotel, and to Mr. W. H. Hamilton Rogers for the loan of the electrotypes of the brasses of Thomas, John, and Ann Mohun, and of the shields with Mohun arms which were made for his book on *The Sepulchral Effigies of Devon.* The plates of the brass of Sir Andrew Luttrell, and of the Town and Castle of Dunster have also appeared in other works. The view in Dunster Churchyard is a reduction of a sketch taken by Mr. Hamilton Aidé some years ago.

The *Notes on some early Charters of Bruton Priory,* promised on page 6, will appear at a future date.

H. C. M. L.

January, 1882.

LIST OF ILLUSTRATIONS.

—

LIST OF ILLUSTRATIONS.

DUNSTER CASTLE

By G. T. CLARK.

THE Castle of Dunster is of high antiquity, and it was for many centuries a place of great military consideration in the western counties. It was the *caput* of an extensive Honour, and the chief seat of a line of very powerful barons. The hill upon which it stands is the eastern extremity of a considerable ridge, from which it is cut off by a natural depression, and thus forms what is known in West Saxon nomenclature as a " Tor." This Tor covers about ten acres of ground, and is about 200 feet high, with a table-top about a quarter of an acre in area. It stands on the northern edge of a deep and broad valley, which contains the park, and on the east expands into a tract of meadow about a mile in breadth, skirting the sea from Minehead to below Carhampton. The park is traversed by a considerable stream, the Avill, one head of which springs from Croydon Hill, and the others from the lower slopes of Dunkery Beacon.

The home view, one of exceeding richness, is limited on the south and west by the Brendon Hills and the high ground rising towards Exmoor, to the east it includes the vales of Cleeve and Williton, bounded by the Quantocks. Seaward, on to the north, the eye ranges over Bridgwater Bay to the headland of Brean Down and Worle, and commands the Welsh or opposite coast from Penarth Point to Aberaven and Swansea. North Hill, behind Minehead, is prominent on the north-west.

On the north and west sides of the Castle hill, under the immediate control and protection of the old fortress, is the town of Dunster, a cluster of old-fashioned houses, many with timber fronts, in the midst of which is the parish church, once connected with the Priory, founded by one of the early Norman lords. The eastern or monastic part of the building now forms the private chapel of the Luttrells, and contains several of their tombs.

The fancy cloths once known as "Dunsters" have long since ceased to be made, and of the fulling-mills the ruins have well nigh perished. The haven at which these manufactures found shipping is silted up, and the privileges conceded to the townspeople being now shared by the community at large, are no longer commemorated. Of the neighbouring hills, that on the west, "Grabhurst," is said to be so named from an entrenched wood, though this use of the word "graff" is unknown or unusual in the South English nomenclature, and "hirst" or "hurst" belongs to Sussex and Kent rather than to Somerset. The fact is that the name of the hill is spelt "Grobefast" in old deeds, and is at this time colloquially "Grabbist." Near it is a lofty detached hill known as "Conygar," thickly planted with trees and crowned by a hollow tower of the last century. The castle mill remains ; it is placed on the verge of the park, concealed, and protected by the castle.

The castle is composed of two parts, due to the natural disposition of the ground. The upper part, the mound, is in form oval, and its summit flat by nature has been further levelled by art, the slopes having also been trimmed and rendered almost impracticable for direct ascent. The summit measures about thirty-five yards east and west, by about seventy yards north and south. The keep which stood here was demolished in the seventeenth century, and no traces of it have been found save a sewer and some foundations at the southern end. The keep was probably polygonal, approached, as at Lincoln, by a direct flight of steps from the lower ward. Its gateway seems to have been defended by a portcullis, as the portcullis mentioned in the records could not have been in either of the gateways of the lower ward. The summit of the Tor was laid down as a bowling green in the early part of the last century, and an octagonal summer-house was constructed at its north-eastern corner, in which there is a window in the Perpendicular style, taken from some earlier structure.

The artificial scarping of the hill sides was confined to the upper eighty or hundred feet. At this level are two

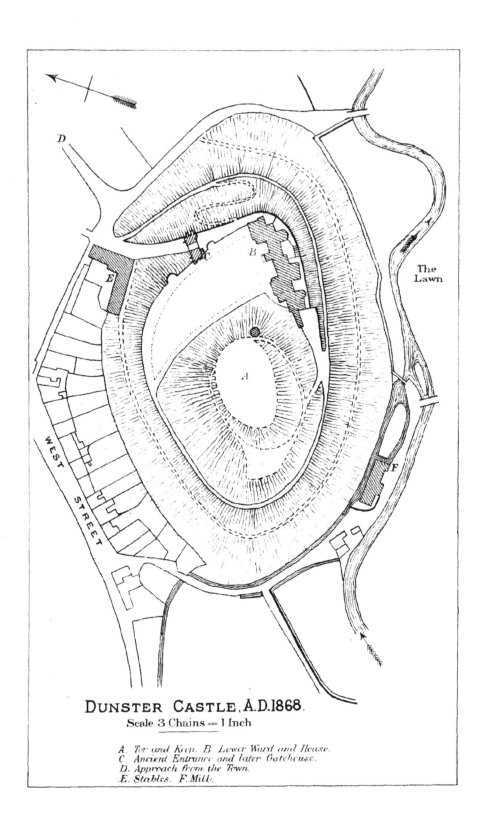

THE LAWN

WEST STREET

DUNSTER CASTLE, A.D. 1868.

Scale 3 Chains = 1 Inch

A. Tor and Keep. B. Lower Ward and House.
C. Ancient Entrance and later Gatehouse.
D. Approach from the Town.
E. Stables. F. Mill.

platforms or shelves, one, a small one, towards the south the other much larger towards the north, and forming the lower ward. The lower ward is of a semi-lunar or semi-oval figure, the hollow side on the south being formed by the natural mound rising to the site of the keep. It measures about thirty-three yards north and south by about one hundred and twenty-six yards east and west, and covers about half an acre of ground. The outer or convex edge, has on the east been cut into a low cliff, supported by a retaining wall, which with its flanking towers and superstructure of parapet protected this ward. At the foot of this wall, part of which supports the present house, the slope recommences, and though now terraced by roads and paths, it formerly descended unbroken to the base of the hill.

The buildings and inhabited part of the old castle were in the lower ward, especially in its eastern part upon the enceinte or curtain wall, and on the site of the present house. The wall was strengthened and flanked by half-round towers, of which the lower parts of several remain incorporated into the later building. Fragments of old wall within the house are known by their great thickness. One of these walls has a core of the natural red sandstone rock enclosed in masonry, but traceable by an occasional exudation of dampness. The gateway of the lower ward remains between two of the flanking towers. It is nine feet broad, with plain chamfered jambs and a low stiff drop arch. There was no portcullis, and probably no drawbridge, the only defence being a massive door made of bars of oak, four inches and a half wide, four inches thick, and four inches and a half apart, forming a grating, planked vertically outside with inch and a half oak boards. Upon each oak bar is laid a bar of iron, and the whole fabric is spiked together with iron fastenings, having diamond-shaped heads. The meeting line of the two valves is guarded by an iron bar. In the right valve, on entering, is a wicket gate four feet four inches high by two feet one inch broad, fastened with a huge iron lock in a wooden shell. This very curious specimen of carpenter's and smith's work, though of later date than the gateway, is old, and not unlike that of Chepstow. The gateway itself belongs to the time of Henry III, or Edward I. In the last century the gates were closed, and behind them was built a wall backed with earth. The gateway has lately been re-opened and restored as far as possible, to its original condition. A flight of steps now gives access through it to the lower ward.

The mural towers flanking the gateway are parts of circles about twenty-two feet in diameter, the lower twelve feet being original. One contains a curious vaulted basement with the usual three loops, and in the rear a doorway which opened into the ward. The other, or eastern flanker had a basement chamber until recently filled with earth, and also three loops. Upon the retaining wall about twenty-five yards to the north-west of the old gateway is another tower of similar character. The towers, the curtain, and the entrance gateway are in substance all of one date, and what ashlar remains is of good quality and well jointed.

The approach to the Castle from the town was very steep, and to enter the old gateway the road made a sharp turn. Just below the gateway, and spanning the road, has been built a gate-house which projects from the curtain, and partly incorporates the western flanking tower of the old gateway. This structure still remains in good condition, and though evidently intended more for ornament than defence, it gives much of a mediæval character to the whole castle. It is 63ft. broad on its outer face, 23ft. deep, and about 45ft. high, sixty-two steps leading to its battlements. It is pierced by an open passage 10ft. 6in. broad, having a plain pointed waggon vault, and at each end a not very highly pointed arch, with good moulded jambs continued round the head. There are not now any lodge doors opening into the archway, nor any traces of portcullis or drawbridge. The fronts are plain, save that the outer front has two flanking buttresses, and over the entrance a rectangular panel containing nine heraldic shields, in three rows—one, four and four. The inner front is flanked by two half hexagonal turrets, of which the eastern contains a well staircase, entered by a small four-centered doorway, and communicating with each floor. The doorway on the other side of the passage was originally a window. Against the eastern

GATEWAY OF THE LOWER WARD

DUNSTER CASTLE.

end of the gate-house are two buttresses of irregular shape, probably added to support the wall which stood on a steep slope and showed signs of settlement. The gate-house is of three stages, each of which formerly contained two rooms about 13ft. high. The whole upper floor has recently been converted into a handsome hall with an open roof. It is now entered from the lower ward by a doorway which does not seem older than the reign of Henry VIII. The windows are mostly of two lights, divided by a transom, with the upper lights cinque-foiled. Some are later than others. The gate-house has been thought to be the "novum ædificium castri de Dunster," with the construction of which Henry Stone was charged in the 9th year of Henry V, though the lower part is in the style prevalent under Richard II. It is probable that the gate-house was for some time used in combination with the gateway by its side. The approach and entrance, however inconvenient for daily use, were so strong as almost to preclude any regular attacks by battering machines, or even by escalade.

The history of Dunster begins with Domesday, in which it is recorded that William de Moion held "Torre," and that there was his castle. Aluric, says the record, held it in the time of King Edward. Mohun no doubt found the Tor strongly fortified after the English manner, for it must have been exposed to the piratical invasion of the Northmen, who gave name to the opposite islands of the Holms, and the not very distant port of Swansea. The place was in fact a natural burh on a large scale, such as Æthelflæd and Eadward the Elder were wont to throw up, though on a smaller scale, in the early part of the tenth century. There was the conical hill with its flat top for the *aula* or *domus defensabilis*, and the court-yard below for the huts and sheds of the dependants and cattle. The many manors belonging to William de Mohun were in his time or soon afterwards combined into an Honour, and Dunster became the *caput honoris*. The Honour of Dunster was one of about eighty-six Honours in England, but it is not precisely known in what respect they differed from baronies. The nucleus of either was almost always an estate held before the Conquest, and enlarged by the Norman who acquired it.

In all cases it extended into more than one county, and was held of the king *in capite* by homage, fealty, and military service. The term is said to have been first used by the Conqueror in his charter to the Abbey of Ramsey. Most of the Honours seem to have gradually fallen into disuse, but the records show that the rights of the Castle of Dunster were maintained in full vigour for many centuries.

To what extent the Mohuns were content with the earlier defences of the castle is unknown, but it is remarkable that no fragments of Norman mouldings or ornament have been found in or about the Tor, although there is original Norman work in the parish church. From the configuration of the ground the lines of the old fortress must have been where they still are, so that there would have been no reason for pulling down the earlier works to enlarge the area. On the other hand it is difficult to suppose that works as durable as those of the Norman period generally were, could have fallen into decay by the time of Henry III or Edward I, the date of the oldest parts extant. However this may be, it is certain that the Castle of Dunster was one of the most important fortresses in the West of England. In the lawless days of Stephen it was held for the Empress against the King, by William de Mohun, the second baron. To him was perhaps due the polygonal keep. His descendant Reginald de Mohun in 1254 founded a mass for the weal of his relations to be said daily by a monk or secular priest in the Chapel of St. Stephen in the Castle, or in the Chapel of St. Lawrence in the Priory, in time of war. Leland mentions St. Stephen's Chapel as connected with the keep. John de Mohun, who died in 1279, may have built the curtain and the mural towers of the lower ward, of which the bases remain. The keep was probably left unaltered, and indeed from the inconvenient height at which it stood it was not likely to be much used. The purely defensive parts of castles when not inhabited by the owner, were often neglected in times of peace. No well has been discovered in the area of the keep. Leland says that the great gate-house was erected by Sir Hugh Luttrell, who lived in the reign of Henry

VII, and that his son Sir Andrew "built a new piece of the castle wall by the east," but the former of these statements appears to be erroneous. George Luttrell built a great part of the present dwelling house on the eastern side of the lower ward, between the years 1589 and 1620. After the surrender of the Castle to the Parliamentary forces under Blake, the keep was demolished and the curtain lowered. It is said that the gate-house was also injured, but its present condition shows that the injury could not have been of a very serious character. More than a century later the Luttrells raised the surface of the lower ward with earth obtained by scraping the adjacent slope of the Tor Other alterations have been made at different times, especially in 1869, when under the judicious advice of Mr. Salvin, the Elizabethan house was greatly enlarged. Still the present residence represents very fairly the ancient fortress. Like it, sheltered by the Tor, and dominating over the park, the town, and the sea coast, it commands a very extensive view, and as becomes the representative of so important a military port, it is itself visible from the broad tract of country of which it was sometimes the terror, but more frequently the protection.

Exterior of North Wing,

"Luttrell Arms Hotel,"

Dunster.

DUNSTER AND ITS LORDS.

By H. C. MAXWELL LYTE.

PART I.

DUNSTER must have been known to the Roman occupiers of Britain, for some copper coins of the reigns of Maximian and Constantine were discovered in the Park about eighteen years ago, close to the old Carhampton road. Nothing however is recorded as to its history before the time of Edward the Confessor, when it belonged to a certain Aluric, who seems to have been a great landowner in the West of England. It then bore the not uncommon name of Torre, and it may here be remarked that the natural mound on which the castle stands is to this day always called " the Tor."

Soon after the Norman invasion, Dunster passed into the hands of William de Moion, the progenitor of the noble family which held it for nearly three centuries and a half from that time. The de Moions derived their surname from the village of Moyon, near St. Lo in Normandy, where they had considerable possessions. They, in their turn, gave their name to Hammoun in Dorsetshire, to Ottery Mohun and to Tor Mohun in Devonshire, and to Grange Mohun in the county of Kildare. The name was spelt indifferently Moion, Moiun, Moyon, Moyun, Mohun, Moun, Moune and Mooun; and just as the illustrious name of Bohun was corrupted into Boone, so was that of Mohun corrupted into Moon.[1] On the other hand, it should be noted that the mediæval chroniclers and lawyers were always careful to distinguish the Moyons or Mohuns from the Moignes or Moynes.

[1] For the sake of uniformity the name will be generally given as Mohun in the following pages, although this way of spelling it was seldom used before the middle of the thirteenth century.

The domain of Moyon formed part of the estates assigned for the dower of Adela, wife of Duke Richard III. of Normandy, in the year 1027, but before long, both the fee and the advowson of the church were acquired by the de Moions, who continued to hold them until the conquest of Normandy by the French.[1] The remains of an ancient castle were to be seen on the west side of the church of Moyon fifty years ago, if, indeed, they do not still exist.[2] It has been suggested that Ralph Mowin, the supposed murderer of Duke Robert, was a member of the family which owned the domain of Moyon.[3] However this may be, it is certain that William de Mohun stood high in the favour of William the Conqueror. He accompanied him in his expedition to England, and fought under his banner on the field of Senlac. Dugdale states that he had " in his retinue not less than forty-seven stout knights of name and repute," and this statement has been repeated by many subsequent writers. It would appear, however, that " forty-seven " is a misprint for " fifty-seven," for that is the exact number of noble followers assigned to William de Mohun by an old French document which has been preserved by Leland in his *Collectanea*.[4] We there read :—

" Be it known that in the year of the grace of our Lord Jesus Christ one thousand and sixty-six on Saturday the feast of St. Calixtus came William the Bastard Duke of Normandy cousin of the noble king St. Edward, the son of Emma of England, and killed King Harold and took away the land from him by the aid of the Normans and other men of divers lands. Among whom came with him Sir William de Moion the old the most noble of all the host. This William de Moion had in his retinue in the host, all the great lords after named as it is written in the book of the Conquerors."

Then follows a list of fifty-seven names, among which we may notice those of Taisson, Marmion, Montfitchet, Bigot, Mowbray, Mortimer, Painel, Basqueville, de Corcy, and Lacy. But the very eminence of the persons described in it as followers of William de Mohun is of itself sufficient to raise a doubt as to its authenticity. And when we turn to the *Roman de Rou*, we there find

[1] "Magni Rotuli Scaccarii Normanniæ" (ed. Stapleton) vol. i, p. lxxxii; vol. ii, p. x.
[2] "Memoires de la Société des Antiquaires de Normandie," 1re Serie, vol. v, p. 214.
[3] Planché. "The Conqueror and his Companions."
[4] Vol. i, p. 202.

the same names standing in the same order, but with this important difference, that of William de Mohun we only read :—

> *" Le viel Willam de Moion*
> *Ont avec li maint compagnon."*

Wace does not even hint that the knights whose names immediately follow that of William de Mohun were in any way dependant on him, and we can scarcely doubt that the whole document given by Leland was the production of some ignorant or dishonest writer, who in a subsequent age wished to gratify the vanity of the Mohuns. As Mr. Planché remarks, the copyist might " have included half the army if an unmistakeable full stop and change of subject had not pulled him up short with the death of Robert Fitz Erneis which he writes incorrectly Herveis . . . Le Livre des Conquerors turns out to be the Roman de Rou."[1]

While however we absolutely reject the oft-repeated assertions that William de Mohun was the noblest man in the Norman army, and that he had an extraordinary number of great lords in his retinue, we must not forget that he really was a very important personage. It would appear from the Exon Domesday that he was Sheriff of Somersetshire, and he was certainly one of the largest landowners in the West of England during the reign of William the Conqueror.[2] At the time of the survey of A.D. 1085 he held no less than sixty-eight manors, of which fifty-five were situated in Somersetshire, eleven in Dorsetshire, one in Devonshire, and one in Wiltshire. His was one of the two castles mentioned as then existing in Somersetshire, Montacute being the other. The entry about Dunster in the Exchequer Domesday is as follows:—

" He himself holds Torre, and there is his castle. Aluric held it in the time of King Edward, and payed geld for half a hide. The land is sufficient for one plough. Two mills there render ten shillings, and there are fifteen bordars, and five acres of meadow, and thirty acres of pasture. It was formerly worth five shillings, but now fifteen shillings."

The Exon Domesday states rather more positively that the improvement in the value of the property had taken

---

[1] " The Conqueror and his Companions," vol. ii, p. 122.

[2] " Exon Domesday," p. 99. Morgan's " England under the Normans," p. 201.

place since it had been in the possession of its Norman
lord.   William de Mohun also held in his own demesne
the manors of Alcombe and Staunton, which are situated
within the parish of Dunster, and the manors of Stockland,
Sedtamtone, Cutcombe, Minehead, Broadwood, Exford,
West Quantockshead, Kilton, Newton, Wolverton, Broomfield, Lydeard St. Lawrence, West Bagborough, Stoke
Pero and Brewham in the county of Somerset, and the
manors of Spettisbury, Pulham, and Ham, in the county
of Dorset.   The manor of Carhampton, too, was before
long added to these, probably by means of an exchange
with the king.

Within a short time after the Domesday Survey, or at
any rate between the years 1090 and 1100, William de
Mohun, by consent of his wife Adelisa, granted the
advowson of the Church of St. George of "Dunestora"
and other valuable property to the monks of St. Peter's
at Bath.   His charter was confirmed both by William
Rufus and by Archbishop Anselm, and the Benedictine
monks thus acquired fisheries at Dunster and at Carhampton, the whole vill of Alcombe, the tithe of the
vineyards, ploughlands, market and flocks of Dunster,
and the tithes of several other places in the neighbourhood.[1]   It is worthy of remark that vines were certainly
cultivated at Dunster in the second half of the fourteenth century, and that a field on the south side of the
steep hill called Grabbist is to this day known as "the
Vineyard."[2]   The avowed desire of William de Mohun in
granting endowments to the Abbey of Bath was that the
monks should "build and raise" the Church of St.
George, and we find that they lost little time in estab-
lishing a cell at Dunster for members of their own
community.   Some few remains of the Priory may still
be traced on the north side of Dunster Church, and the
great tithe-barn of the monks is a prominent feature in
the landscape from many points of view.   The existing
Church of St. George is for the most part in the
Perpendicular style of architecture, but the bases of the
four piers that carry the central tower, and two shafts
with rude capitals at the east end of the nave may with

[1] See Appendix B.
[2] Dunster Castle Muniments.   Box ix, No. 2, and Box i, No. 4.

all probability be referred to the early part of the twelfth
century. The recent restoration of the whole fabric has
moreover brought to light a large Norman doorway which
had been embedded in the wall under the Perpendicular
window at the west end of the church. William de
Mohun gave his body to the monks of Bath Abbey, and
we may here notice that none of his direct descendants
seem to have cared to be buried in the Priory Church
which stood under the very shadow of their own castle.
He had issue at least three sons, of whom the eldest,
William by name, succeeded him in his ample domains.

William de Mohun the second was one of the great
nobles who espoused the cause of the Empress Matilda,
and Dunster Castle was reckoned among her chief strong-
holds. In describing the events of the year 1138, the
author of the *Gesta Stephani* writes :—

"At that time William de Mohun, a man not only of the highest rank,
but also of illustrious lineage, raised a mighty revolt against the King,
and assembling some bands of knights and foot-soldiers in his stronghold
which he had placed in a fair and impregnable situation by the sea-shore,
began to roam over that part of England in hostile manner sweeping it as
with a whirlwind. At all places and at all times laying aside his loyalty
he sought to do cruel deeds, to overcome by violence not only his
neighbours but also other persons living at a distance, to trouble in-
cessantly with robbery and pillage, with fire and sword, any who resisted,
and pitilessly to subject any wealthy persons whom he met to chains
and tortures. By so doing he changed a realm of peace and quiet, of
joy and merriment into a scene of strife, rebellion, weeping and lamen-
tation.

"When these things were after a time reported to the King he collected
his adherents in great numbers and proceeded by forced marches in order
to check the ferocity of William. But when he halted before the
entrance of the Castle, and saw the impregnable defences of the place,
inaccessible on one side where it was washed by the sea, and very strongly
fortified on the other by towers and walls, by a ditch and outworks, he
altogether despaired of pressing on the siege, and taking wiser counsel he
surrounded the Castle in full sight of the enemy so that he might the
better restrain them and occupy the neighbouring country in security.
He also gave orders to Henry de Tracy, a man skilled in war and approved
in the events of many different fights, that acting in his stead, as he
himself was summoned to other business, he should with all speed and
vigour bestir himself against the enemy. Henry therefore in the King's
absence sallied forth from Barnstaple his own town, and by the King's
special license made vigorous and valiant attacks on his adversaries, so
that he not only restrained their wonted incursions and plundering raids
in the neighbourhood, but also captured a hundred and four horsemen in
a single encounter. At length he so reduced and humbled William that

he desisted from attacking him any further and left the country in greater peace than before, and entirely free from his disturbance."[1]

In a subsequent passage, the same writer records that at the siege of Winchester in 1140, the empress bestowed on William de Mohun the title of Earl of Dorset.[2] In this instance he seems to have been misinformed about the proceedings of the hostile party; for while we find that William de Mohun and one of his descendants were styled Earls of Somerset, there is no evidence to show that any member of the family was ever styled Earl of Dorset.[3] In a charter of the Empress Matilda, and in charters of his own son and grandson, William de Mohun the second is described simply as "Earl William de Moion," or "Earl William," without any territorial title. To him, rather than to his son of the same name, must be ascribed the foundation of the Priory of Regular Canons at Bruton, in the eastern part of Somerset, in the year 1142.[4] He appears also to have given some land at Hanelham to the monks of Dunster for the soul of his son Ralph.[5] It is very difficult to distinguish between the different William de Mohuns who held Dunster in the twelfth century, but it was almost certainly the second of that name who, with Agnes his wife, granted the Church of Whichford to the Priory of Bridlington.[6] In the reign of Henry I, the number of his knights' fees was forty.[7] He had issue a son and heir of his own name, and four younger sons, who all became clerks.

---

[1] "Gesta Stephani" (ed. Sewell), p. 52. Readers who know how Dunster Castle is situated will, perhaps, be surprised at finding it described as "by the sea-shore," and again "as bounded by the sea on one side." It is quite possible, however, that the level ground, now known as "the Lawn," on the eastern side of the Tor, was, in the middle of the twelfth century, occasionally covered by water. The old road to Carhampton and Watchet certainly ran further inland and on a higher level than the present one. Its course may clearly be traced through the Park, and there is still a right of way for foot passengers on it from the southern end of Dunster. On the other hand, the situations of the mill and of the haven preclude any idea of the sea having extended over the Lawn at low water within historical times.

[2] Ibid., p. 81.

[3] At the same time it must be remembered that for some purposes Somerset and Dorset were often treated as forming one county.

[4] Notes on "Some early charters of Bruton Priory" will appear in a subsequent part of this volume.

[5] See Appendix B.

[6] Dugdale's "Antiquities of Warwickshire," p. 585. The advowson, however, reverted to the Mohuns afterwards, and, by the marriage of one of the Mohun heiresses to Lord Strange, passed to the Stranges.

[7] "Liber Niger Scaccarii," (ed. Hearne), vol. i, p. 91.

William de Mohun the third was, like his father, a benefactor to the Benedictine monks of Dunster as well as to the Augustinian Canons of Bruton.[1] To him we may probably ascribe the grant of the manor of Lydeard St. Laurence to the Priory of Taunton.[2] His wife Godehold or Godelind, seems to have held the vill of Brinkley, in the county of Cambridge, in her own right, and to have died at an advanced age in 1208.[3] The number of knights' fees belonging to the Honour of Dunster varied from time to time. A return issued in 1166 in connection with the aid for the marriage of the king's eldest daughter places the total number at forty-four, and gives the names of the tenants.[4] William Fitz Durand, who appears in the list as tenant of five knights' fees and a half, was probably a son of Durand de Moion, who is mentioned in a writ of Henry I, respecting the Abbey of Bath.[5] William de Mohun, the son of the Earl of Somerset, left issue three sons, William, Geoffrey, and John, of whom the second and third successively died seised of land at Brinkley, and also of the manor of Ham in Dorsetshire, which for several centuries afterwards continued to be held under the Lords of Dunster by a younger branch of the Mohun family.[6]

William de Mohun, the eldest son, appears to have inherited the bulk of his father's estates in 1177, after a vexatious escheat to the crown. Richard of Ilchester, Bishop of Winchester, who was at the same time guardian of the Honour of Montacute, rendered an account to the Exchequer in that year, from which we learn that he had charge of the Honour of Dunster for about eighteen months. He had however been ordered by the king to pay £18 to William de Mohun. The sale of corn and wine from the demesne lands during his administration yielded the sum of £19.[7]

To the Canons of Bruton William de Mohun granted

---

[1] See Appendix B.

[2] Dugdale's "Monasticon," vol. vi, p. 166.

[3] "Placitorum Abbreviatio," p. 60. Reginald de Mohun was found to be her next heir. She is mentioned as a witness in several charters of her husband.

[4] "Liber Niger Scaccarii," vol. i, p. 91.

[5] Madox's "History of the Exchequer,"

vol. i, p. 77. Durandus de Moion is also mentioned in Leland's "Collectanea," vol. i, p. 445.

[6] "Rotulus Cancellarii," 3 John, p. 142. "Rotuli de oblatis," vol. i, p. 136. "Excerpta e Rotulis Finium," vol. i, pp. 77, 79." "Calendarium Rotulorum Clausarum," vol. i, p. 300.

[7] See Appendix C.

several charters, one of which gave them the right to elect their own prior, provided that they presented the person so elected to him or his heirs whether in England or in Normandy. So faithfully was this condition carried out that long after the main line of the Mohun family had become extinct, the Canons of Bruton maintained the custom of presenting their Prior-elect to the Lord of Dunster for the time being.[1] William de Mohun the fourth seems to have died between the years 1190 and 1194, and his eldest son of the same name must have died either in his lifetime or very shortly after him. Lucy de Mohun, widow of the former, received for her dower seven knights' fees, chiefly in the counties of Somerset and Dorset.[2] She also obtained from the crown a lease of the ancestral estates of her husband's family at Moyon in Normandy.[3] She was, like him, a warm friend to the Canons of Bruton.

During the later years of the reign of Richard I, and in the early years of the succeeding reign, the Honour of Dunster was an escheat in the King's hands. It was successively administered by William of St. Mary Church, William de Wroteham, Nicholas Puinz, Hubert de Burgh, Hugh de Gurney, and Reginald de Clifton. The outgoings were very small, and consisted chiefly of the salaries of a porter and a watchman at the Castle, and a pension of £2 a year which had been granted by William de Mohun to a clerk named Richard.[4] In 1203, Hubert de Burgh, the Great Chamberlain of England, was ordered to induce Reginald de Mohun to exchange his lands at Lyon, near Caen in Normandy, for lands in England.[5] This Reginald, who was son of William de Mohun the fourth by Lucy his wife, obtained livery of Dunster Castle and his other ancestral domains in 1204.[6] Six years later, we find him serving with the English army in Ireland, and borrowing money for the purpose.[7] At the time of his death, which occurred before 1213, he was barely thirty years of age. His wife Alice, one of the

[1] Dunster Castle Muniments. Box xxxvii.
[2] "Rotulus Cancellarii," 3 John pp. 143, 209. "Rotuli de Oblatis," vol. i, p. 135. Pipe Roll, 4 John.
[3] "Magni Rotuli Scaccarii Norman-"nie (ed. Stapleton), vol. ii, p. ix.

[4] Pipe Rolls, 6—10 Richard I, and 1 —7 John. See also "Rotulus Cancellarii," 3 John, pp. 143, 198, 205-211.
[5] Patent Roll, 4 John, m. 1.
[6] Patent Roll, 6 John, m. 10; Close Roll, 6 John, m. 16.
[7] "Rotuli de Liberate," pp. 181, 204, 216.

five daughters of William Briwere the elder, eventually brought a great inheritance to the Mohuns.[1]

Their eldest son Reginald, being under age at the time of his father's death, was placed under the care of Henry Fitz-Count, son of the Earl of Cornwall, but was afterwards placed under the care of his own grandfather, William Briwere.[2] During the greater part of his minority, however, the King retained Dunster in his own hands; and when an attempt was made to establish a market at Watchet, in rivalry of the Dunster market, it was promptly suppressed by royal order.[3] For several years, the King maintained archers and horsemen in Dunster Castle.[4]

Reginald de Mohun the second was in 1242, and again in 1252, appointed to the high office of Justice of the Forests south of Trent.[5] Henry III. also gave him the right to have a weekly market at Dunster, to have free warren in his manors of Dunster, Ottery and Whichford, and to hunt hares, foxes, cats and other animals in all the king's forests in the county of Somerset.[6] He, in his turn, gave the burgesses of Dunster the right to hold a fair and a market in North Street, without any impediment from him or his heirs.

By another charter he granted to them that they should not, against their will, be made bailliffs or farmers of the sea-port, or of the toll of the borough, or of the mills, that they should be free from all tallage, and that they should have the common on Croydon enjoyed by their predecessors.[7] He released the buyers and sellers in Dunster market

[1] "Excerpta e Rotulis Finium," vol. i, pp. 7, 78, 242. Close Roll, 17 John, m. 13. She married secondly William Paganell. "Excerpta e Rotulis Finium. vol i, p. 167.

[2] "Excerpta e Rotulis Finium," vol. i, p. 79. Close Roll, 15 John, m. 4. Close Roll, 8 Henry III., m. 2.

[3] Close Roll, 7 Henry III., part 1, m. 29, 23.

[4] "Calendarium Rotulorum Clausarum," vol. i., pp. 418, 492, 503, 503, 512, 524, 535.

[5] Patent Roll, 26 Henry III., m. 6. Ibid, 36 Henry III., m. 1. Matthew Paris' "Chronica Majora."

[6] Dunster Castle Muniments, Box viii, No. 3,—an old certified extract from the Charter Roll of 37 Henry III. The original roll is no longer to be found among the public records in London.

[7] Savage's "History of Carhampton." p. 386, gives a translation. A copy of the original is preserved among the Muniments at Dunster Castle in a volume of transcripts of some records in the Parish chest in Dunster Church. I shall hereafter quote this MS. simply as "Dunster Church Book." Most of the original documents have unfortunately disappeared from the Church chest since the 18th century, when the transcript was made. It would seem that they were given by a former Vicar to his different antiquarian friends! "Gentleman's Magazine," 1808, p. 873.

from all toll on transactions under the value of a shilling, and the fishermen and merchants from all toll whatsoever. He abandoned all claim to take more than four lagens from any brewery, at the rate of a farthing a lagen, and he forbad the brewing of strong beer (*cervisia præponi*) in Dunster   Finally, he promised not to exact more than 6d. as a fine for any offence except an attack on a member of the household of the castle, and he gave a general confirmation of the customs hitherto observed by the burgesses of Dunster.   He granted the first of these two charters in consideration of a tun of wine worth two pounds; and the second in consideration of twenty marks, and for the benefit of the soul of his eldest son, John, lately deceased.[1]

In 1254, he gave fifty marks to the Prior and Convent of St. Peter at Bath, in order to provide for a mass for the soul of his late son John, for his own soul, and for the souls of his wives, of his ancestors and successors, and of all faithful departed.   The prior and convent, on their side, undertook that this mass should be celebrated daily to the end of time by one of the monks of Dunster, or by an honest secular priest in the upper chapel of St. Stephen in Dunster Castle, unless access thereto was forbidden by an ecclesiastical interdict, by a besieging force, or by the castellan of Dunster, in either of which cases, they promised that the mass should be said in the lower chapel of St. Laurence, belonging to the Priory of Dunster.   The founder undertook that all necessary books, vestments, tapers, &c., should be supplied by him and his heirs or other owners of the castle.[2] To the canons of Bruton Reginald de Mohun surrendered all his right in the revenues of the priory during the vacancy of the office of prior, and he also granted lands at Slaworth and at Stortmanford to the neighbouring Cistercian Abbey of Cleeve.[3]

But he chiefly deserves to be remembered as the founder of the Cistercian Abbey of Newenham, on the borders of Devonshire and Somersetshire.   His ancestors on both sides had already done much for the English

---

[1] Dunster Church Book.
[2] Dunster Castle Muniments, Box 733.
xvi, No. 1.
[3] Dugdale's "Monasticon." Vol. v, p.

church.   His grandfather and guardian, William Briwere,
had founded the Abbey of Torre, the Abbey of Dunkes-
well, the Priory of Mottisfont, the Nunnery of Polslo,
and the Hospital of St. John at Bridgwater; and his
mother had contributed a great deal of marble to the
fabric of Salisbury Cathedral.   Inspired by their examples,
and encouraged by his younger brother, William de
Mohun, he resolved to establish a lasting memorial of his
piety and munificence.   The site was dedicated in July,
1246, and six months later a colony of Cistercian monks
came to take formal possession of it in the presence of
Reginald and William de Mohun, and of a great concourse
of people.   The foundation stone of the church was laid
in July 1250, by Prior Walter.   There was another grand
ceremony at Newenham in September, 1254.   The abbot
and the monks went in solemn procession from their
temporary chapel to the site of the conventual church,
chaunting psalms suitable to the occasion; and Reginald de
Mohun laid a corner stone and two other stones.   William
de Mohun also laid a stone, and Wymond de Raleigh
another.   Then the monks stopped their chaunt, and the
abbot, the deacon and the sub-deacon duly vested for
mass, and the rest of the community knelt before the
founder and prayed him to adopt their church as his place
of burial.   He readily promised to do so, and gave
instructions to that effect in a document dated at Dunster,
on the 29th of June 1255.   During the later years
of his life, Sir Reginald gave a hundred marks a year to
the building fund, and, by his will, he bequeathed a
further sum of seven hundred marks to the Abbey.[1]   An
old French history of the Mohun family, the same,
apparently, as that which gave the apocryphal list of the
companions of William de Mohun, has the following
story:—

"When Sir Reginald saw that (*i.e.* the Consecration of the Abbey)
done, he passed to the Court of Rome, which then was at Lyons, to
confirm and ratify his new Abbey to his great honour for ever, and he
was at the Court in Lent when they sing the office of the Mass *Lætare
Jerusalem*, on which day the custom of the Court is that the Apostle
(*i.e.*, the Pope) gives to the most valiant and most honourable man who
can be found at the said Court a rose or a flower of fine gold.   They

[1] Davidson's "History of Newenham Abbey."

therefore searched the whole Court and found this Reginald to be the
most noble of the whole Court, and to him Pope Innocent gave this rose
or flower of gold, and the Pope asked him what manner of man he was
in his own country. He answered 'a plain knight bachelor.' 'Fair son,'
said the Pope, 'this rose or flower has never been given save to Kings, or
to Dukes, or to Earls, therefore we will that you shall be Earl of
Este,' that is of Somerset. Reginald answered and said 'O Holy Father,
I have not wherewithal to maintain the title.' The Apostle therefore gave
him two hundred marks a year to be received at the Choir of St. Paul's
in London, out of the (Peter's) pence of England, to maintain his position;
of which donation he brought back with him bulls which still have the
lead attached, etc., together with ten other bulls of confirmation of his
new Abbey of Newenham. After this day he bore the rose or flower in
his arms."[1]

Whatever may be the real historical value of this
curious narrative, this much is certain, that the second
Reginald de Mohun sometimes styled himself "Earl of
Somerset and Lord of Dunster," and that he bore for
his arms, a dexter arm habited in a maunch, the hand
holding a fleur-de-lys.[2]

In addition to his paternal estates Reginald de Mohun
held considerable property in the county of Devon, partly
inherited from his uncle, William Briwere the younger,
who died without issue in 1232, and partly derived from
the Flemyngs. Thus it was that he lived sometimes at
Ottery Flemyng, which was afterwards known as Ottery
Mohun, and sometimes at Torre, which in contradis-
tinction to the many places of that name in the west of
England, came to be known as Torre Mohun or Tor-
Moham, a name which it has retained to our own time.
He confirmed to the Præmonstratensian Canons of Torre
the benefactions of his grandfather William Briwere, and
his arms may still be seen in the ruins of Torre Abbey.
But the site of his court-house, in which, by special permission of the abbot, he had a private chapel, can
no longer be recognized amid the upstart villas of
modern Torquay.[3]

One of the monks of Newenham has left us the
following account of Reginald de Mohun's last days:—

"In the year of our Lord 1257, on Sunday, 20th of January, the feast
of Saints Fabian and Sebastian, Reginald de Mohun, the Lord of Duns-

---

[1] Fuller's "Church History," book iii, § 5.
[2] See Appendix A. "On the Arms and Seals of the Mohun family."
[3] Oliver's "Monasticon Dioecesis Exon."

torre, and founder of Newenham Abbey, entered the way of all flesh, at
Torre, in Devonshire. His end was this. On being attacked by severe
illness at Torre, he sent for a Franciscan friar, called Henry, at that time
a learned professor of theology at Oxford. The said friar arrived at Torre
on the Wednesday before Reginald's death, and received his humble,
entire, and sincere confession. Early on the Friday morning, as the said
friar entered the bedroom, Reginald thus addressed him : 'I have had a
vision this night; I imagined myself to be in the church of the White
Monks,[1] and when on the point of leaving it, a venerable personage,
habited like a pilgrim presented himself and accosted me thus : 'Reginald,
I leave it to your option either to come to me now in safety and without
hazard, or to await until the week next before Easter exposed to danger.'
My reply was, 'My Lord, I will not await, but will follow you forthwith.'
As I was preparing to follow him he said, 'No, not as yet, but you shall
securely join me on the third day.' This was my dream and vision.'
The confessor, after administering motives of consolation, returned to his
own chamber, and during a short slumber, dreamed that he was present
in the aforesaid Cistercian Monastery and beheld a venerable person
attired in white, conducting a boy more radiant than the sun and vested
in a robe brighter than crystal, from the baptismal font towards the
altar. On enquiry whose beautiful child this was, the person answered
'this is the soul of the venerable Reginald de Mohun.' The third day
arriving, Reginald requested Henry to recite *Prime* and *Tierce*, 'as my
hour' he said 'is approaching;' for he was in the habit of hearing the
whole divine office repeated. The friar having done so, went into the
Abbey Church to celebrate Mass. The Introit was *Circumdederunt me*,
etc. Mass being over, the said friar returned in his priestly vestments,
bringing with him the *Viaticum* to fortify the Lord Reginald, with the
receiving of the body and blood of Christ. As he entered the bed-
chamber Reginald was anxious to rise, but could not from excessive
weakness. About ten persons were present, to whom he said, 'Why
not assist me to meet my Saviour and Redeemer?' And these were his
last words. Henry then gave him the Communion, and afterwards the
extreme unction, and then began with the priests and clerks the recom-
mendation of a departing soul. At the end of these prayers, Reginald
being still alive, they began to repeat them; and whilst they were
reciting the words 'All ye Saints pray for him,' without a groan or
apparent agony, he fell asleep in the Lord. His corpse was removed to
Newenham, and deposited on the left side of the High Altar."

"When the pavement of the Sanctuary of our Conventual Church
was relaid, in the year of our Lord 1333, the body of the said founder
(seventy five years after its interment) was found in the sarcophagus
perfectly incorrupt and uninjured, and exhaling a fragrant odour. For
three days it lay exposed to public view. I both saw it and touched it."

Reginald de Mohun the second was twice married. In
one of his charters to Cleeve Abbey, and again in the
Register of Newenham Abbey, his first wife is simply

[1] *i.e.* at Newenham.
[2] Oliver's "Ecclesiastical Antiquities in Devon," vol. i, pp. 206-208. I have taken the liberty of altering a word or two in the translation for the sake of euphony.

styled Avice or Hawys de Mohun, which of course was
the name which she bore after her marriage.[1]   But
some ingenious antiquaries not satisfied with this, have
chosen to read the M as a B, and to describe her as
sister of Humphrey de Bohun.[2]   Others, with little
better authority, have described her as a sister of John
Fitz-Geoffrey.[3]   It is more probable that she was the
heiress of the Flemyngs of Ottery.[4]   But whatever was
her maiden name, her memory seems to have been long
preserved at Dunster, for in the middle of the fifteenth
century one of the towers of the Castle was known as
" Damhawys toure."[5]

The oldest parts of the existing castle, that is to say,
the entrance gateway, the series of projecting semi-circular
towers and the thick wall that connects them, were,
apparently, built at this period, though it is not easy to
understand why the lower ward of the Norman castle
should have required to be rebuilt so soon.   The eastern
part of Dunster Church was also destroyed in the
thirteenth century, and was replaced by a handsome
chancel in the Early English style.

Reginald de Mohun's second wife, Isabel, widow of
Gilbert Basset and daughter of William Ferrers, Earl of
Derby, was, through her mother, one of the eventual
coheiresses of the Marshals, Earls of Pembroke.[6]   By her
he had a son William, who inherited part of the Marshal
property, and also received the manor of Ottery Mohun,
which, at his death in 1280, passed to one of his daughters
and coheiresses, Mary, the wife of John de Carew, and
became afterwards known as Carew's Ottery.   Nicholas
Carew, the only son of John and Mary, died without

---

[1] " Proceedings of the Somersetshire
Archæological Society," vol. vi, p. 28.
See Appendix E.

[2] Dugdale's " Baronage," p. 497.

[3] Pedigrees by Robert Glover, Harl.
MS. 807, f. 73.   "The Visitation of
Cornwall 1620," (Harleian Society).

[4] Reginald de Mohun certainly acquired
a great part of the Flemyng estate in
Devonshire. See Pole and Lysons passim.
The Flemyng arms appear next after
those of Briwere in a shield of the quar-
terings of the Mohun family, in Lanteglos
Church, and in the Heralds' Visitation of
Devon in 1620.

On the other hand it must be observed
that the Flemyng property passed to Sir
Wm. Mohun, son of Reginald de Mohun, by
his second wife.

[5] Dunster Castle Muniments, Box
xi, No. 3.   "In 1 magna clave empta de
Hugone Lokyer et in emendatione 1 seræ
pro damhawys toure 4s.   In Johanne
Bolkinam conducto per 1 diem ad pur-
gandum damhawys toure ad cibum domini 2d."

[6] Dugdale's "Monasticon," vol. v, p.
271.   "Calendarium Genealogicum," vol.
i, p. 94.   Patent Roll, 18 Edw. III, p. 2.
m. 9.

SHIELDS WITH THE MOHUN ARMS.

1

2

3

4

1. At Ottery Mohun.　　2. At Axminster.　　3. At Bruton.
4. At Wolveton.

To face p. 15.

issue, but the Carews who succeeded him in his estates quartered the arms of Mohun on their shield as if they had inherited the blood as well as the property of William de Mohun. Beatrix de Mohun, widow of William, paid no less than £100 for leave to choose a second husband in 1288.[1]

It is stated in almost every account of the Mohun family that Reginald the second was succeeded by his son John de Mohun, but a careful examination of contemporary documents proves conclusively that he was succeeded by his grandson, and that a whole generation has been omitted by Dugdale and other genealogists.[2] John de Mohun, the eldest son of Reginald and Hawys, died, as has already been observed, during the life of his father. His body was conveyed from Gascony, where he met his end, to Bruton Priory, and his heart was buried at Newenham Abbey.[3] By Joan, his wife, daughter of William Ferrers, Earl of Derby, a younger sister of his step-mother, he left two sons, of whom the elder, John, succeeded Reginald as Lord of Dunster. The title of Earl of Somerset was never again assumed by any member of the Mohun family.

There is little to be remarked about John de Mohun the second, beyond the fact that he granted a charter to the townsmen of Dunster, which has generally been ascribed to his son of the same name.[4] The records of the time do not show which side he espoused in the Barons' War, though there was some fighting in his neighbourhood in 1265. Rishanger says, " In that year, on the Sunday before the battle of Evesham, a multitude of Welshmen having as their captain, William de Berkeley, a knight of noble birth but of infamous character, landed at Minehead, near the castle of Dunster, in order to ravage the county of Somerset. The warden of the castle, Adam Gurdon by name, came out to meet them, slew many of them with the sword and putting many others to flight, among whom was the captain, caused them to be drowned."[5]

---

[1] " Rotulorum Originalium Abbreviatio," pp. 42, 100. " Calendarium Genealogicum," vol. i, pp. 94, 227, 318, 345, 539, 546, 547. " Placitorum Abbreviatio," pp. 277, 293. Rot. Fin., 16th Edward I, m. 7.

[2] For proofs see Appendix D.

[3] Oliver's "Monasticon Dioecesis Exon," pp. 362, 363.

[4] As for instance in Savage's " History of Carhampton," p. 387.

[5] " Willelmi Rishanger Chronica," Rolls Series, p. 41.

On the death of the last of the sons of William Marshal Earl of Pembroke, the illustrious Protector, a large share of the Marshal estates passed to Sibilla, wife of William Ferrers Earl of Derby, and a large share of her inheritance came to John de Mohun and to William de Mohun his uncle, through their respective mothers, Joan and Isabel.[1] John de Mohun the second died in 1279, leaving by Eleanor Fitz-Piers, his wife, a son and heir of his own name, who was then about nine years of age, and who remained a ward of Edward I. during the greater part of his minority.[2] Eleanor, his widow, had for her dower no less than twenty-seven knights' fees in the counties of Somerset, Devon and Dorset; and she afterwards married William Martin. Fifty-five knights' fees were at that time held of the Honour of Dunster.[3]

John de Mohun the third served in the wars of Edward I. in Flanders and in Scotland, and sat in several parliaments as a peer of the realm.[4] He was one of the English barons who in 1300 wrote a letter to Boniface VIII., declaring that their king ought not to submit to the papal judgment, and in that famous document he is styled " John de Mohun, Lord of Dunster."[5]

In 1312, he was a party to the execution of Piers Gaveston, the unworthy favourite of Edward II.[6] To the burgesses of Dunster he, in 1301, granted a general confirmation of the charters of his ancestor Reginald, and of his father John, at the same time giving them the right to take furze, broom, turf, firebote and heath, sufficient for their fuel, from Croydon Hill.[7] Six years later he gave them leave to dig slime for manuring their lands, and common of pasture in his marshes near the sea,

[1] " Calendarium Genealogicum," (Ed. Roberts), vol. i, p. 227.

[2] Inquisitiones post mortem, 7th Edw. I, No. 13. Dunster Castle Muniments, Box i, No. 1; Box iv, No. 1; Box viii, No. 5. Oliver's "Monasticon Dioecesis Exon," p. 362. Savage's "History of Carhampton," p. 345.
In 1289, a payment was made on behalf of the king, "Johanni de Mooun infanti existenti in custodia Regis, et socio suo, pro sellis, frenis, ocreis, calcaribus, et alio minuto harnes quod eis competit pro instanti seysona hiemali in anno xviij°, per manus Johannes Launcelewe magistri sui apud Clarendon xxs." Ward-

robe Books (Tower), 18th Edw. I. Soon after the death of John de Mohun in 1279, the custody of his lands was committed to John de Saunford the King's Escheator in Ireland. " Rotulorum Originalium Abbreviatio," vol. i, p. 36.

[3] " Calendarium Genealogicum," vol. i, p. 371. Inq. post mortem, 7th Edw. I, No. 13.

[4] " Parliamentary Writs," ed. Palgrave, vol. i, p. 740, and vol. ii, part 3, pp. 1176, 1177, " Documents Illustrative of the History of Scotland."

[5] Nicolas's " Historic Peerage."

[6] " Parliamentary Writs."

[7] Dunster Church Book," f. 3.

except in East Marsh, which he reserved for himself.[1] One of the boundaries mentioned in the deed was "the road which leads to the sea-port of Dunster;" and perhaps this is the most suitable place for calling attention to the existence of this port in the middle ages. As early as the year 1183 the reeve of Dunster was fined 106s. 8d. for exporting corn from England.[2] A charter of Reginald de Mohun, already noticed, alludes to the bailiffs of the sea-port, and in the reign of Edward III, writs were sent to the bailiffs of Dunster, forbidding them to allow any friars or monks or any treasure to leave the realm by the sea-port.[3] The place where the river Avill widens out before joining the sea is still called "the Hone," or more properly, "the Hawn," which is an obvious corruption of the Haven. John de Mohun also assigned to his burgesses, twenty out of the twenty-four lagens of beer annually due to him from every brewery in the town.[4] To the Priories of Dunster and of Bruton he confirmed the gifts of his ancestors.[5] In 1299 he exchanged Grange Mohun and other lands in Ireland for the manor of Long Compton, in Warwickshire.[6]

By Ada, his wife, daughter of Payn or Robert Tiptoft, he had issue seven sons and one daughter. John, the eldest son, was knighted during his father's lifetime, and took part in the battle of Boroughbridge.[7] He died shortly afterwards in Scotland without having inherited the estates of his ancestors, and he is said to have been buried far away from them, in the church of the Grey Friars at York.[8] His wife Christian, daughter of Sir John Segrave, brought him a marriage-portion of £400 in 1305, and bore him an only son named John, who eventually succeeded to the lordship of Dunster.[9]

Sir Robert de Mohun the second son of John, Lord of

[1] Dunster Church Book.
[2] Madox's History of the Exchequer, vol. i, p. 558.
[3] Rymer's "Fœdera," vol. ii, p. 701, and vol. iii, p. 728.
[4] Dunster Church Book, f. 6. There is a translation in Savage's "History of Carhampton," p. 388.
[5] Dunster Castle Muniments, Box xvi, No. 4. Patent Roll, 20th Edw. III, p. 2, m. 24.
[6] "Placitorum Abbreviatio," p. 241.

"Rot. Pat. et Claus. Hiberniæ."
[7] "Parliamentary Writs" (ed. Palgrave), vol. ii, part 2, p. 198.
[8] "The Visitation of Devon, 1620" (Harleiah Society). The date of his death is put down at 1322, but the whole account of the Mohuns given there is so full of blunders that the Visitation scarcely deserves to be quoted as an authority.
[9] The settlement made on the marriage is given in Patent Roll, 33rd Edward I, p. 1, m. 9.

Dunster, is said to have married Elizabeth Fitz-Roges of Porlock, and to have been killed by her contrivance.[1] The Mohuns of Fleet, near Weymouth, a branch of the family which flourished until the latter part of the last century, claimed him as their ancestor.

Baldwin de Mohun, the third son, took holy orders, and became parson of Whichford in Warwickshire, the advowson of that church having somehow reverted to the Mohuns from the monks of Bridlington.[2]

Payn de Mohun, the fourth son, was a minor at the time of his mother's death, and, as such, had great difficulty in obtaining from his father a choir-cope wrought with gold which she had expressly bequeathed to him.[3]   He subsequently received a legacy from Lady Anne Maltravers.[4] In 1366 he was appointed by the king guardian of the lands of William of Wymondham, at Staundon, in the county of Hertford.[5]

Sir Reginald de Mohun, the fifth son, married the heiress of Sir John Fitz-William of Cornwall, and settled either in that county or in Devonshire. One of his descendants, Reginald Mohun of Boconnoc, was created a baronet in 1612, and his son, Sir John, was in 1628 advanced to the peerage under the title of Baron Mohun of Okehampton.   The Barony of Mohun of Dunster having been long extinct, this younger ennobled branch of the family assumed as its motto :—" *Generis revocamus honores.*" Two of the Lords Mohun of Okehampton attained some celebrity, the first as a leader of the royalist forces in the civil war, and the fifth as one of the most dissolute courtiers of the early part of the eighteenth century. The once illustrious name of Mohun is, by most people, remembered only in connection with the fatal duel between Lord Mohun and the Duke of Hamilton in Hyde Park in 1712. It so happens that the present owner of Dunster Castle, Mr. George Fownes Luttrell, is the direct representative of the Mohuns of Boconnoc, his ancestor, John Fownes, having married the heiress of Samuel Maddock, whose wife was the daughter and eventual heiress of the third Lord Mohun of Okehampton.[6]

---

[1] "The Visitation of Cornwall, 1620" (Harleian Society).
[2] Dugdale's " Antiquities of Warwickshire," p. 586.
[3] Register of Bishop Drokensford at Wells, f. 217, b.
[4] Nicolas, "Testamenta Vetusta," p. 91.
[5] " Rotulorum Originalium Abbreviatio," vol. ii, p. 94.
[6] See Appendix E.

Brass of Thomas de Mohun, at Lanteglos-by-Fowey, co. Cornwall.

Patrick, the sixth son of John Mohun, Lord of Dunster, seems to have lived either at Bradworthy or at Carhampton,[1] and Lawrence the seventh son is said to have been the progenitor of the Mohuns of Tavistock.[2]

John de Mohun, Lord of Dunster, married a second wife named Sibilla, and died in 1330.[3] There is no reason to doubt he was buried with his ancestors at Bruton.[4] The right of inheritance passed to his grandson John, son of his eldest son Sir John de Mohun. This John, the fifth of that name in direct succession, being only ten years old at the time of his grandfather's death, was given as a ward to Henry de Burghersh, Bishop of Lincoln, and afterwards to Sir Bartholomew de Burghersh, brother of that prelate.[5] He received livery of his lands in 1341, and in the same year took part in the war against the Scots. He subsequently fought in the different foreign campaigns of Edward III., serving sometimes under Sir Bartholomew de Burghersh, sometimes under John of Gaunt, and sometimes under the Black Prince.[6] On the establishment of the Order of the Garter in 1350, Sir John de Mohun was nominated one of the twenty-five original knights, and a brass plate setting forth his title and his arms is still to be seen in St. George's Chapel, at Windsor. In 1349, we find the Black Prince giving him a horse called Grisel Gris.[7]

Before he was twenty-two years of age Sir John de Mohun married Joan, the daughter of his former guardian, Sir Bartholomew de Burghersh, a lady who plays a very important part in the history of Dunster. One story indeed that is told of her, and that reminds one partly of Dido and partly of Lady Godiva, rests solely on tradition. Camden and Fuller relate that she obtained from her husband as much common land for the poor of Dunster as she could walk round in one day barefooted.[8] No charter corresponding to any such grant is to be found

---

[1] Dunster Castle Muniments, Box xvii, No. 1. Inq. p. m., 6th Henry IV, No. 33.

[2] Appendix E.

[3] "Rolls of Parliament," vol. ii, p. 71. Inq. p. m., 4th Edward III, No. 35.

[4] The monument on the north side of the Chancel of Dunster Church which is generally said to be that of this John de Mohun, is really that of Sir Hugh Luttrell. See Part II.

[5] Inq. p. m., 4th Edward III, No. 35. "Rolls of Parliament," vol. ii, p. 71.

[6] Dugdale's "Baronage," vol. i, p. 984.

[7] Beltz's "Order of the Garter."

[8] Camden's "Britannia;" Fuller's "Worthies," under Somerset.

among the muniments at Dunster, and if there be any
truth in the story the real heroine of it was more probably
the wife of Reginald de Mohun.   The chief charter of
the last Lord Mohun of Dunster was a grant to the
prior and monks of that place, of common of pasture on
Croydon and Grabbist Hills, and of twelve cartloads a
year of dead wood and wind-fall wood from his park of
Marshwood in the parish of Carhampton, and his outer
woods at Dunster.   He also confirmed to them the different grants of his ancestors, and remitted certain annual
payments due to him.[1]   During his life the town of
Dunster returned members to Parliament for the first
and last time, in 1360.[2]   He himself was regularly summoned to the upper house as a baron.[3]

At different dates after his marriage, Sir John de
Mohun executed a series of entails and conveyances of
his landed property, generally for the purpose of securing
a larger income to his wife ; sometimes, apparently, for the
purpose of raising money.[4]   His expenses at the court
and in the camp of Edward III. must have been considerable ; and his will, only a few lines long, contains an
ominous reference to creditors in London.[5]   He eventually,
in 1369, conveyed his chief estates to feoffees on condition
that they should dispose of them according to the instructions of his wife.[6]   He died on the 14th of September, 1376, without leaving any male issue, and was buried
according to his own desire in the Priory Church of
Bruton.[7]   No sooner was he dead than his widow obtained from the feoffees a reconveyance of the estates to
herself for life, with remainder to the Lady Elizabeth
Luttrell in fee.[8]   Thus on the only occasion since the
Norman Conquest, on which Dunster Castle has passed
by sale, it was sold by one woman and bought by another.

The sum paid for the right of succession to the great
Barony of Dunster amounted to five hundred marks

---

[1] Dunster Castle Muniments, Box
xvi, Nos. 2, 3.

[2] " Parliaments of England," (1878).

[3] "Report from the Lords' Committee
on the Dignity of a Peer."

[4] Dunster Castle Muniments, Box i,
Nos. 4, 5, 6. Box iv, No. 17.

[5] Ibid, Box xxxvii, No. 4, A.D. 1342.

[6] Ibid, Box i, No. 4.

[7] Ibid, and Box xxxvii, No. 4.

[8] Ibid, Box i, No. 4.   During the life
of her husband, in 1374, Lady Joan
Mohun had agreed to sell the estates to
Lady Elizabeth Luttrell, and had re-
ceived from her a deposit of £200.
Dunster Castle Muniments, Box i, No. 7.

(£3333 6s. 8d.), and the original receipt of Lady Joan de Mohun for this sum is one of the most interesting documents in the possession of Mr. Luttrell. In one way at least Lady Joan de Mohun had the best of the bargain for she lived nearly thirty years after the payment of the purchase-money. She had the less scruple in selling Dunster and the manors dependent on it, inasmuch as all her three daughters had made brilliant marriages. Elizabeth, the eldest, was the wife of William de Monta-cute, Earl of Salisbury. Philippa, the second, was the wife of Sir Walter Fitz-Walter, and Matilda, the youngest, was the wife of Sir John Strange, Lord of Knockyn. Each of these three ladies inherited from their father some portion of the Mohun property. Lady Joan de Mohun afterwards surrendered to her two elder daughters for forty marks a year her own life interest in the more valuable estates which she had alienated to Lady Elizabeth Luttrell.[1] Having thus practically severed her connection with Dunster, she seems to have gone to live in London, where she and her daughter, the Countess of Salisbury, used to figure at court arrayed in the robes of the Order of the Garter.[2] In 1386 she obtained from the king a grant for life of the manor and hundred of Macclesfield, which about three years later she exchanged with Anne, the Queen-Consort, for an annuity of £100 sterling.[3] She built for herself a sumptuous chantry near the altar of St. Mary in the crypt or "undercroft" of the Cathedral Church of Canterbury, and in 1395 she gave to the prior and convent the sum of 350 marks, a high red hearse worth £20, a set of vestments also worth £20, and a missal and chalice.[4] According to a formal agreement made in

---

[1] Inq. p. m. 6 Henry IV., No. 33.

[2] Beltz's "Order of the Garter," pp. 248, 249, 255. Dunster Castle Muniments. Box ix, No. 3.

[3] Thirty-sixth Report of the Deputy-keeper of the Public Records. Appendix i, pp. 346, 347.

[4] "Pro uno lecto albo rubeo de Camaka coopertorio inde duplicato cum blodio serico cum chiefciel et celura unius sectæ, et tribus curtinis de Sendal de Gene, et uno travers rubeo de Sendal de Tripe, et quatuor cusshynis de secta dicti lecti, unde valor estimative viginti

libræ, et vestimento palleato rubeo et nigro velvet et Camaka duplicato cum viridi Sendal, videlicet quantum pertinet ad unum capellanum, diaconum, et subdiaconum de una et eadem secta, et duabus capis dictis quercopis de veste aurea, valor estimative viginti libræ, et uno missali pretii centum solidorum, et uno calice pretii quadraginta solidorum."

The living persons to be mentioned in the daily mass were, Richard, King of England, Lady Joan Mohun, Elizabeth (probably Elizabeth de Burghersh her mother), and Elizabeth le Despencer (daughter of Sir

that year one of the monks was to say mass daily for her soul and for the souls of other persons connected with her, at the altar of St. Mary, except on certain great festivals when he was to celebrate at the altar of St. John the Baptist, near the tomb of St. Thomas of Canterbury. For this service he was to receive £2 a year, and the clerk in charge of the chapel was to receive 5s. a year for keeping the tomb clean and in good condition. *Placebo* and *Dirige* were to be sung on the eve of the anniversary of her death and a solemn mass of *Requiem* on the morrow, the celebrant receiving 6s. 8d. and the deacon and sub-deacon 3s. 4d. apiece. A hundred poor people were also to receive one penny apiece on the day of her obit.

"Joan de Moune Lady of Dunster" made her will on the second of October, 1404, in the guest-house called "Mayster onerys," within the precincts of Christ Church, Canterbury. By it she gave to her daughter Elizabeth, Countess of Salisbury, the cross which she had promised to give to the daughter whom she loved best, and a copy of the *Legenda Sanctorum*. Matilda, the third daughter, had predeceased her mother, and Philippa, the second, received only the maternal blessing and some choice red wine. This lady had been married three times, firstly to Sir Walter Fitz-Walter, secondly to Sir John Golafre, and thirdly to Edward Plantagenet, Duke of York. Her third husband was alive in 1404, and received, under his mother-in-law's will, a copy of the *Legenda Sanctorum* and an illuminated book. Lady Joan de Mohun also left to her singular Lord Archbishop Arundel, a Psalter bound in white; to her esteemed cousin, Lady le Despencer the elder, a green bed; to the Prior of Canterbury, some old green tapestry embroidered with lions and some "ystayned" tapestry; to her confessor, Friar John, of the Franciscan order, ten marks; and various other legacies to other persons, not forgetting Philip Caxton, her clerk, and her six damsels and attendants.[1] She died two days after the date of her will, and was duly buried

---

Bartholomew de Burghersh the younger). The dead persons to be mentioned were:— John (de Mohun), Edward (probably Edward III.), Edward (le Despencer), Bartholomew (de Burghersh), and Philippa and Anne Queens of England. Arundel MS. lxviii, ff. 59-60

[1] Register of Archbishop Arundel, at Lambeth, f. 218. For "Maysteronerys" see "Archæologia Cantiana," vol. vii, p. 96.

Stothard.

JOAN DE MOHUN, "LADY OF DUNSTER".
DIED 1404

in the undercroft at Canterbury.[1] The effigy on her tomb shows her habited in the close-fitting tunic known as a *cote hardie*, but both the arms have been broken off.[2] The inscription round it was :—"𝔓our dieu prie𝔷 por l'ame 𝔍ohane 𝔅urwasche 𝔮e feut 𝔇ame de 𝔐ohun."[3]

Philippa, Duchess of York, the last surviving daughter of the last Lord Mohun of Dunster, died in 1431, and was buried in Westminster Abbey, where her monument may still be seen in the Chapel of St. Nicholas.[4]

There is in a canopied niche on the south side of the chancel of Dunster Church a recumbent effigy of a lady attired in the costume of the thirteenth century, and it is probable that she was the wife or the daughter of one of the early lords of the place. There is also in the church of Stoke-Flemyng in Devonshire an effigy of a lady, who may likewise have been a member of the Mohun family. But with these two doubtful exceptions, the tombs of Lady Joan de Mohun at Canterbury and of the Duchess of York at Westminster are the only sepulchral memorials of the Mohuns of Dunster that have escaped the hand of the destroyer. The fair Abbey of Newenham is now a shapeless ruin, and of the Priory Church of Bruton not a vestige remains. On the other hand, "the right goodly and stronge Castelle of Dunestorre" has for eight centuries maintained its position as one of the chief secular buildings in the County of Somerset.

---

[1] Inq. post mortem 6 Henry IV, No. 33.

[2] There is an engraving of the tomb in Dart's "Canterbury." The photo-lithograph opposite has been copied from the etching in Stothard's "Monumental Effigies."

[3] Willement and Powell give the spelling of some of the words differently.

[4] There is an engraving of it in Gough's "Sepulchral Monuments," and another in Stothard's "Monumental Effigies."

Mohun Arms, from an old tile in Dunster Church.

Appendix A.

The Arms and Seals of the Mohun Family.

There is fair ground for believing that the original bearing of the Mohun family was either a maunch, or a human hand holding a fleur-de-lys, almost all early examples of heraldic art being very simple in character. We have no evidence however on the point that will take us back beyond the time of Henry III. A deed of Reginald de Moyone preserved among the muniments at Dunster Castle (Box xxvi, No. 1) has attached to it a green seal, of which a woodcut is given on the opposite page, No. 1.[1] On this seal the hand holding a fleur-de-lys, and habited in a maunch, is represented as a device rather than as a regular heraldic charge. The motto inscribed round it consists of five words, of which the second is "sunt," the third "que," and the fourth apparently "malo," the other two being unfortunately illegible. This may possibly be the seal of the first Reginald de Mohun of Dunster, but it is more probably the seal of his son and successor, the second Reginald.

The third seal figured on the opposite page is unquestionably that of the second Reginald de Mohun, the founder of Newenham Abbey, who died in 1257. There is now only one impression of it among the muniments at Dunster Castle; but in the last century there was another impression of it, attached to a charter in the parochial chest in Dunster Church. The legend is "SIGILL. REGINALDI DE MOUN,"-and the hand holding a fleur-de-lys and habited in a maunch is represented on a shield in heraldic style. It is scarcely probable that this baron had two different seals in use during the last few years of his life, and if it could be shown that either of the above-mentioned seals was in use before the consecration of Newenham Abbey, we might absolutely reject as mythical the old story that Reginald de Mohun, "Earl of Este," added a fleur-de-lys to his arms in allusion to a golden rose, supposed to have been given to him by Innocent IV. when he went to Lyons for Papal Bulls confirming his new foundation.

In Glover's Roll, which dates from the time of Henry III, the arms of Reginald de Mohun are certainly blazoned as "*De goules ov ung manche d'argent.*" An ingenious theory has lately been started to the effect that "the fleur-de-lys was added either by John de Mohun or his son, after the marriage of the former with the heiress Joan de Aguylon, when the bearing of her family was combined with the Mohun maunch.'[2] Against this it might be argued almost conclusively that the heiress, Joan Ferrers, did not marry Robert Aguylon until after the death of John de Mohun, who was her first husband; but no such arguments are necessary to refute it when we have before us the original seals of Reginald de Mohun with the fleur-de-lys clearly shown.

In the Register of Newenham (f. 39 b.) there is the following entry :— "*Reginaldus de Moun fundator hujus domus portavit, de Goules les escu ove la manche dargent ermyne e en la mayn de argent une florete de or. Willelmus frater ejus et fundator portavit : les escu de goules ove la manche de argent ermyne et croizeles.*"

---

[1] All the woodcuts of seals are the same size as the originals.

[2] Hutchins's "History of Dorset" (ed. 1861), vol. i, p. 272, and Planché's "Pursuivant of Arms," p. 169.

SEALS.

1.

Reginald de Mohun.

2.

John de Mohun.

3.

Reginald de Mohun, Earl of Somerset.

William de Mohun, the son of the second Reginald, in the later part of the thirteenth century bore for arms :—" *Gules*, a maunch *argent*, a label *azure*."[1]

The second seal figured in our series of woodcuts is that of John, son of Richard de Moyon, who held lands at Watchet in the early part of the reign of Henry III. The original, in white wax, is attached to a deed preserved among the muniments at Dunster Castle. The only clues to the date are the style of writing used in the deed, and the name of one of the witnesses—William, Abbot of Cleeve. The device is an eagle displayed, and the legend round it is—"Sig. Johis filii Ricardi."

Eleanor, wife of William Martin, and widow of the second John de Mohun, who died in 1279, is said to have used a seal showing three different shields, viz. :—Two bars and a label for Martin, a hand issuing from a maunch and holding a fleur-de-lys for Mohun, and three lions rampant for Fitz-Piers.[2]

The Mohuns of Ham, who appear to be descended from a younger brother of the first Reginald, assumed the arms of the elder branch of the family, with the tinctures reversed :—*Ermine* a dexter arm habited in a maunch *gules*, the hand *proper* holding a fleur-de-lys *or*.[3]

For some reason unknown, John de Mohun, Lord of Dunster, who died in 1330, abandoned the arms of his ancestors, and adopted a totally different bearing. The register of Newenham Abbey states positively :—"John de Moun the third changed the ancient arms of those who used to bear a maunch ermine. This John the third bore a gold shield with a sable cross engrailed."[4] So, again, in the lists of the English knights who were present at the siege of Carlaverock in 1300, we read :—

> " *Jaune o crois noire engrelee*
> *La portoit John de Mooun.*"[5]

The seal of this John de Mohun attached to the letter of the English barons to Pope Boniface VIII. gives his newly adopted shield, with a lion on each side of it, and a eagle displayed above. The inscription round it is :—"S. Johanis de Moun." The woodcut on the opposite page—No. 4—is copied from the original in the Public Record Office.[6] The fact that an eagle displayed occurs on the seals of two different members of the Mohun family, seems almost to indicate that this was their badge or crest.

The Augustinian Priory of Bruton and the Cistercian Abbey of Newenham alike followed the example of Sir John de Mohun by assuming for their arms :—" *Or* a cross engrailed *sable*."[7] The shield borne by his eldest son, Sir John, at the battle of Boroughbridge in 1322, was blazoned :—" *Dor ove 1 croiz engrele de sable ovec 1 label de gul.*"[8] It is remarkable, however, that some of the younger sons adhered to the ancient bearing of their ancestors. Thus the Mohuns of Fleet, who claimed des-

---

[1] "Archæologia," vol. xxxix, p. 423.

[2] Nicolas's "Siege of Carlaverock," p. 159. The reference there given is to Cotton MS. Julius, c. vii., but the seal in question is not tricked in that volume. Sir H. Nicolas must have had some other good authority for his statement.

[3] Hutchins's "History of Dorset" (ed. 1861), vol. i, p. 272.

[4] See Appendix D.

[5] Nicolas's "Siege of Carlaverock."

[6] The engraving of it in "Vetusta Monumenta" is not accurate.

[7] There are some rough woodcuts of the seals of three Abbots of Newenham in Davidson's "History of Newenham Abbey."

[8] "Parliamentary Writs" (ed. Palgrave), vol. ii, part 2, p. 198.

cent from Sir Robert Mohun of Porlock, bore " *Gules*, a dexter arm habited in a maunch *ermine*, the hand *proper* holding a fleur-de-lys *or*, within a bordure *argent*," the bordure being, of course, intended as a mark of cadency. The Mohuns of Aldenham, in Hertfordshire, bore the maunch like them, but without any bordure.[1]

Sir Reginald de Mohun, the fifth son of Sir John, is described as bearing "*de goules ove une maunche d'ermyn*," about the year 1337.[2] His descendants, however, preferred to have the cross engrailed on their shield, and only used the maunch as a crest. When one of them, Sir John Mohun, was created a peer as Baron Mohun of Okehampton, he took as supporters " two lions rampant, guardant, *argent*, crowned with earl's coronets, *or*, the balls, *argent*." [3] The Mohuns of Tavistock bore the cross with a mullet for difference.

Reverting now to the last Lord Mohun of Dunster, who died in 1376, we find that he bore on his seal a cross which we should describe as " lozengy " if we did not otherwise know that it should be described as " engrailed." The inscription is: "SIGILLUM JOHANNIS DE MOUN." The woodcut of it—No. 5—is taken from the seal attached to a deed of the year 1345, preserved among the muniments of Dunster Castle (Box xxiv). There are also at the same place two impressions of the seal of his wife, the Lady Joan, one of which is attached to the receipt given by her to Lady Elizabeth Luttrell, the purchaser of the Castle and Honour of Dunster. This seal shows the arms of Mohun and Burghersh impaled according to the old fashion by being placed side by side on separate shields. The inscription is: "S. Johanne de Mo-un." In a register of Christ Church, Canterbury, now preserved in the British Museum, the arms of this lady are given on one shield, quarterly 1 and 4, Mohun, 2 and 3, Burghersh.[4]

A seal of her daughter Philippa shews the arms of Fitz-Walter—a fesse between two chevronels, impaled in the modern way with those of Mohun—a cross engrailed. The inscription is—" Sigillum Philipp . e . ffitz. wauter." The woodcut—No. 7—is copied from a seal attached to a deed of the year 1398, preserved among the muniments at Dunster Castle. The arms of Mohun, Fitz-Walter, Golafre, and Plantagenet, appear on the monument of the Duchess of York in Westminster Abbey. Though the ancient family of Mohun is now believed to be extinct, several families of the name of Moon or Moone bear as arms either the maunch or the cross engrailed.

APPENDIX B.

THE EARLY CHARTERS OF DUNSTER PRIORY.

Leland states that the Priory of Dunster was founded by William de Moion, the companion of the Conqueror, and his statement has been accepted implicitly by Dugdale and other subsequent writers. Inasmuch however as no original authority has yet been quoted to give the history of the foundation, it seems desirable to print *in extenso* some of the

[1] Heralds' Visitation of Hertfordshire, A.D. 1572.

[2] "Collectanea Topographica et Genealogica," vol. ii, p. 326.

[3] Lysons's "Magna Britannia, Cornwall," p. lxxxiii.

[4] Arundel MS. lxviii, f. 59.

SEALS.

4.
John de Mohun.
d. 1330.

5.
John de Mohun.
d. 1376.

6.
Joan de Mohun.
d. 1404.

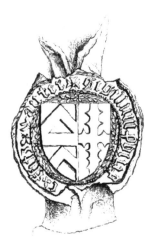

7.
Philippa Fitzwalter.
d. 1431.

earliest charters that bear on the subject. Nos. 1 and 2 are copied from a valuable chartulary of Bath Abbey, preserved among the MSS. of Archbishop Parker in the Library at Corpus Christi College, Cambridge.[1]

1. "Notum sit omnibus catholicæ ecclesiæ fidelibus tam præsentibus quam futuris quia ego Willelmus de Moione, timore Dei compunctus dono et concedo perpetualiter pro salute animæ meæ, regisque Anglorum Willelmi atque omnium antecessorum meorum et successorum ecclesiæ beati Petri de Bathonia et Johanni episcopo ejusdem monasterii et monachis tam præsentibus quam futuris ecclesiam Sancti Georgii de Dunestore, et me ipsum, et decimam ejusdem villæ tam vinearum quam carrucarum, et mercati necnon omnium pecudum, et totam villam Alcume, et omnia sibi pertinentia libere et quiete ab omni servitio, scilicet unam hidam terræ, et dimidiam partem decimæ de Mancheafe, et totam decimam de Bradenude, et omnem decimam de Carentuna quantum mihi inde pertinet, et totam decimam de Niwetuna, et dimidiam decimam de Brunfeld, et totam decimam de Stokelande, et totam de Kilvestune, et duo piscatoria, unum pertinens ad Dunesthorram et aliud ad Carentunam, et totam decimam equarum mearum de moris. Et hæc omnia concedo supradictæ ecclesiæ de Bathonia per consensum uxoris meæ Adelisæ, ut ecclesiam beati Georgii præsul et monachi ejusdem ædificent et exaltent. Hujus beneficii sint etiam testes ex mea parte, Henricus de Port, et Durandus dapifer, et Ogis, et Geoius, et Walterus de Celsui, et Rodbertus Flavus, et Gaufridus et Rodbertus filii mei, et Wilmundus frater meus, et Odo Dealtribus, et Willelmus de Hermodvilla, et Rodbertus filius Ricardi, et Hunfridus de Petreponto, et Radulfus filius Osberni, et Herebertus de Kent, et Ricardus Flavus, et Picotus, et Engelram filius Ivelini, et Alexander de Perceio. Hi sunt ex parte episcopi, scilicet Girenuardus mo-[nachus?], et Girebertus archidiaconus, et Dunstanus sacerdos, et Gillebertus sacerdos, et Willelmus clericus, et Adelardus dapifer, et Turaldus, et Sabianus."

2. "Teobaldus dei gratia Cantuariensis archiepiscopus Anglorum primas et Apostolicæ Sedis legatus, omnibus sanctæ matris ecclesiæ fidelibus per episcopatum Bathoniensem constitutis salutem Ea quæ a venerabilibus fratribus nostris episcopis seu principibus ecclesiis et locis religiosis in elemosinam misericordiæ intuitu conferuntur, ut eisdem locis inconvulsa et inmutilata præserventur merito sunt auctoritatis munimine roboranda. Eaque ratione inducti, inspectis etiam cartis dominorum fundi et honoris de Dunestorra et confirmatione sanctæ memoriæ Anselmi Cantuariensis archiepiscopi, et illustris regis Anglorum Willelmi Ruffi, quæ ecclesiam de Dunestorra cum omnibus ad eam pertinentibus, terris, decimis, et capellis, in liberam elemosinam monachis Bathoniensibus esse concessam et datam astruebant, eisdem monachis confirmamus ecclesiam prænominatam cum terris et decimationibus de Karentona et Stochelande et Kelvetona, et Anelhame, et Stantona, et dimidiam decimam Menehafe, et dimidiam decimam Exeforde, et cæteris eis jure adjacentibus et

præsentis scripti patrocinio corroboramus. Auctoritate itaque quâ fungimur inhibemus ne quis ecclesiam Bathoniensem vel monachos in ea jugem Deo famulatum exhibentes, super æcclesia de Dunestorra quæ eis in liberam elemosinam auctoritate sancti Anselmi Cantuariensis archiepiscopi confirmata est et regiis cartis corroborata temere præsumat inquietare vel ullam attemptet inferre molestiam. Quod si quis attemptaverit injuste Dei omnipotentis indignationem et nostram se noverit incursurum. Valete."

John de Villula, to whom the former of these charters is addressed, was Bishop of Bath from 1090 to 1122, and William Rufus died in 1100. It may, therefore, be referred to the decade of years between 1090 and 1100. The modern names of the places mentioned are:—Dunster, Minchead, Broadwood, Carhampton, Newton, Broomfield, Stockland, Kilton, Stanton, and Exford. Durand and Ogis were tenants under William de Moion at the time of the Domesday Survey.

3. "Willelmus de Moion hominibus suis tam his qui sunt quam his qui futuri sunt salutem. Sciatis me acceptam habere donationem quam avus meus et pater meus fecerunt ecclesiæ de Dunestore, scilicet totam villam de Alecumbe cum omnibus pertinentiis suis liberam et quietam ab omni servitio, et decimam totius villæ de Dunestore tam vinearum quam carrucarum et molendinorum et mercati, necnon etiam omnium pecudum et virgulti, et dimidiam partem decimæ de Manehafda, et totam decimam de Bradwude, et omnem decimam de Carentome, et totam decimam de Niwetona, et dimidiam decimam de Branfeld, et totam decimam de Stocland, et ecclesiam de Chelvetune cum omnibus pertinentiis suis et decimis, et duo piscatoria, unum pertinens ad Dunestore, et aliud ad Charentunam, et totam decimam equarum mearum de Moris, et decimam de Exford, terram etiam de Aseleam *(sic)* quam pater meus dedit pro salute animæ fratris mei Radulfi de Moyon, iii. etiam ferlingos terræ apud Nordcume liberos et quietos ab omni servitio pro salute animæ meæ et patris mei eidem ecclesiæ concedo et monachis in ea Deo serventibus. His testibus, Hewano de Mouum et Ricardo clerico fratre ejus, Radulfo de Piron, Ricardo de Langheham, Hugone Norreis, Radulfo capellano, et Johanne capellano, Ricardo Russe, et multis aliis."

This charter, of which an early copy is preserved among the muniments at Dunster Castle (Box xvi, No. 7), may safely be referred to the third William de Moion, the son of the Earl of Somerset, as the names of the witnesses correspond closely with those of some of the witnesses to his different charters to Bruton Priory. Ivan de Moion and Richard his brother, were sons of the Earl of Somerset.

4. "Omnibus Christi fidelibus præsens scriptum visuris vel audituris Johannes de Mohun miles, Dominus de Donestorre salutem in Domino sempiternam. Noveritis me cartam Domini Reginaldi de Mohun antecessoris mei inspexisse sub tenore qui sequitur.

Reginaldus de Mohun universis hominibus suis præsentibus et futuris salutem. Sciatis me acceptam habere donationem quam pater meus et antecessores mei fecerunt ecclesiæ Sancti Georgii de Donestorre et monachis ibidem Deo servientibus, scilicet totam villam de Alecumba cum omnibus pertinentiis suis liberam et quietam ab omni servitio, et decimam totius villæ de Donestorre tam vinearum quam carucarum et molendinorum et mercati, necnon etiam omnium pecudum et virgulti, et dimidiam partem decimæ de dominio de Mennehevede, et totam decimam de Brodwode, et totam decimam de Carampton, et totam decimam de Nyweton, et dimidiam partem decimæ de Bromfeld, et totam decimam de Stoclond, et ecclesiam de Kelveton cum omnibus pertinentiis suis et decimis, et duo piscatoria unum pertinens ad Donestorre, et aliud ad Carampton, et totam decimam equarum mearum de Moris, et decimam de Exefond, terram etiam de Anellam quam Willelmus de Mohun dedit pro salute animæ Radulfi de Moion, tres etiam ferlingos terræ apud Northecumbe liberos et quietos ab omni servitio in puram et perpetuam elemosinam. Ut hoc ratum et firmum habeatur imperpetuum sigilli mei munimine præsens scriptum roboravi et confirmavi. Hiis testibus, Roberto capellano de Castello, Radulfo capellano de Dunstorre, Roberto clerico de Mennehevede, Willelmo clerico de Dunstorre, Johanne de Regny, Willelmo de Punchardon, Roberto filio Roberti, Willelmo de Pentir, Roberto Bonzam, Willelmo de Kytenore, Hugone de Avele, Ricardo de Holne, Radulfo le Tort, Willelmo Vinetar, Roberto Coule, Ricardo Russel et multis aliis.

Inspexi insuper aliud scriptum ejusdem Reginaldi in quo continetur quod idem Reginaldus concessit pro se et heredibus suis Priori de Donestorre et monachis et eorum successoribus decimam bestiam porcorum suorum de Donestorre, Caramptone, et Kelveton nomine decimæ, secundum quod contigerit eas capi vivas vel mortuas. Quas quidem concessiones et confirmationes pro me et heredibus meis in omnibus ratifico et confirmo imperpetuum per præsentem. In cujus rei testimonium sigillum meum præsenti cartæ est appensum. Hiis testibus, Dominis Johanne de Meriet, Andrea Loterel et Symone de Roges, militibus, Johanne de la Croys et Rogero Arundel, Johanne de Hiwys, Vincentio de Stoke, et multis aliis. Datum apud Whycheforde die Sancti Laurentii, Anno regni Regis Edwardi vicesimo septimo." [1]

5. The Prior and Convent of Bath undertake to provide for the celebration of masses at Dunster for the soul of John eldest son of Reginald de Moyon, A.D. 1254.[2]

6. Thomas, Prior of Bath, grants to the Prior and Monks of Dunster the Church of Carhampton, with its appurtenances, to be held of him and his successors for ever on payment of 20 marks a year, of which half-a-mark is to be paid to his chamberlain on the Feast of St. Carentoc, and half-a-mark on the anniversary of St. Martin.[3]

7. Confirmation by John de Mooun, Lord of Dunster, of the grants of his ancestors to the Church of Dunster, 15 Edward III.[4]

8. Confirmation by Pope Honorius.[5]

9. John de Mohun grants to the Church of Dunster a yearly rent of 8s. 6d., common of pasture on Croydon, pasture on Grobefast, and twelve cartloads of wood from Marshwood Park, etc. Friday, after the Feast of St. Peter ad Vincula, 16 Edward III.[6]

10. Confirmation of No. 9 by John de Mohun, in French. The Feast of St. Barnabas, 33 Edward III.[7]

---

[1] Dunster Castle Muniments. Box xvi, No. 4.
[2] Box xvi, No. 1.
[3] Box xvi, No. 3.
[4] Patent Roll, 20 Edward III, p. 2, m.
30, printed in Dugdale's "Monasticon," vol. iv, pp. 201-202.
[5] Dunster Castle Mun. Box xvi, No. 2.
[6] Box xvi, No. 3.
[7] Box xvi, No. 6.

The following list of the Priors of Dunster, although obviously imperfect, is the fullest that has yet appeared :—

Martin, in the later part of the reign of Henry III.[1]
Robert de Sutton, appointed in 1332.[2]
John Hervey, in 1376.[3]
William Bristow, in 1412.[4]
John Henton, appointed in 1425.[5]
Richard, in 1449.[6]
John Abingdon, in 1489.[7]
Thomas Brown, in 1499.[8]
John Griffith, in 1535.[9]

Appendix C.

Dunster in the Reign of Henry II.

The following are the most important notices of the Honour of Dunster that occur in the unpublished Pipe Rolls of the reign of Henry II:—

A.D. 1162. "De scutagio Willelmi de Moun. In thesauro £22. Et in pardon per breve Regis [13s. 4d.]"

A.D. 1168. "Willelmus de Moiun reddit compotum de 41 marcis pro 41 militibus de veteri feoffamento. In thesauro 37 marcæ. Et debet 2 marcas de veteri feoffamento. Idem debet de novo 5 marcas et dimidiam pro 5 militibus et dimidio."

A.D. 1169. "Willelmus de Moun reddit compotum de 2 marcis pro militibus veteris feoffamenti. In pardon per breve Regis Hugoni de Gundovill 2 marcæ. Et quietus est. Idem debet 5 marcas et dimidiam de novo feoffamento."

A.D. 1176. "Willelmus de Moiun debet 5 marcas et dimidiam de novo feoffamento. Sed requirendi (sic) sunt ab Episcopo Wintoniæ qui custodit terram et heredem."

A.D. 1177. "Ricardus, Episcopus Wintoniæ reddit compotum de 5 marcis et dimidia de novo feoffamento de honore Willelmi de Moiun. In thesauro 5 marcæ, et quietus est."

"Vicecomes reddit compotum . . . . de 18 marcis de auxilio terræ Willelmi de Moyona."

"Terra Willelmi de Moun. Ricardus, Wintoniæ episcopus, Jordanus de Turri clericus ejus, et Willelmus Poherius pro eo, reddit compotum de £22 1s. 8d. de veteri firma maneriorum ejusdem honoris de dimidio anno, et de £44 3s. 4d. de hoc anno. Summa £66 5s. In thesauro £34 14s. 8d. Et in decimis constitutis monachis de Sancto Georgio de Dunestora £2 14s. de anno et dimidio. Et in defalta molendini de Carletona (Carhampton) 15s de prædicto termino. Et in wasto villæ de Dunestora 16s. 6d. de prædicto termino. Et in defalta thelonii et molendini ejusdem villæ £5. Et in emendatione

---

[1] Dunster Castle Muniments. Box xvii, No. 1. Box viii, No. 2.
[2] Dugdale's "Monasticon," vol. ii. p. 259.
[3] Dunster Castle Muniments. Box i, No. 4.
[4] Dunster Church Book. f. 44.
[5] Harl. MS. 6966, f. 156. It has been

erroneously stated that he was appointed to succeed John Telesford, who was really Prior of Bath, not of Dunster.
[6] Dunster Castle Muniments.
[7] Harl. MS., 6966. f. 147.
[8] Register of Bishop King, at Wells.
[9] Valor Ecclesiasticus.

molendini et operatione vineæ, et liberatione servientium, et aliis minutis exitibus £4 4s. 9½d. Et in liberatione Willelmi de Moiun £18, de eodem termino per breve Regis.

Idem reddit compotum de £19 de bladis et vino de dominio vendito. In thesauro liberavit, et quietus est.

Idem reddit compotum de £2 7s. 1d. de prædicto termino de exitu de Toteberga quam Willelmus de Moiun habuit in custodia. In thesauro liberavit, et quietus est.

Et reddit compotum de £4 19s 4d de prædicto termino de exitu de Wicheforda quod idem Willelmus habuit in custodia. In thesauro liberavit, et quietus est."

A.D. 1178. "De auxilio ad maritandam filiam Regis. Episcopus Wintoniæ reddit compotum de dimidia marca de honore Willelmi de Moiun de novo feoffamento."

There is no record of any payment having been received by the Exchequer by way of relief or primer seisin from the Honour of Dunster between 1156 and 1176, and so it may fairly be assumed that one person, William de Moiun, held the property continuously through that period. The entry which states that the Bishop of Winchester had the custody of the land and of the heir in 1176, is somewhat perplexing. It would at first sight seem to show that William de Moiun had recently died leaving an heir under age. In such an event the custody of the land and of the minor would, in the ordinary course, have fallen into the hands of the King, who would have been free to deal with them according to his own pleasure. The entry on the Pipe Roll for 1177 indicates that the heir was another William de Moiun, but it is difficult to understand how any one of that name could have been a minor at that date, inasmuch as both William the son of the Earl of Somerset, and William the son and heir of William de Moiun, the husband of Godehold, were old enough to appear as witnesses to important charters during the lifetime of their respective fathers. And moreover some of the charters of William de Moiun the husband of Lucy were attested by his son and heir who was also called William.[1] The Honour of Dunster was, we know, again escheated to the crown at some time between 1190 and 1195, and if William de Moiun the husband of Lucy was under age in 1166 he could scarcely have had a son of full age, even by the latest of these dates—1195. The hypothesis of a minority in 1176 seems to require that two different Williams should have appeared as witnesses to charters while still under age.

On the other hand it is possible that the King may have had cause to distrust the loyalty or good faith of the heir of William de Moiun in 1176, and may, consequently, have deputed the Bishop of Winchester to exact prompt payment of a year's revenue by way of relief or primer seisin. The restitution to the heir of about one third of the gross receipts after the land had been in the custody of the Bishop for a year and a half seems to favour this hypothesis. The main objection to it is that it does not satisfactorily explain how the heir himself, if of full age, came to be placed under the custody of the Bishop.

---

[1] See "Notes on some early Charters of Bruton Priory" in a later part of this volume.

APPENDIX D.

The Heir of Reginald De Mohun.

The ordinary books of reference so consistently state that the second Reginald de Mohun of Dunster was succeeded by his eldest son, that it seems desirable to collect in one place some of the strongest proofs that he was, on the contrary, succeeded by his grandson in 1257. They are as follows :—

1. Reginald de Mohun in 1254 established a mass at Dunster for the soul of his eldest son John, who was then deceased.[1]

2. The following passage occurs among the "Parliamentary Writs" of 1277 :—"Johannes de Mohun recognovit servitium trium feodorum militis pro terris quæ fuerunt Reginaldi de Mohun, avi sui."[2]

3. In the "Placita de quo warranto" it is distinctly stated that John de Mohun, who was a minor in the reign of Edward I, was the great-grandson of Reginald, the founder of Newenham.[3]

4. At an inquisition held at Odyham, 16 May, 1327, it was found that John de Mohun, who was then over forty years of age, was "cousin" and heir of Reginald de Mohun, being the son of John, who was the son of John, who was the son of the said Reginald.[4]

5. The genealogy of the Mohun family, given in the Register of Newenham Abbey, states that John de Mohun, who married Ada Tiptoft, was the third of that name.[5]

APPENDIX E.

Pedigree of the Mohun Family.

The following account of the Mohuns of Dunster, written by a monk of Newenham in the middle of the fourteenth century, deserves a place here, because it has been very incorrectly given in the large edition of Dugdale's "Monasticon," and also in Oliver's "Monasticon" of the Diocese of Exeter.[6]

"Alicia de Moun quarta filia Willemi Brewer ad cujus participationem inter quinque filias heredes dicti Willelmi Brewer cecidit mancrium de Axeminster cum pertinentiis. Quæ Alicia prædicta nupta fuit domino Reginaldo de Moun domino de Dunstorre in qua procreavit Reginaldum de Moun heredem ipsorum Reginaldi et Aliciæ ; et ille Reginaldus filius Reginaldi prædicti fundavit Abbatiam de Nyweham in manerio de Axeminster anno gratiæ mccxlvi, octavo idus Januarii die dominica, luna xv., epacta prima, concurrente prima, sub papa Innocentio quarto, regnante in Anglia Henrico Christianissimo Rege filio Johannis Regis ; regnante in Francia Lodowyco filio Lodowyci filii regis Philippi ; vacante imperio

---

[1] Dunster Castle Muniments, Box xvi, No. 1.
[2] Vol. i, p. 202.
[3] Oliver's "Monasticon Dioecesis Exon," p. 365.
[4] Inq. post mortem 1 Edw. III, No. 51.
[5] See Appendix E.
[6] From the original in Arundel MS., xvii. f. 38.

Romano, Frederico deposito ; gubernante ecclesiam Cantuariensem Bonefacio, ecclesiam vero Exoniensem Magistro Richardo Albo de eadem civitate Exoniensi nato ; abbatizante apud Bellum Locum dompno Acio de Gysortis, cum dicta domus Belli Loci esset quadraginta duorum annorum et dimidii ; abbatizante apud Forda domino Adamo. Qui supradictus Reginaldus de Moun habuit duas uxores, scilicet Hawysiam de Moun et Isabellam Basset. Et in dicta Hawysia procreavit unum filium nomine Johannem heredem ipsius. Qui Johannes habuit unum filium nomine Johannem heredem ipsius. Qui Johannes prædictus in Gasconia moriebatur ; cujus cor jacet coram magno altare inter sepulchrum Reginaldi de Moun et Willelmi de Moun domini de Moun Otery de Nyweham, corpus vero apud Brutonam. Qui Johannes de Moun heres prædicti Johannis habuit unum filium nomine Johannem heredem ipsius. Qui Johannes de Moun secundus habuit unum filium heredem nomine Johannem. Qui Johannes modo tertius fuit in custodia domini Regis in tempore quo justiciarii domini Regis itinerantes in Devonia sederunt. Qui Johannes de Moun tertius sumpsit uxorem Audam Typetot in qua procreavit septem filios et unam filiam quorum nomina patent. Idem Johannes de Moun tertius mutavit arma antiqua eorum qui solebant portare manicam erminatam. Iste Johannes tertius portavit scutum aureum cum nigra cruce engrellata.

Filii Johannis de Moun tertii
{
Johannes, heres ipsius,
Robertus, dominus de Purloc,
Baldewynus, rector de Wyccheford,
Paganus,
Reginaldus miles,
Patricius,
Hervicus et Laurentius.
}

Filia supradicti Johannis de Moun tertii Elianora nupta Radulfo de Wyleton. Johannes de Moun quartus habuit unum filium heredem ejus et duas filias pro data. Filius dicti Johannis quarti Johannes heres ejusdem. Filiæ dicti Johannis quarti Margareta nupta Johanni de Carru, Elizabetha quæ moriebatur sine exitu. Dominus Johannes de Moun quartus moriebatur in Scocia per plurimos annos ante Johannem tertium patrem suum, et filius ejus et heres Johannes modo quintus post mortem avi sui fuit in custodia Domini Henrici de Burghwash Lincolniensis Episcopi. Qui Johannes quintus sumpsit uxorem Johannam filiam domini Bartholomæi de Burghwasch fratris dicti episcopi Lincolniensis."

The following genealogical tables scarcely require any explanation. That of the Mohuns of Dunster is based on original authorities already quoted in this paper. That of the Mohuns of Ham is based on Hutchins's "History of Dorset" (ed. Shipp) and on a pedigree from the Plea Rolls given in "Collectanea Topographica et Genealogica," vol. i, p. 140. That of the Mohuns of Fleet is based on Hutchins's "History of Dorset," and family papers in the possession of the Rev. J. Maxwell Lyte. That of the Mohuns of Cornwall is based on the Visitations of Cornwall and Devon in 1620, printed by the Harleian Society, on notices in Hamilton Rogers's "Monumental Effigies in Devon," in Westcote's "Devonshire," in the "Topographer and Genealogist," and in the "Gentleman's Magazine," and on family papers in the possession of G. F. Luttrell, Esq. That of the Mohuns of Tavistock is based on the "Visitation of Devon" 1620.

PEDIGREE OF THE MOHUNS OF DUNSTER.

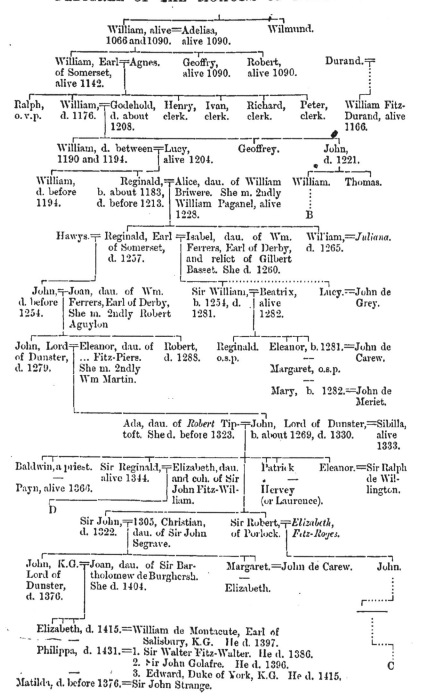

William, alive=Adelisa,
1066 and 1090. alive 1090.   Wilmund.

William, Earl=Agnes.   Geoffry,   Robert,   Durand.⊤
of Somerset,   alive 1090. alive 1090.
alive 1142.

Ralph,   William,=Godehold,   Henry,   Ivan,   Richard,   Peter,   William Fitz-
o.v.p.   d. 1176. | d. about   clerk.   clerk. clerk.   clerk.   Durand, alive
                  | 1208.   1166.

William, d. between=Lucy,   Geoffrey.   John,
1190 and 1194. | alive 1204.   d. 1221.

William,   Reginald,=Alice, dau. of William   William.   Thomas.
d. before   b. about 1183, | Briwere. She m. 2ndly
1194.   d. before 1213. | William Paganel, alive
                             | 1228.   B

Hawys.⊤ Reginald, Earl=Isabel, dau. of Wm.   Wil'iam,=Juliana.
        of Somerset, | Ferrers, Earl of Derby, d. 1265.
        d. 1257. | and relict of Gilbert
                       | Basset. She d. 1260.

John,=Joan, dau. of Wm.   Sir William,=Beatrix,   Lucy.=John de
d. before | Ferrers, Earl of Derby, b. 1254, d. | alive   Grey.
1254. | She m. 2ndly Robert   1281. | 1282.
          | Aguylon

John, Lord=Eleanor, dau. of   Robert,   Reginald.   Eleanor, b. 1281.=John de
of Dunster, | ... Fitz-Piers. d. 1288.   o.s.p.   Carew.
d. 1279. | She m. 2ndly   Margaret, o.s.p.
            | Wm Martin.
                                            Mary, b. 1282.=John de
                                                            Meriet.

            Ada, dau. of Robert Tip-=John, Lord of Dunster,=Sibilla,
            toft. She d. before 1323. | b. about 1269, d. 1330. | alive
                                                                  1333.

Baldwin, a priest.   Sir Reginald,=Elizabeth, dau.   Patrick   Eleanor.=Sir Ralph
—   alive 1344. | and coh. of Sir .—   de Wil-
Payn, alive 1366. | John Fitz-Wil-   Hervey   lington.
                                  | liam.   (or Laurence).
D

Sir John,=1305, Christian,   Sir Robert,=Elizabeth,
d. 1322. | dau. of Sir John   of Porlock. | Fitz-Royes.
         | Segrave.

John, K.G.=Joan, dau. of Sir Bar-   Margaret.=John de Carew.   John.
Lord of | tholomew de Burghersh.
Dunster, | She d. 1404.   Elizabeth.
d. 1376.

Elizabeth, d. 1415.=William de Montacute, Earl of
                     Salisbury, K.G. He d. 1397.
Philippa, d. 1431.=1. Sir Walter Fitz-Walter. He d. 1386.
                    2. Sir John Golafre. He d. 1396.
                    3. Edward, Duke of York, K.G. He d. 1415.
Matilda, d. before 1376.=Sir John Strange.

C

PEDIGREE OF THE MOHUNS OF HAM MOHUN.

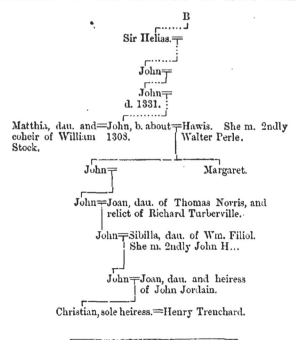

B

Sir Helias.

John

John
d. 1331.

Matthia, dau. and = John, b. about = Hawis. She m. 2ndly
coheir of William   1303.   Walter Perle.
Stock.

John   Margaret.

John = Joan, dau. of Thomas Norris, and
       relict of Richard Turberville.

John = Sibilla, dau. of Wm. Filiol.
       She m. 2ndly John H...

John = Joan, dau. and heiress
       of John Jordain.

Christian, sole heiress. = Henry Trenchard.

PEDIGREE OF THE MOHUNS OF TAVISTOCK.

Thomas Mohun of Tavistock, (said to have
been son of Lawrence Mohun, son of John,
Lord Mohun of Dunster, but more probably
his great-grandson.)

Thomas.

Thomas, Serjeant-at-Arms = Agnes, dau. of William Amidis. She m.
to Henry VIII.   2, Thomas Stoford, 3, John Charles, 4,
                            William Abbot, of Hartland.

Thomas. = Joan, dau. of William
          Kedley, alias Pointer.

Grace, dau. of = Thomas. = Joan   Charles,   Joan. = 1. Richard Edgcumbe.
Richard Single-   da. of   o.s.p.   2. Christopher Wo-
ton.   John   bridge.
                          Harris.   3. Erasmus Drew.
                                                           4. Alexander Mains.

Thomas, b. about 1600.   Frances, = William   Deonis. = 1. Ralph Taylor.
                          b. 1598.   Moore.   2. John Elliot.
William, b. about 1607.
                          Deonis, b. 1601.   Dorothy. = William Carden.
Peter, b. about 1609.
                          Alice, b. 1618.   Eleanor. = 1. Thomas Harris.
Ellis, b. about 1615.   2. William Grafton.
                                                 Ann,
Edward, b. about 1617.   o.s.p.

PEDIGREE OF THE MOHUNS OF BAUNTON AND FLEET.

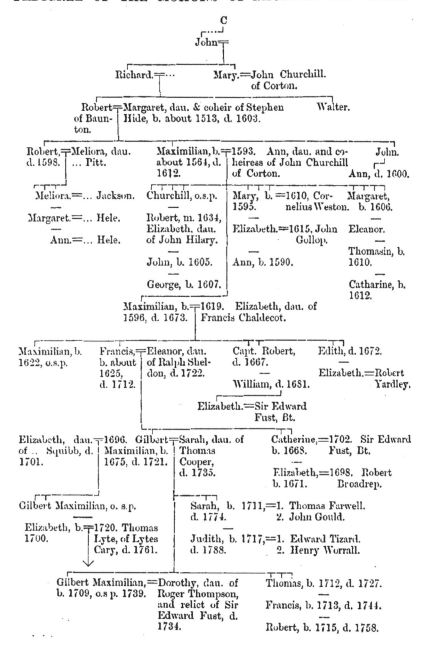

C

John=

Richard.=...   Mary.=John Churchill. of Corton.

Robert=Margaret, dau. & coheir of Stephen   Walter.
of Baun-| Hide, b. about 1513, d. 1603.
ton.

Robert,=Meliora, dau.   Maximilian, b.=1593. Ann, dau. and co-   John.
d. 1598. | ... Pitt.   about 1564, d. | heiress of John Churchill
     1612.   of Corton.   Ann, d. 1600.

Meliora.=... Jackson.   Churchill, o.s.p.   Mary, b. =1610, Cor-   Margaret,
     1595.   nelius Weston.   b. 1606.

Margaret.=... Hele.   Robert, m. 1634,
     Elizabeth, dau.   Elizabeth.=1615, John   Eleanor.

Ann.=... Hele.   of John Hilary.   Gollop.
                 Thomasin, b.
     John, b. 1605.   Ann, b. 1590.   1610.

     George, b. 1607.   Catharine, b.
                       1612.

Maximilian, b.=1619. Elizabeth, dau. of
1596, d. 1673. | Francis Chaldecot.

Maximilian, b.   Francis,=Eleanor, dau.   Capt. Robert,   Edith, d. 1672.
1622, o.s.p.   b. about | of Ralph Shel-   d. 1667.
     1625, | don, d. 1722.   Elizabeth.=Robert
     d. 1712.   William, d. 1681.   Yardley.

     Elizabeth.=Sir Edward
     Fust, Bt.

Elizabeth, dau.=1696. Gilbert=Sarah, dau. of   Catherine,=1702. Sir Edward
of .. Squibb, d. | Maximilian, b. | Thomas   b. 1668.   Fust, Bt.
1701.   1675, d. 1721. | Cooper,
     d. 1735.   Elizabeth,=1698. Robert
            b. 1671.   Broadrep.

Gilbert Maximilian, o. s.p.   Sarah, b. 1711,=1. Thomas Farwell.
     d. 1774.   2. John Gould.

Elizabeth, b.=1720. Thomas   Judith, b. 1717,=1. Edward Tizard.
1700. | Lyte, of Lytes   d. 1788.   2. Henry Worrall.
     Cary, d. 1761.

Gilbert Maximilian,=Dorothy, dau. of   Thomas, b. 1712, d. 1727.
b. 1709, o.s p. 1739.   Roger Thompson,
     and relict of Sir   Francis, b. 1713, d. 1744.
     Edward Fust, d.
     1734.   Robert, b. 1715, d. 1758.

Brass of John and Ann Mohun, at Lanteglos-by-Fowey, co. Cornwall, A.D. 1508.

To face p. 37.

PEDIGREE OF THE MOHUNS OF CO. CORNWALL.

┌─D.

John.=Joan, dau. of ... St. Aubyn.

Thomas.=Elizabeth, dau. and heiress of Richard Hayre.

William.=Joan, dau. of ... Cavell.

William.=Isabel, dau. and eventual coheir of Sir Hugh Courtenay.

John, d. 1508.=Ann, dau. of Richard Goode, d. 1508.

Reginald.=Joan, dau. of Sir   John,   Isabel.=John Nicolls.
Wm. Trevanion.   o.s.p.

Joan.=... Rosuggan.

Elizabeth,=Sir Wil-=Ann (or   Hugh, o.s.p.   Isabel.=Matthew Trewin-
dau. and   liam d.   Margaret)   —   ward.
heiress of   1587.   dau. of Wil-   Reginald, o.   Jane.=John Teffry.
Sir John   liam Res-   s.p.   —
Horsey.   kymer.   Ann.=Francis Belot.
   John, o.s.p.   Honor.

Edith.=Sir   William.=Honor, dau. and   William.   Jane.=Sir John
d.   Ralph   coheir of Robert   Speccot.
1628.   Hor-   Trencreke.   Thomas.
   sey.   —   Bridget.=Sir
   Nathaniel,=Jane, dau.   Philip, o.s.p.   Arundel,   Tho-
   1624.   of Thos.   —   o.s.p.   mas
   Trefusis.   Thomas b.   Arun-
   about 1604.   del

1, Mary, dau.=Sir Reginald,=2, Philippa,=3, Dorothy,
of Sir Henry   Kt. and Bart.,   dau. of John   dau. of John
Killigrew.   d. 1637.   Hele.   Chudleigh.

William, o.s.p.   Reginald.   Dorothy.   Penelope, b 1609.
1613.   Ferdinand.   Bridget.=1636, John   Margaret, b. 1619.
   Nicholls.
   George.

Sir John, created=Cordelia, dau. of Sir John   Elizabeth.=John Trelawney.
Lord Mohun,   Stanhope, and relict of   —
d. 1644.   Sir Roger Aston.   Penelope.=William Drew.
   d. 1637.

John,   Warwick,=Catherine,   Charles,   Cordelia.=John Harris.
Lord   Lord   dau. of ...   b. 1622,   —
Mohun,   Mohun,   Welles.   d. 1642.   Theophila.=James Campbell.
o.s.p.   d. 1655.   Philippa, b, 1623.
   Philadelphia, d. 1733.

Charles,=Philippa, dau. of Arthur, Earl   James,   Isabel.=Samuel
Lord   of Anglesey. She m. 2ndly   d. 1699.   Maddock,
Mohun.   Wm. Coward, and d. 1714.   d. 1713.

1. Charlotte,=Charles, =2. Elizabeth, dau. of   Elizabeth,   Christian.=Nicholas
dau. of James   Lord   Dr. Thomas Law-   d. 1709.   Docton.
Mainwaring.   Mohun,   rence, and relict of   Ann, d.=John
   d. 1712.   Col. Griffith. She m.   1772.   Fownes.
   3rdly Charles Mor-   ↓
Charles, b. 1692, o.s.p.   daunt, and d. 1725.

Part II.

The name of Luttrell first occurs in history in the later part of the twelfth century. Like the generality of ancient surnames, it has been spelt in many different ways, the most ordinary forms being Loterel, Luterel, and Luttrell. The fact that a certain Robert Lotrel was in Normandy in 1195, rather favours the theory that the family was of Norman origin.[1] However this may be, it is not from him but from his contemporary, Geoffrey Luttrell, that the Luttrells of Dunster Castle trace their descent. During the absence of Richard I in Palestine, this Geoffrey Luttrell took part in the unsuccessful rebellion of John, Earl of Mortain, and was consequently deprived of his estates in the county of Nottingham.[2] He was reinstated, however, on the accession of the Earl of Mortain to the English throne, and from that time until his death he seems to have been constantly employed in the King's service.[3] In 1201, he was appointed one of the overseers of the expenses incurred in the enclosure of the royal park of Bolsover.[4] In 1204, he was sent into Ireland with a recommendatory letter to the archbishops and bishops, and received £10 for his maintenance.[5] In the following year he went to Poictiers in charge of the King's treasure, and in 1210, he held the responsible office of paymaster of the navy.[6] In 1215, he

[1] "Magni Rotuli Scaccarii Normanniæ" (ed. Stapleton), vol. i, p. cxxx. It is almost needless to remark that the so-called Roll of Battle Abbey, in which the name of Lotterell appears, has no real historical value.

[2] Thoroton's "History of Nottinghamshire," p. 62. Pipe Rolls, 6 and 7 Richard I, co. Notts.

[3] Thoroton, p. 63. Pipe Roll, 1 John.

"Rotuli de Oblatis," vol. i, pp. 51, 460, 552, 556, 565.

[4] Pipe Roll, 2 John, co. Notts. Charter Roll, 2 John, m. 7.

[5] "Rotuli de Liberate," p. 83. Patent Roll, 6 John, m 6.

[6] Close Roll, 7 John, m. 5. "Rotuli de Liberate," pp. 176, 179, 185, 188, 194, 202, 206, 208, 213, 227-230.

was sent on an embassy to Pope Innocent III, partly to explain the arrangement that had been made about the dower of Queen Berengaria, and partly to denounce the barons who had extorted Magna Charta from the reluctant king. In one of these commissions he is styled "*nobilis vir.*"[1] He received several grants of land from his royal patron, but the real foundation of the future wealth of the Luttrell family was laid by his marriage with Frethesant, daughter and coheiress of William Paganel.[2] Although this lady's father only belonged to a younger branch of the Paganel family, she received as her inheritance from him, seven knights' fees and a half, in the counties of York, Nottingham, and Lincoln.[3]

Sir Geoffrey Luttrell appears to have died on his journey to Rome in 1216, leaving a widow and a son named Andrew, who was under age at the time. The widow, Frethesant, soon married a second husband, Henry de Newmarch, and the custody of the heir was granted to Philip Marc, a man of some importance in the midland counties, who had been one of the confidential advisers of King John.[4] As might have been expected, the young Andrew Luttrell was made to marry a daughter of his guardian, Petronilla by name.[5] He had livery of seisin in 1229, when he succeeded not only to the estates of his father and mother, but also to the whole inheritance of his grandfather William Paganel, whose second daughter Isabella had died without issue.[6] A few months later, he unexpectedly received a considerable accession of property on the death of his third cousin, Maurice de Gaunt, the heir of the elder branch of the Paganel family.[7]

It has already been remarked that Dunster Castle has only once passed by sale from one family to another since the Norman Conquest. The manor of East Quantockshead,

[1] Rymer's "Fœdera," vol. i, pp. 137-140.
[2] Close Roll, 7 John, m. 6. Fine Rolls, 5 and 6 John. Pipe Rolls 13 and 15 John, co. Warwick. Patent Roll, 17 John, m. 18.
[3] Pipe Roll, 13 John.
[4] "Excerpta e Rotulis Finium," vol. i, pp. 9, 83. "Testa de Nevill." Close Rolls 2 Henry III, p. 2, m. 8, and 3 Henry III, m. 7. Pipe Roll, 3 Henry III, co. Warwick.
[5] Close Roll, 2 Henry III, p. i, m. 10,

and r. 2, m. 8. Patent Roll, 3 Henry III, p. 2, m. 2. Dugdale's "Monasticon," vol. vi, p. 877. Petronilla Luttrell presented Robert Luttrell to the living of Bridgeford A.D. 1267. Register of Archbishop Giffard, quoted in Dodsworth's MS.
[6] Close Roll, 14 Henry III, m. 20.
[7] Pipe Roll, 15 Henry III, co. Lincoln. Close Roll 16 Henry III, m. 11. Dugdale's "Baronage," vol. i, p. 725. Dugdale's "Monasticon," vol. vi, p. 878.

nine miles to the east of Dunster, affords a yet more remarkable instance of the continuity of land tenure in England, its present owner, Mr. G. F. Luttrell, being the lineal descendant of Ralph Paganel, who held it in the reign of William the Conqueror. At the time of the Norman invasion, Merlosuen, Sheriff of Lincolnshire, held the manor of Irnham and other estates in that county, several manors in Yorkshire and in Devonshire, and the manors of Stockland, East Quantockshead, East Bagborough, Hewish, and Newhall, in the county of Somerset. Before the year 1085, his estates had fallen into the hands of Ralph Paganel, a Norman, at whose death the greater part of them passed to his eldest son William, the founder of the priory of Drax. William Paganel left issue an only daughter Alice, who married, firstly, Richard de Courcy, and secondly, Robert de Gaunt, brother of Gilbert de Gaunt, Earl of Lincoln. By her second husband this lady had an only daughter Avice, who married Robert, son of Robert Fitz-Harding, and by him had a son Maurice, sometimes called Maurice de Gaunt, and sometimes Maurice Paganel. Though twice married, Maurice de Gaunt left no children, and on his death in 1230, his estates were divided. Those which he had inherited from his father passed to Robert de Gurney, son of his half-sister Eva, whilst those which he had inherited from his mother passed to Andrew Luttrell, whose mother, Frethesant, had been grand-daughter or great-grand-daughter of Alexander, the youngest son of Ralph Paganel the Norman.

The fine paid by Andrew Luttrell for the right of succession, amounted to one hundred marks.[1] In 1243 he paid £55 towards the aid for making the king's eldest son a knight, £25 being charged on the twelve knights' fees and a half of Maurice de Gaunt, and £30 on the fifteen knights' fees of William Paganel of Hooton Paganel.[2] In 1242, he was summoned to perform military service against the French.[3] He was Sheriff of Lincolnshire for about six months, in the thirty-fifth year of Henry III, but in the following year he paid three

[1] See the elaborate paper on "Holy Trinity Priory, York," by Mr. Stapleton, in the York volume of "Proceedings of the Archæological Institute."

[2] Pipe Roll, 38 Henry III, co. York.

[3] Rymer's "Fœdera," vol. i, p. 246.

Brass of Sir Andrew Luttrell, at Irnham, co. Lincoln, A.D. 1390.

To face p. 41.

marks in order to be excused from serving as justiciary, sheriff, bailiff, or juror during the remainder of his life.[1] He also obtained from the King right of free-warren on his father's estates at Gamston and Bridgeford in Nottinghamshire, and right to hold a weekly market at Irnham, the head place of the barony of Maurice de Gaunt.[2] It is probable that he for the most part resided at one or other of these places, and that he transferred the manor of Hooton Paganel to his eldest son Geoffrey during his own life time.[3]

There are at Dunster Castle three small undated deeds by which Andrew Luttrell granted the manor of East Quantockshead with the advowson of that church to his younger son Alexander and his heirs in tail, on condition that they should render yearly a pair of gilt spurs or 6d. at Whitsuntide.[4] This grant was confirmed by Geoffrey Luttrell, and in October 1269, Sir Roger de Somery, son of Maurice de Gaunt's widow, released all his right in East Quantockshead to Alexander Luttrell.[5] Thus was established the Somersetshire branch of the Luttrell family.

Andrew Luttrell died in 1269, and was succeeded by his eldest son Geoffrey already mentioned.

There is no need, however, in this place to follow the history of the main line any further. It will suffice to say that the Luttrells held the barony of Irnham until 1417, when Sir Geoffrey Luttrell died without male issue. The inheritance passed through successive heiresses to the families of Hilton, Thimelby, Conquest, and Arundell, and the Lord Clifford, who sold the manor of Irnham a few years ago, was the direct representative of Andrew Luttrell and of Ralph Paganel. There is in the parish church of Irnham a monument, which may be that of Geoffrey Luttrell, who died about the year 1269, and a very fine sepulchral brass of his great-grandson, Sir Andrew Luttrell, who died in 1390. But to the artist and to the antiquary, by far the most interesting memorial

[1] Thoroton's "History of Nottinghamshire," p. 63.

[2] Charter Rolls, 30 Henry III, m. 6, and 36 Henry III, m. 10.

[3] Patent Roll (Gascony), 37 and 38 Henry III, p. 2, m. 8.

[4] Box xxii, No. 1.

[5] Ibid. A translation of Geoffrey Luttrell's charter is given by Mr. Stapleton p. 143.

of the Luttrells of Irnham is the famous Psalter, which
was illuminated for a third Sir Geoffrey Luttrell about
the year 1330, and which now belongs to Mr. Weld, of
Lulworth Castle.[1]

Alexander Luttrell, of East Quantockshead, held land
at Hickling in Nottinghamshire as well as in his own
county.[2] In 1266 he received from the King the custody
of the person of his elder brother, who had lost the use of
his reason.[3] Sir Geoffrey Luttrell died about four years
later, and Alexander being thus released from the duty
of looking after him, embarked for the Holy Land in the
retinue of Prince Edward.[4] He died either in the
Crusade of 1270 or very shortly after his return.[5] His [6]
widow, Margaret, who married secondly Giles de Fishbourne, had for her life a stone-roofed house opposite to
the hall of the manor of East Quantockshead.[6] Sir
Alexander Luttrell had two sons, Andrew and John, and
a daughter, Annora.[7]

Sir Andrew Luttrell, the eldest son, was in 1301
summoned to perform military service against the
Scots.[8] His wife Elizabeth was probably a daughter of
Warin de Ralegh.[9]

His son and successor, another Alexander, was in 1326
called upon to account for his neglect to take knighthood.[10] Three years later he presented to the living of
East Quantockshead an acolite named Andrew Luttrell,
who obtained leave of absence from the bishop in order
that he might prosecute his studies at the University.[1]
In 1341 Sir Alexander was appointed collector of the
duties on wool in the county of Somerset, and in 1363 he
and some of his neighbours borrowed money from the

[1] The best accounts of the Luttrells
of Irnham are those given by Mr. Stapleton in the paper already noticed, and
that given in the "Vetusta Monumenta,"
vol. vi, where there are six plates of en-
gravings from subjects in the Luttrell
Psalter.
[2] Heralds' College MS., Vincent, vol. vii,
ff. 53, 88.
[3] Patent Rolls, 50 Henry III, m. 25,
and 52 Henry III, m. 3.
[4] Patent Roll, 54 Henry III, m. 8, 11.
Rymer's "Fœdera," vol. i, p. 484.
[5] Fine Roll, 1 Edward I, m. 21. Close
Roll, 2 Edward I, m. 3.

[6] "Rolls of Parliament," vol. i, p. 5
Pipe. Roll, 6 Edward I, co. Somerset.
Close Roll, 1 Edward I, m. 5.
[7] Heralds' College MS. Picture of
Our Lady, f. 97. Fine Roll, 1 Edw. I,
m. 20.
[8] "Parliamentary Writs," vol. i, p. 351.
[9] Dunster Castle Muniments, Box
xxii, No. 1.
[10] "Parliamentary Writs" (ed. Palgrave) vol. ii, part i, pp. 743, 751.
[11] Registers of Bishops John de Drokensford and Ralph de Salopia at Wells.

Sir Geoffrey Luttrell
arming for the Tournament.

Sir Geoffrey Luttrell at table.

J Akerman Photo-lith

Scenes from the Luttrell Psalter.

Company of the Bardi, the great Florentine financiers.[1]
On the marriage of his eldest son Thomas with Joan, the
daughter of Sir John Palton in 1343, he undertook to
give them a yearly rent of £10 from East Quantockshead,
and to settle certain lands on them, on condition that
Sir John Palton should become responsible for their
maintenance and should pay him the sum of two hundred
marks.[2]   Five years later he conveyed to Sir John
Palton, and to his son and his daughter-in-law, Thomas
and Joan Luttrell, the manor, and the advowson of the
church, of East Quantockshead for an annual rent of forty
marks and of a robe worth forty shillings.   He at the
same time reserved to himself for life a hall with chambers
adjoining, a stable in the outer court at East Quantockshead, and the right to gather hay and fuel, and to take one
half of the fines and heriots of the manor.[3]

In 1360, Thomas Luttrell settled the manor of East
Quantockshead on himself and his second wife Dionysia
and his own heirs.[4]   The date of his death is unknown,
and there is no evidence to show whether Sir John
Luttrell, who succeeded him, was his son or his brother.
This Sir John Luttrell was created one of the original
Knights of the Bath when that illustrious Order was
established by Henry IV, two days before his coronation
in 1399.[5]   Five months later, the same king assigned to
his "beloved and faithful knight," Sir John Luttrell,
whom he had attached to his own person, an annuity of
£40 for life from the revenue of the county of Somerset.[6]
Sir John Luttrell was Sheriff of Dorset and Somerset in
1400.[7]   In the month of May, 1403, he took up arms in the
king's behalf, "to resist the malice of a certain Henry
Percehay, Knight," and, when on the point of starting, made
a will by which he directed that if he should die without
issue before returning to his mansion at East Quantockshead, his estates should pass to his "cousin," Sir
Hugh Luttrell.[8]   The event showed that he acted wisely in

[1] Close Roll, 16 Edward I, p. 1, m. 15, in dorso. Dunster Castle Muniments.
[2] Dunster Castle Muniments, Box xxii, No. 1.
[3] Ibid.
[4] Ibid, Box xxii, No. 2.
[5] Holinshed's "Chronicle," vol. ii, p. 511.
[6] Patent Roll, 1 Henry, IV, p. 1, m. 26.
[7] Fuller's "Worthies."
[8] Dunster Castle Muniments, Box i, No. 15.

making his will, for he died within the next few weeks.[1] In him the direct line of the Luttrells of East Quantockshead came to an end.

A younger branch of the family had been settled in Devonshire for about sixty years. A certain Sir John Luttrell, who was probably a son of Sir Andrew Luttrell of East Quantockshead, had license in 1337 to buy land at Chilton, in the parish of Thorverton.[2] He styled himself "Lord of Chilton," and his manor was sometimes described as Chilton Luttrell.[3] This Sir John was appointed a Commissioner of Array in 1347 and in 1359, and he sat as one of the members for Devonshire in the Parliaments of 1360 and 1368.[4] His wife Joan survived him, and died in 1378 or 1380.[5]

Their son, Sir Andrew Luttrell, married Elizabeth Courtenay, widow of Sir John de Vere, a lady of the most illustrious lineage.[6] Her father Hugh, Earl of Devon, one of the companions in arms of Edward III, and one of the original members of the Order of the Garter, was head of the noble family of Courtenay. Her mother Margaret was daughter of Humphrey de Bohun, Earl of Hereford and Essex, Lord High Constable of England, "the flower of knighthood, and the most Christian knight of the knights of the world," by Elizabeth his wife, daughter of King Edward I.[7] One

[1] Dunster Castle Muniments, Box xxxvii, No. 43. As East Quantockshead was held under the Luttrells of Irnham and not in chief, there are no inquisitions post mortem for any members of the Luttrell family of that place.

[2] Inquisitiones post mortem, 11 Edward III, No. 9. Dunster Castle Muniments, Box xxiv, No. 1. Sir John Luttrell of Chilton has sometimes been mistaken for his uncle John Luttrell, whose wife's name was Rose. There were apparently two other persons of that name living in the reign of Edward III, viz., John Luttrell, who was Chancellor of the University of Oxford in 1320, and John Luttrell, who is mentioned with his wife Catharine in a deed of 1369. Wood's "Antiquities of Oxford." Heralds' College MS., Picture of Our Lady.

[3] Oliver's "Monasticon Dioecesis Exon," p. 123.

[4] Carte's "Gascon Rolls," vol. ii, p. 39. Patent Roll, 33 Edward III, m. 4, in dorso.

[5] Inquisitiones post mortem, 1 Richard II, No. 22, and 8 Richard II, No. 26.

This lady is in some pedigrees described as a daughter of Lord John Mohun of Dunster, and it is possible that her father may have been John de Mohun the third, who died in 1330. She does not appear, however, in the list of his children made by a monk of Newenham during the early part of her life. See Appendix E. Nor is there any other contemporary evidence to show that she was by birth a Mohun. It is probable that this surname was assigned to her at random by some herald who wished to show a connection by marriage between the two families that have held the Barony of Dunster. Robert Glover, the herald, is certainly wrong in describing the wife of Sir John Luttrell of Chilton as Isabella daughter of John de Mohun.

[6] Dunster Castle Muniments, Box xxxvii, No. 39. Inquisitiones post mortem, 19 Richard II, No. 48.

[7] There is among the muniments at Dunster Castle a table of the descendants of Humphrey de Bohun, drawn up in the reign of Henry VI.

of her brothers, was, like her father, an original Knight of the Garter, another became Archbishop of Canterbury, another Lieutenant of Ireland, and another Governor of Calais. Through her sisters she was connected with the Lords Cobham and Harington. Sir Andrew Luttrell, who was by birth only a cadet of a younger branch of the baronial family of Luttrell of Irnham, was, by his marriage, raised to a higher position in the social scale. In 1359 he and his wife received from Edward III a grant of an annuity of £200 for the term of their joint lives, for the maintenance of their station, and the grant was confirmed by Richard II immediately after his accession to the throne.[1] In 1361, Sir Andrew and Lady Elizabeth Luttrell went on a pilgrimage to the famous shrine of St. James of Compostella.[2] For many years the latter was in close attendance on her cousins, Edward the Black Prince and the Fair Maid of Kent his wife. In consideration of her faithful services to them, she obtained from Richard II a continuance of the annuity of £200 after the death of her husband, which occurred before the year 1375.[3] With part of her savings she purchased the manors of Feltwell, co. Norfolk, and of Moulton, Debenham, and Waldenfield, co. Suffolk, and the right of appointing two of the canons of the priory of Flitcham.[4] In 1373 she received a grant of free-warren in her different manors, but she appears to have sold those of Feltwell and Moulton a few years later.[5]

By far the most important transaction in the life of Lady Elizabeth Luttrell was her purchase of the right of succession to the castle and manor of Dunster, and the manors of Minehead and Kilton, and the Hundred of Carhampton, after the death of Lady Joan de Mohun. For this she paid a deposit of £200 in February, 1374, and a further sum of £3133 6s. 8d. on or before the 20th of November, 1376.[6] Even if these sums were multiplied

[1] Patent Rolls, 33 Edward III, p. 2, m. 25, 1 Richard II, p. 5, m. 37, and 4 Richard II, p. 3, m. 7.
[2] Close Roll, 35 Edward III, m. 22.
[3] Patent Roll, 4 Richard II, p. 3, m. 7.
[4] Dunster Castle Muniments, Box xxxvii, Nos. 38, 39.
[5] Charter Roll, 47 Edward III, m. 11.

Dunster Castle Muniments, Box xxxvii, Nos. 40, 41.
[6] Dunster Castle Muniments, Box i, No. 7. Hamilton Rogers's "Sepulchral Effigies of Devon," p. 198. Her father had many years before bought the Devonshire estates of Sir John de Mohun, Lord of Dunster. Close Roll, 29 Edward III, m. 27.

by twenty to bring them to their present value, the price paid would, at first sight, appear utterly inadequate, but it must be remembered that Lady Joan de Mohun reserved her life interest in the whole of the property. As she did not die until 1404, the Luttrells did not get any advantage from the transaction until nearly thirty years after the payment of the purchase-money. Lady Elizabeth Luttrell herself did not live to take possession of the future home of her descendants, as she died in 1395.[1] She was buried in the Benedictine Church of St. Nicholas at Exeter.[2] Edmund Stafford, Bishop of Exeter, in August, 1395, ordered public prayers to be offered throughout his diocese for the souls of Margaret Cobham and Elizabeth Loterel, sisters of the Archbishop of Canterbury, and as an encouragement to the faithful to pray for them, granted an indulgence of forty days.[3]

Sir Hugh Luttrell, son of Sir Andrew and Elizabeth, may be styled the second founder of the family. He was a man of great worth, and was honourably employed by three successive Kings of England. In consideration of his services to Richard II, he, in 1391, received a grant of a yearly pension of £20, payable out of the confiscated English revenue of the priory of St. Nicholas at Anjou.[4] Seven years later he was warden of the forest of Gillingham.[5] Like his relations the Courtenays, he afterwards attached himself to the cause of the House of Lancaster. In 1401 he was made steward of the household of Queen Joan, and soon afterwards Constable of Bristol Castle and Warden of the forests of Kingswood and Fulwood for life.[6] In 1401-2, he went into Normandy to act as Lieutenant of Calais, and while there he was appointed one of the commissioners to treat with the French.[7] At the end of 1403 he was sent as Ambassador to the Duke of Burgundy.[8] Several of his letters from abroad on state affairs have been preserved.[9] In the following

[1] Inquisitiones post mortem, 19 Richard II, Nos. 47, 48.
[2] Dunster Castle Muniments, Box, xxxvii, No. 42.
[3] Hamilton Rogers's "Sepulchral Effigies of Devon," p. 330.
[4] Patent Roll, 15 Richard II, p. 1, m. 31.
[5] Patent Roll, 22 Richard II, p. 2, m. 20.
[6] Lipscombe's "History of Bucks,"

vol. iii, p. 523. Patent Roll, 14 Henry IV, m. 22.
[7] Carte's "Gascon Rolls," vol. ii, pp. 185, 186. "Royal and Historical Letters," vol. i, p. 188.
[8] Carte's "Gascon Rolls," vol. ii, p. 186.
[9] "Royal and Historical Letters," vol. i, pp. 170, 177, 186, 188, 194, 197, 202, 204. British Museum, Add. Charter 1397.

April he was sworn a member of the Privy Council, and a few weeks later he was appointed Mayor of Bordeaux.[1] His own affairs ere long required his presence in England.

On the death of Sir John Luttrell in 1403, Sir Hugh became undisputed owner of East Quantockshead, and on the death of Lady Joan de Mohun a year later, he took possession of Dunster Castle. He was not, however, allowed to enjoy it in peace. The heirs of John de Mohun, the last lord of Dunster, namely, Elizabeth, Countess of Salisbury, the Duke and Duchess of York, and Sir Richard Strange, challenged the validity of the sale, and commenced legal proceedings to recover the inheritance of which they had been deprived. On the 14th of May, 1406, the King nominated nine judges to hear the cause. A contest against such powerful adversaries must have sorely tried the courage and the resources of Sir Hugh Luttrell, but he obtained a timely loan of £50 from the Abbot of Cleeve. It was no small advantage to him that he was at the time one of the members for the county of Devon. On the 19th of June the House of Commons sent up a petition that the question at issue might be referred to four peers of the realm and all the justices. Both parties agreed to this on condition that the arbitrators should swear before the King to do justice according to law before the 1st of November, without favour or prejudice. The plaintiffs made choice of the Lords de Ros and Furnivall, and the defendant of the Bishops of Exeter and St. David's, who duly took the prescribed oath. The Chief Justice of the Common Pleas, the Chief Baron of the Exchequer, and five other judges took the oath on the 5th July, before the King and the Lord Chancellor at the London house of the Bishop of Durham. The famous Sir William Gascoigne, chief justice, was for some reason absent. On the 22nd of October, Sir Laurence Drue was substituted for the Bishop of Exeter. The case was heard at some length, but the arbitrators could not be induced to give judgment because the parties were still at issue. The House of Commons again took the matter in hand, with a scarcely disguised bias in favour of Sir Hugh Luttrell, whose "poor estate,"

---

[1] "Proceedings of the Privy Council" (ed. Nicolas), vol. i, p. 233, Carte's "Gascon Rolls" vol. i, p. 189.

they said, could not stand protracted litigation. They, therefore, prayed that the special assize might be discharged if the plaintiffs could not make good their claim within a given time. They prayed, moreover, that if the plaintiffs had recourse to the ordinary process of law, no one should be allowed to serve on the jury who did not possess lands to the value of at least 40s. a year. They ended by declaring that the estates in question were of great value, and that the parties interested were powerful persons, so that " speedy mischief and riot " might arise if special precautions were not taken. To this it was replied that the sheriff of the county of Somerset should be sworn to impanel the most capable and impartial persons that could be found within his bailiwick.[1] The trial took place at Ilchester in Michaelmas term, the plaintiffs contending that the estates had been entailed on the heirs of the body of John de Mohun and Joan his wife, and that his subsequent conveyance of them to the feoffees, who sold them to Lady Elizabeth Luttrell, was, therefore, invalid.[2] Their suit, however, after being argued at considerable length, broke down, and Sir Hugh Luttrell was recognized to be the lawful lord of Dunster.

From 1405 to 1415 Sir Hugh Luttrell appears to have remained in England, where he was successively member for Devonshire, a Commissioner of Array for Somersetshire, auditor of the accounts of the Treasurers of the Wars, member of Parliament for his own county, and a commissioner for the repression of the Lollards.[3] A special messenger was sent to him in haste on the escape of his cousin, Sir John Oldcastle, Lord Cobham, from the Tower of London.[4]

When Henry V determined to prosecute the war against France with new vigour, he was glad to avail himself of the services of so experienced a warrior as Sir Hugh Luttrell. On the fall of Harfleur, Sir Hugh was appointed councillor to the English Governor of that place, and his duties appear to have detained him there while his comrades were distinguishing themselves on the

---

[1] "Rolls of Parliament," vol. iii, pp. 577, 578, 597.

[2] Year Book, Michaelmas, 8th Henry IV.

[3] Patent Roll, 6 Henry IV, p. 2, m.

15, in dorso. "Rolls of Parliament," vol. iii, p. 577. Patent Roll, 1 Henry V, p. 5, m. 23, in dorso.

[4] "Issues of the Exchequer" (ed. Devon), p. 331.

battle-field of Agincourt.[1] In consideration of the sum
of £286, he, in 1417, agreed to serve the king in the
French war at the head of a body of soldiers, consisting
of one knight, nineteen esquires, and sixty archers.[2]
About the same time he was recommended by the Privy
Council as one of the fittest persons for the office of "Knight
Constable."[3] In 1418 he was made Governor of Harfleur.
He was present at the siege of Rouen, and as the tide of
success ran more strongly in favour of the English, he
was deputed to treat for the surrender of the hostile
towns of Monstreville, Dieppe, Fecamp, and Avranches.[4]
He was about the same time promoted to be Great
Seneschal of Normandy, and as such, he, in 1420, received
authority over all the English officers in France and
in Normandy.[5] He seems to have returned to England
in the course of that year, as he was chosen one of the
members of Parliament for the county of Devon. In the
following year he was nominated steward of the household of the queen of Henry V.[6]

During Sir Hugh Luttrell's long periods of absence in
Normandy, his wife Catherine Beaumont, widow of John
Strecche, remained in England, staying sometimes at
Dunster Castle, and sometimes at her mother's house at
Saunton in Devonshire. John Luttrell, their eldest son,
acted as treasurer and overseer of the accounts, and as
such, enjoyed a yearly allowance of £10. He was from
time to time assisted by the advice of Peter Courtenay,
Thomas Beaumont, Hugh Cary, and other relations and
friends. A receiver-general and a steward, who each
received £5 a year besides their board, collected the rents
and payments due to their lord, and maintained the
establishment at Dunster. The receiver-general also
transmitted great quantities of provisions and other
necessaries to Normandy. Fish of various kinds, salmon,

---

[1] Hall's "Union of the families of
Lancaster and York," p. 45.
[2] Heralds' College MS., Vincent, vol.
xxix, f. 55.
[3] "Proceedings of the Privy Council,"
vol. ii, pp. 204, 232.
[4] Carte's "Gascon Rolls," vol. i, pp.
277—279, 295, 296, 325, 333. Norman
Roll 6 Henry V, p. 1, m. 13, in dorso,

p. 2, m. 1, and m. 9. Harleian MS.
1586, f. 85.
[5] Norman Roll, 8 Henry V, p. 1,
m. 28, in dorso. There are at Dunster
several letters from "Hugh Luttrell,
Knight, lord of Dunsterr and Gret Senes-
chall of Normendie," addressed to his
receiver-general at Dunster.
[6] Lipscombe's "History of Bucks,"
vol. iii, p. 523.

ling, "scalpin," conger, hake, and milwell, was salted and
packed in barrels for convenience of transport, and when,
in 1420, six oxen and thirty "muttons" were placed on
board ship, they were stowed into large "pipes." The
"lardyner" received 20d. "for syltyng and dyghtyng of
al the flessh." On the same occasion 3s. 7d. was paid for
"mattys and naill boght for to make a caban in the ship
for savyng of the corne and of the malt." On other
occasions the wheat and the barley-malt were packed in
barrels, like the beans, the green peas, the oats, and the
candles. The provisions were embarked sometimes at
Poole, sometimes at Southampton, and sometimes at
Minehead, Roger Kyng a shipman of the last place being
frequently employed. On one occasion a barge, known
as the "Leonard of Dunster," was specially chartered to
sail from Minehead to Bordeaux. It would appear that
Sir Hugh himself was on board, and that he took with
him five live oxen, and two pipes of beer for consumption
on the voyage. The expenses of the trip to Bordeaux and
back, including the repair of the anchors, sails, etc.,
amounted to £42 3s. 1d., but as Philip Clopton the
master of the barge received £40 10s. from certain merchants for the freight of their wine on the return journey
from Bordeaux to England, Sir Hugh had only to pay the
difference between these two sums. Roger Kyng, too,
used to bring back wine with him, which Lady Catherine
Luttrell was glad enough to buy.[1]

The fishermen of Minehead used to exercise their
vocation, not only in the Bristol Channel, but also off the
eastern coasts of Ireland. Several of them, tenants of
Sir Hugh Luttrell, were in 1427 captured near Carling-
ford, by a Spaniard named Goo, and carried to Scotland,
when they were imprisoned in Bothwell Castle. They
were not released until a special letter was sent to the
King of Scotland in the name of Henry VI.[2]

Sir Hugh Luttrell came home from time to time, but
his visits to Dunster were generally of short duration.
When he was there in 1416 or 1417, he had his chariot
repaired, and various payments were made on his behalf
for the stuffing of saddles, for stirrups, poles, reins,

---

[1] See Appendix H.   [2] Rymer's "Fœdera" (Tonson), vol. x, p. 382.

buckles, and a whip. One of his horses that fell ill was doctored with verdigris and white wine. He was in England again at the end of 1419, and he spent Christmas with his family at Dunster. He left again by way of Domerham, Southampton, and Portsmouth.

On this, or on another of his journeys to Harfleur, he took with him all the portable ornaments of his private chapel, and a good deal of plate. Among the pieces of silver that he left at Dunster was "a coppe ynamed Bath," a "coppe ynamed Courtenay," "an hie coppe ycoveryd with fetheris yplomyd," the Courtenay crest, "a coppe with an egle ygylt in the pomell," "a tastour," "an ymage of Synd Jon of sylver and gylt," and "a spone and a verke for grene gyngyn."[1] Part of his plate had come to him from his grandmother, the Countess of Devon, and part probably from his uncle, Archbishop Courtenay.[2] In 1416 he had himself paid £54 to the executors of Sir Ivo Fitzwarren, for certain silver vases.

Various repairs and alterations were made in the fabric of Dunster Castle in Sir Hugh Luttrell's time. In 1417 a mason was summoned from Bridgewater to advise about the re-building of the hall, and two years later part of the walls of the hall and of the Castle was pulled down. A new building was at the same time begun near the hall. Free-stone was brought from Bristol, and lias-stone delivered at Watchet, was conveyed thence to Dunster, by sea. Sir Hugh's own horses and oxen were employed to drag it up the steep hill to the Castle. The workmen were provided with "crowes, mattokkes, pycoyses, wegges, spades, shovylles," and "sleigges" made for the purpose, and were placed under the direction of an overseer.[3] It can scarcely be doubted that the "*novum ædificium*" then begun was the gatehouse which spans the approach to the Castle from the north-west. Some antiquaries, having regard only to the architectural features and the character of the mouldings, have assigned this building to the time of Richard II. Others again, taking Leland as their authority, have referred it to the time of Henry VII, nearly a whole century later. It would appear, however,

---

[1] See Appendix H.
[2] Wills at Somerset House, "Rouse,"
f. 15. Somner's "Canterbury" (1703), Appendix, p. 331.
[3] See Appendix H.

that the true date lies midway between the two which have been suggested. On the one hand, it is highly improbable that Lady Joan de Mohun, who was the owner of Dunster Castle throughout the reign of Richard II. would have made a costly addition to the fabric, after having arranged that the property should, at her death, pass into the hands of strangers. On the other hand, it is easy enough to account for Leland's mistake. On the occasion of his hurried visit to Dunster, he was doubtless informed that the gatehouse was built by Sir Hugh Luttrell, and he may have ascertained by personal observation that the last of the series of shields over its western arch bore the arms of a Sir Hugh Luttrell, who married Margaret Hill, and died in the twelfth year of Henry VIII. He accordingly wrote, without hesitation :—"Sir Hugh Luterelle, in the tyme of Dame Margarete, his wife, sister to the olde Lord Dalbeney, made a fair tourre by north, cummyng into the Castelle."[1] It did not occur to him that there had been two Sir Hugh Luttrells, and that the sculptured shield might be of a later date than the rest of the structure. The gatehouse seems to have been designed as much for domestic as for military purposes. It abuts against, and partly incorporates one of the flanking towers of the older Edwardian gateway.

The household accounts of Sir Hugh Luttrell mention an upper and a lower Castle, the former of which, generally known as " le Dongeon," contained a chapel and a kitchen, and had at least one tower. In the lower ward, near the new gatehouse, stood the Hall, separated from a second chapel by wooden " enterclos" and " haches," and lit by glazed windows. There was a lantern on the steps leading to the hall, and a bell hung overhead. The accounts also make mention of Dame Hawys's Tower, the tower over the entrance, the portcullis, the room between the gates, the gatekeeper's room, the lord's room, the constable's room, the store-house, and the stables.[2] A street on the west of the gate house was known as "Castel-bayly," and twelve acres of sloping ground on and around the Tor were known as " Casteldyche pastour."[3] The Park on

---

[1] "Itinerary," vol. ii, p. 71.
[2] See Appendix H.
[3] Dunster Castle Muniments, Box viii,

No. 2. Dunster Church Book, f. 14.
Inquisitiones post mortem, 6 Henry VI,
No. 32.

EXTERIOR OF THE GATE-HOUSE.

DUNSTER CASTLE.

the south of the Tor, lying partly in the parish of Dunster, and partly in that of Carhampton, was, in the 14th, 15th, and 16th centuries, always described as "the Hanger Park," or "le Hanger," obviously in reference to its hanging woods. Mention is occasionally made of a "New Park." Like his predecessors, the Mohuns, Sir Hugh Luttrell had a larger park at Marshwood, in the parish of Carhampton, near the sea.[1] The accounts show that he built a new lodge at the rabbit-warren ("*cunicularium*"), of which the name only remains in Conygar, a hill on the north side of the town of Dunster. He kept his dogs at a house hired for the purpose.[2]

The number of retainers living in the castle varied according to circumstances. When Sir Hugh Luttrell first took up his abode there, he had a steward, a chamberlain, and a cook, and fifteen henchmen and servants, who received wages ranging from 10s. up to £2 a year apiece. Lady Catherine Luttrell had one damsel in attendance on her, and there was one laundress for the whole establishment. Master John Odeland and John Scolemaster who were successively staying at the castle in 1424, may probably have come to teach some of the younger members of the family.

Sir Hugh's married daughters and his daughter-in-law, the wife of John Luttrell, sometimes came as guests, but when Lady Elizabeth Harington took up her quarters at the castle for several months in 1424, she had to settle with the steward for the board of her whole retinue.[3] Messengers who brought letters or presents of venison, boar, capons, porpoises, salmon or melet, were entertained and amply rewarded. It is worthy of remark that in 1405 the Prior of Dunster was able to offer Lady Catherine

[1] Dunster Castle Muniments, Box i, No. 4, Box ix, No. 2, Box xvi, No. 3. Inq. p.m., 6 Henry VI, No. 32.

[2] The following places in Dunster are mentioned in deeds prior to the reign of Henry VI :—"Gallokestrete," "Dodde brugge," "Est strete," St. George's street, the well of St. Leonard on the north side of Grobbefast, "la Chipyngstret," "Water street," "Machonnes brigge," "Skybardsclyf" "Portmanes Acre," "Fountegary," "Algore," "Waglonde," "Develane," "Crokkeslane (Dunster Castle Muniments, Box viii, No. 2), "le Chesell de Karemore,

(Box x, No. 1), "deux acres de terre en la hangre qui gisent entre la fosse de les vignes de l'une partie, et le chemin qest appelle Brooklane de l'autre partie," "Prestlonde" (Box, i, No. 4), "le Conynger" (Dunster Church Book, f. 7).

[3] Savage describes this lady as cousin and next heir of Sir John Luttrell of East Quantockshead. It does not, however, appear how she was related to him. She was the wife of John Harington, the fourth baron of that surname. Her husband was son of Sir Hugh Luttrell's first cousin.

four bushels of green peas on the 20th of December. Seven days later Sir Hugh gave 8s. 4d. to three tenants of John Cobleston, and six of his own tenants, and to a number of children from Minehead, who played before him. At the following feast of the Epiphany he gave 1s. "to the Clerks of St. Nicholas." Richard Popham, a lawyer, received 6s. 8d. for his professional services. One of the rolls of accounts preserved at Dunster gives details of all the food bought from day to day in the course of a twelve-month from the 27th of June, 1405.[1]

Sir Hugh Luttrell had two sons, John and William,[2] and four daughters Elizabeth, Ann, Margaret and Joan. When in 1406 the first-named of these daughters married William Harleston, Sir Hugh settled on them and the heirs of their bodies the manor of Debenham in Suffolk, the bridegroom on his side settling rents worth 40 marks a year on the lady, and paying down the sum of 125 marks.[3] Two years later Ann Luttrell was married to William Godwin the younger, and each party brought into settlement rents worth £20 a year, and Sir Hugh undertook to pay 100 marks in instalments.[4] In 1412 Margaret Luttrell was betrothed to a certain John de Cotes, and her father undertook to provide them their two servants and their two henchmen (chivalers) with meat and drink for the first year after the marriage. He also promised to give £20 to his daughter "pour sa chambre," and 100 marks to his future son-in-law, who in return undertook to settle lands worth £20 a year on the issue of the marriage.[5] The fourth daughter took the veil at Shaftesbury.[6]

Sir Hugh Luttrell died on the 24th of March, 1428, and was buried at Dunster in a manner fitting his rank. Among the persons who attended the funeral were sixteen poor men and women who wore jupes and capes of black

---

[1] See Appendix H.

[2] Robert Luttrell, ancestor of the Luttrells of Luttrellstown, co. Dublin, is stated by Lodge and Burke to have been a younger son of Sir Hugh Luttrell of Dunster. This however is extremely doubtful. Mr. Stapleton suggests that the Irish Luttrells were descended from an illegitimate son of Geoffrey Luttrell, the minister of King John. When Simon Luttrell, of Luttrellstown, was raised to the peerage in the reign of George III, he chose as his titles Baron Irnham and Earl of Carhampton, as if he were connected with the Luttrells of Lincolnshire and of Somersetshire.

[3] Dunster Castle Muniments, Box xxxvii, No. 6.

[4] Ibid., No. 48.

[5] Ibid., No. 44.

[6] See Appendix H.

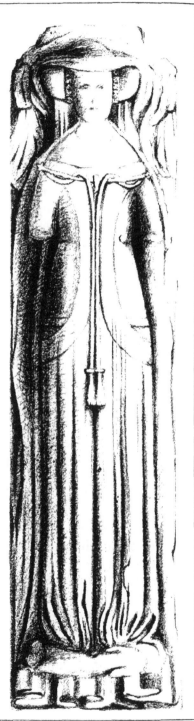

EFFIGIES
of
SIR HUGH LUTTRELL.
AND HIS WIFE.
In Dunster Church.
A.D. 1428-1435.

and white cloth.[1] A monument was erected to his memory on the north side of the high altar, in the thickness of the wall that separated the chancel from a small outlying chapel.[2] Two of the lancet windows that formerly gave light to the chancel were blocked up to make room for it, and the northern chapel was about the same time rebuilt in the Perpendicular style The only evidence indeed of the existence of an earlier chapel on the site is a massive stone altar which can hardly be later than the first part of the thirteenth century. There are fair grounds for believing that this was "the lower chapel of St. Laurence;" mentioned in the agreement of 1254 between Reginald de Mohun and the Prior and Convent of Bath. The effigy of Sir Hugh Luttrell, beautifully carved in alabaster and relieved with gilding, shows him accoutred in plate armour. The arms and legs have been broken off, and other parts have been shamefully mutilated. On the left side of this effigy lies that of Lady Catherine Luttrell, also wanting the arms, and much defaced. The lady is represented as wearing a sideless dress, through the openings of which may be seen the girdle of the kirtle, and over all a mantle fastened in front by cords which pass through open "fermeules" or loops. A long veil hangs down from the top of the head.

It might have been expected that the name of the Great Seneschal of Normandy, the first of the Luttrells that lived at the castle, the builder of the gate-house, would have been so well known at Dunster, that there could be no question as to the fact that he and his wife were the originals of the alabaster figures on the north side of the chancel of the conventual church. Yet every modern writer, without exception, who has mentioned the monument of Sir Hugh and Lady Catharine Luttrell, has described it as that of Sir John de Mohun and his wife. The mistake appears to have arisen out of the exaggerated respect that has been so generally paid to the authority of John Leland. It has been pointed out already that Leland fell into error as to the date of the

---

[1] Inquisitiones post mortem, 6 Henry VI, No. 32. See Appendix II.

[2] The open cresting along the top of the monument has been copied from a fragment found in the ground close by during the recent restoration of the Church. One of the carved cusps was found in the Priory garden, the others are new.

gate-house at Dunster, and his account of the monuments in the church shows that he cannot have committed his notes to paper on the spot. He writes:—

"The late Priorie of Blake Monkes stoode yn the rootes of the north-west side of the Castelle, and was a Celle to Bathe.

"The hole Chirch of the late Priorie servith now for the Paroche Chirch. Aforetymes the Monkes had the Est Parte closid up to their use.

"In the north part of this was buried undre an Arche by the high Altare one of the Luterelles, or, as I rather thynke, of the Moions, for he hath a Garland about his helmet, and so were Lordes of old Tymes usid to be buried.

"There ly ij images on the South Side of the Chauncelle of one of the Moions and his wife; and therby lay an image of one of the Everardes Gentilmen first there set up by the Moions, yn token wherof they had a parte of the Castelle to defende by service; the image lyith now bytwixt ij arches or Boteres in the Chirch Yarde.

"The Maner Place of the Everardes was and yet ys at Aller in Carnetun Paroche a mile from Dunster Castelle.

"Carntoun is shortly spoken for Carantokes Towne, wher yet is a Chapel of this Sainct that sumtyme was the Paroche Chirche.

"There lyith one Elizabeth, wife of one of the Luterelles, afore the high Altare under a playne stone." [1]

Not one of the four monuments here mentioned is accurately described. The Everarde monument, of which no traces now exist, can scarcely have been placed between two arches in a churchyard. The incised slab of Lady Elizabeth Luttrell, who died in 1493, is at Dunster —not at Carhampton. The only early monument on the south side of the chancel at Dunster is that of a nameless lady of the thirteenth century, without any husband by her side, while that on the north has the figures of a knight and his lady. Such being the case, Leland's hesitating words " I rather thinke " are not worth much as evidence.

James Savage, the author of the "History of the Hundred of Carhampton," tried to show that the effigies of the knight and the lady were those of John de Mohun, whom he wrongly styles "the second," and Ada Tiptoft his wife. A living antiquary perceiving that they could not possibly be of so early a date as the year 1330, has suggested that they may have been intended to represent the last of the Mohuns of Dunster and his wife Joan de Burgwash.[2] Against this it may be urged that the nobleman in ques-

---

[1] "Itinerary," vol. ii, p. 71.　　　[2] Hamilton-Rogers's "Sepulchral Effigies of Devon," p. 112.

tion gave distinct instructions for his burial at Bruton; that his widow made elaborate arrangements for her burial in her own chantry at Canterbury; and that she would have had no inclination to set up a cenotaph for him and for herself at Dunster after selling to a stranger the right of succession to all her estates in the West of England.[1] The costume, moreover, of the knight, the "orle" or wreath round his bascinet, the "demi-placcates" covering his breast, the sword-belt hanging diagonally across his body, the six overlapping "taces" or plates round his waist and hips, and the "tuiles" that protect his thighs, show clearly that he lived in the first part of the fifteenth century. The collar of SS. round his neck, furthermore marks him out as a person attached to the court of one of the Lancastrian kings. No Lord of Dunster, except Sir Hugh Luttrell, answers to this description.

Inquisitions were held in the counties of Somerset, Devon, Wilts, Dorset, and Suffolk, after the death of Sir Hugh Luttrell, and it was found that his son and heir John was upwards of thirty-four years of age.[2]

Sir John Luttrell had not long been in possession of his estates before he received the following letter from Sir John Stourton, claiming repayment of the money disbursed by him on account of the inquisition on Sir Hugh Luttrell taken in Wiltshire:—

"My ryght worshipfull and with all myne herte wel-belovid cosyn y recomande me to yow beseching yow that ye woll be remembrid of the litell money that I dude paic by the hondes of Robert Colyngborn whiche yo toward me in your name as for the speed of your diem claus-it extremum in the counte of Wiltes and by the advys of your cervaunt whiche laborud for hit in your name which drawith in all to the summe of iiijli ixs id which y praie yow that ye do sende me in as hasty tyme as ye godely may consideryng my nede ate this present hoeure that I have for my goyng obir see. And the holy Trinite yow evir conserve to his plesaunce and your ryght greet joy and confort

      "Your cosyn John
      "Stourton Knyzght."

The little bill was duly discharged, and the valet of William Wadham, who brought it to Dunster, received a

---

[1] "Lego animam meam Deo, et corpus meum do sepeliendum in Prioratu canonicorum regularium de Bruton." Will of Sir John de Mohun dated 3 nones September, 1342. Dunster Castle Muniments, Box xxxvii, No. 4.

[2] Inquisitiones post mortem, 6 Henry VI, No. 33.

gratuity of 20d. One of Sir John Luttrell's first acts was to buy a barge for his own use, and to stock it with provisions. The price of it was £80, which he arranged to pay, in instalments, to an Irishman, named Foughler, In 1429 or 1430, he made a very minute addition to the fabric of the Castle, which can be identified with tolerable certainty. Finding the gatehouse erected by his father somewhat insecure, he resolved to strengthen it by building the two buttresses, which are still to be seen on the north side. Most of the stone was brought from Croydon Hill, about two miles distant, a small quantity only being quarried for the purpose in the Hanger Park. The building was accomplished in a fortnight, by two masons, from Wootton, and one labourer, whose wages were, respectively, 18d., 14d., and 11d. a week. The hire of a cart and four horses, with the wages of the carman, amounted to 1s. a day. About the same time one of the rooms adjoining the gateway was lined with cement, so that it should serve as a storehouse for salt. Among the visitors who stayed at Dunster in Sir John's Luttrell's time we may notice his sister Joan, and another nun of Shaftesbury, his cousin, Lady Elizabeth Courtenay, and a certain Walter Portman, who came to speak about a law suit against Philippa, Duchess of York, and other business. Sir John was on good terms with his Bishop, John Stafford, of Bath and Wells, and on one occasion he bought four hundred buckhorns at Exeter, as a present for him. He did not, however, long enjoy his ample worldly possessions, for he died on the 30th of July, 1430, having only survived his father by a little more than two years. He left behind him a widow, Margaret, who was by birth an Audley, and an only son, James, then about three years of age.[1] His funeral seems to have taken place at Dunster, though in the following year his anniversary was solemnly observed at Bruton by the Prior, fifteen canons, two secular priests, and various townsmen. There is no monument at Dunster or elsewhere, to his memory, or to to the memory of his widow, who survived him by about seven years.[2]

[1] Inquisitiones post mortem, 9 Henry VI, No. 51. Dunster Castle Muniments, Box i, No. 29.

[2] Inquisitiones post mortem 17 Henry VI, No. 14.

Scale _____ 1ft. _____ 2ft.

HERALDIC TABLET
carved in stone
on the gatehouse
DUNSTER CASTLE.

During the first part of the minority of the heir the estate was burdened with the maintenance of two widows, Lady Catharine Luttrell, his grandmother, being in receipt of an annuity of £100, derived chiefly from the manors of Minehead and East Quantockshead. Lady Margaret, his mother, seems to have been rather pinched for money, for she had to make over some of the family plate to her mother-in-law, and certain other silver vases and worsted-work to her receiver-general in part payment of his bill. She resided, for the most part, at Carhampton.[1] Soon after he came of age, James Luttrell effected an entail of the castle and manor of Dunster, of the manors of Minehead, Carhampton, and Kilton, and of the hundred of Carhampton, with a view to his marriage with Elizabeth, daughter of his guardian, Sir Philip Courtenay, of Powderham.[2] The wedding took place in the private oratory, or chapel of Powderham Castle, by special permission of Bishop Lacy, in 1450.[3] Two of the shields sculptured over the western arch of the gatehouse at Dunster show the arms of Luttrell impaled with those of Courtenay. The first commemorates the marriage of Andrew Luttrell with Lady Elizabeth Courtenay, who purchased Dunster from Lady Joan Mohun ; the second commemorates the marriage of their great-grandson with another Elizabeth Courtenay, and heralds may notice that in the second instance the label on the Courtenay shield bears nine labels as a mark of cadency, the Courtenays of Powderham, being a younger branch of the family then represented by the Earl of Devon.

It was in James Luttrell's time that the laymen of Dunster resolved to build or rebuild the central tower of their parochial church. They seem to have been collecting money for the purpose for several years, for as far back as 1419, a certain William Pynson bequeathed forty shillings towards the new bell-tower, twenty shillings towards a new bell, and half-a-mark towards a new rood-loft.[4] In 1443 a contract was made between

[1] See Appendix H.
[2] Dunster Castle Muniments, Box i, Nos. 19, 23, 24. Patent Roll, 27 Henry VI, part 3, m. 1.
[3] Oliver's "Ecclesiastical Antiquities in Devon," vol. i, p. 28.
[4] Dunster Church Book, f. 123

the parish of Dunster and a certain John Marys of
Stokgursy, for the erection of a tower an hundred feet
high, within the next three years. The "patron" or
design, which was supplied by a freemason named Richard
Pope, showed a French buttress at three of the angles
and a "vice" or corkscrew staircase at the fourth, with
battlements and four pinnacles on the summit. There
were to be two windows on the first floor and four
windows at the bell-bed, and three gurgoyles. The
parish undertook to provide all ropes, pulleys, wynches,
and other necessary implements, and to deliver the
building materials in the transept of the church from
time to time. Inasmuch, therefore, as Marys was not
put to any expense in this respect, his remuneration was
fixed at the low rate of 13s. 4d. a foot.[1] Some alterations
must have been made in the contract afterwards, for the
present tower does not attain to the full height of an
hundred feet, nor do the windows quite correspond to the
specifications of 1443.

In one of the later years of the reign of Henry VI,
Alexander Hody, who was probably the son of Thomas
Hody, who had been receiver-general of Sir Hugh
Luttrell, drew up a statement of complaint against
James Luttrell, Esquire. According to the account there
given, Luttrell sent a man to Hody's wife to ask where
her husband was to be found, and she, suspecting no
deceit, told him where he would be for the next three
days. Luttrell then seized one of Hody's servants "and
putte hym in his castell of Dunster by the space of a
nyghte, so that the seyd servaunt should not make
knowliche to the seyd Alisaunder of the unfeythfull
disposission of the seyd Jamys." The story proceeds:—

" In the mornyng there upon the seyd Jamys with the nombir of xxxv
persones and moo with bowys beyng bente and arowys in ther hendys by
hym unlawfully gaderyd, wente to the house of Thomas Bratton Squyer
fadir in lawe to the seyd Alisaunder, where and atte which tyme she
saide here husbande would be, and there sowght hym purposyng to have
murderyd and sleyne the seyd Alisaunder.

" Item the seyd Jamys ande his servaunts to the nombir of 24 persones
arrayed with dobeletts of defence, paletts, bowys, arrowys, gloyvys and
speris to . . . . . and ther John Coker servaunt to the seyd Alisaunder
bete and woundyd so that the seyd John was in dispeyre of his lyfe."

[1] Dunster Church Book, f. 10. See Appendix I.

DUNSTER CHURCH.
from the South West

"Item the seyd Jamys with his servaunts and othir to the nombir of 44ᵗⁱ persones and moo of grete malice forthought purposyng to murdyr and slee the seyd Alisaunder, entryd the castell of Taunton and ther the Constabillarye of the same and all the dorys ther brake, and entrid serchyng after the seyd Alisaunder, and 7 sponys of silver of the seyd Alisaunder and 5 ivery knives and other godis of the seyd Alisaunder toke and bare aweye and apon the wyfe of the seyd Alisaunder asaute made, bete, and with here daggers manasyd to slee, and so would have do, ner by grace of God one of ther felishipp lette hit, and Walter Peyntoir servant to the seyd Alisaunder cowardly with dagger nye to the dethe smote, and apon Sir Roberd preste to the seyd Alisaunder asaute made and hym by the here to the grounde pluckyd betyng hym with the pomelles of ther swerdis."

"Item the seyd Alisaunder askyth of the seyd Jamys 100 marke in money of the dette of Richard Luttrell whos administrator of goodis and catall the seyd Jamys ys.

"Item he askyth of the seyd Jamys 17s. 6d. remaynyng unpayyd for potts of silver & gilte for a gretter summe of moneye by the seyd Alisaunder to him sold."[1]

James Luttrell was soon afterwards engaged in a strife of far greater moment, for in 1460 he took up arms on behalf of the House of Lancaster. He fought against the Duke of York at Wakefield on the last day but one of that year, and he was knighted on the field of battle.[2] Seven weeks later he again served under the victorious banner of Queen Margaret at the second battle of St. Albans, but he there received a wound of which he died on the fifth day. He left a widow and two sons, Alexander and Hugh, both under age and apparently well provided for by various entails and settlements.[3] The first parliament of Edward IV however passed a sweeping decree against all the chief adherents of Henry VI, Sir James Luttrell being reckoned among those who "with grete dispite and cruell violence, horrible and unmanly tyranage murdered" the Duke of York at Wakefield, was included among the traitors who were to "stand and be convycted and attainted of high treason and forfeit to the King and his heires all the castles, maners," and other lands of which they were possessed.[4] Edward IV had evidently anticipated this decree, for the accounts of the receipts and expenses of his bailiff at

[1] Dunster Castle Muniments, Box xxxvii, No. 16.
[2] Heralds' College MS., Le Neve (quoted by Narcissus Luttrell).
[3] Inquisitiones post mortem, 1 Edward IV, No. 43. William of Worcester's "Annales," printed in "Wars of the English in France," Rolls' Series, vol. ii, p. 776.
[4] "Rolls of Parliament," vol. v, pp. 177, 179.

Dunster begin as early as the 16th of March, 1461, twelve days only after the accession of the House of York.[1]   In June, 1463, the king granted to William Herbert, Earl of Pembroke, and his heirs in tail, the honor, castle, manor and borough of Dunster, and the manors of Minehead, Kilton, East Quantockshead, and Iveton, together with the hundred of Carhampton, and other lands in the county of Somerset, the manors of Chilton and Blancombe in Devonshire, the manors of Stonehall and Woodhall in Suffolk, and all other lands and tenements in those counties lately forfeited to the crown by the treason of Sir James Luttrell.[2]   The Earl of Pembroke was beheaded by the Lancastrians in 1469, and in 1472 the king committed the custody of Dunster and of other estates just mentioned to Ann, Countess of Pembroke, during the minority of her son.[3]   In 1475 the young earl obtained quiet possession of all his lands, and the cause of the Luttrells seemed hopeless indeed.[4] During the long years of their adversity we only hear of them twice, firstly when Lady Elizabeth Luttrell, the widow of Sir James, stood as godmother to a son of the Duke of Clarence, born at Tewkesbury in 1476, and secondly when Edward IV in a relenting mood allowed Hugh Luttrell son of Sir James, to receive the reversion of a moiety of the manor and market of Debenham in Suffolk, which had been settled by Sir Hugh Luttrell on the issue of his daughter Elizabeth Harleston.[5]   Alexander Luttrell, the eldest son of Sir James, died in obscurity.

[1] Dunster Castle Muniments, Box i, No. 27.
[2] Pat. Roll, 3 Ed. IV, part 2, m. 16.
[3] Inquisitiones post mortem 9 and 10 Edward IV, No. 21.   Patent Roll 12 Edward IV, part 2, m. 23.
[4] Pat. Roll, 15 Edw. IV, part 3, m. 7.
[5] Dugdale's "Monasticon" (1819), vol. ii, p. 64.   Patent Roll, 22 Edward IV, part 1, m. 26.

Arms on bench-end in Thorverton Church.

PART III.

The great victory of the Lancastrian party on the field
of Bosworth revived the hopes of the Luttrell family.
Henry VII had not occupied the throne many weeks
before "Hugh Loterell, son and heir to James Loterell,
Knight," presented a petition in parliament setting forth
that his father had been attainted "only for the trouth
and liegauns that the seid James owed to his prynce and
sovereyn lord that tyme Kyng Henry the VI, late Kyng
of England," and praying that the attainder might consequently be reversed. His prayer was readily granted,
and so after an enforced absence of twenty four years he
returned to Dunster Castle to take possession of his
ancestral domains.[1] The ejectment of the Herberts however did not put an end to his troubles, for his mother,
the Lady Elizabeth, laid claim to the manors of East
Quantockshead, Kilton and Minehead as her jointure.
Moreover, she and her second husband Thomas Malet
refused to give up the plate and other personal property
valued at 800 marks which Sir James Luttrell had
bequeathed to his eldest son.[2] At last, after legal
proceedings had been commenced, the two parties agreed
to a compromise. East Quantockshead was assigned to
the Malets, and Minehead to Hugh Luttrell, who undertook to pay eighty marks a year for it to his mother for
the rest of her life. The Malets then delivered to him
"2 basons of silver, 2 ewers, 2 gilte cuppes covered
standyng, 2 pottes of silver and gilt with a pot of silver,
2 saltes with one cover, 3 bolles with one cover, a chafyng
disshe of silver, 2 doseyn spones, a chaleys, a masse boke,

[1] "Rolls of Parliament," vol. vi, p. 297.
[2] Dunster Castle Muniments, Box i. No. 24.

a peire of vestementes," and a list of the other goods which should descend to him on the death of his mother.[1] The Lady Elizabeth lived for several years after this, and at her death in 1493 was buried near the high altar of Dunster Church. An incised stone slab, which has lately been removed to the south aisle of the chancel, represents her attired in a sideless dress, faced or fronted with ermine, and a mantle lined with ermine, the neck being bare and the head covered with a veil falling below the shoulders. The inscription, which it may be remarked makes no mention of her second husband, runs :—-

"Orate queso pro aia dne Elizabeth lutterell que obiit primo die mensis Septembris anno dni Millio cccc Nonagesio tercio. Nunc Xre te petimus miserer' qs qui bristi redime pbitos noli dampnare redemptos."

This may be translated :—

"Pray, I beseech you, for the soul of Lady Elizabeth Lutterell, who died on the first day of the month of September in the year of our Lord 1493. Now O Christ we pray thee, have mercy we beseech thee. O thou who didst come to redeem the lost, do not condemn the redeemed."[2]

Hugh Luttrell of Dunster was created a Knight of the Bath at the coronation of Elizabeth of York, wife of Henry VII, in November, 1487, and a few days later he received from his uncle, Peter Courtenay, Bishop of Winchester, a grant of the office of Master of Poundisford Park, with an annuity of £10 for life.[3] He was Sheriff of Dorset and Somerset in 1488.[4] Nine years later he attached himself to the suite of the Duke of Buckingham, and went with him to take the field against Perkin Warbeck.[5] When the Princess Catharine of Aragon came to England in 1501, in order to marry the Prince of Wales, Sir Hugh Luttrell was one of the seven knights and gentlemen of Somerset who were appointed to escort her from Crewkerne to Sherborne.[6] In 1513 he was on board the ship of Leonard Fiscaballis, a vessel of 300

[1] Ibid., Box xxviii, No. 18.

[2] Leland describes this slab as existing at Carhampton, and Collinson does not appear to have discovered the error. A good deal of the pitch, or black composition with which the incised lines were filled has disappeared.

[3] Anstis's " Knights of the Bath,"

p. 37. Dunster Castle Muniments, Box xxxvii, No. 17.

[4] Fuller's "Worthies."

[5] Holinshed's "Chronicle," vol. iii, p. 784.

[6] "Letters and Papers of the reigns of Richard III. and Henry VII." (ed. Gairdner), vol. i, p. 406.

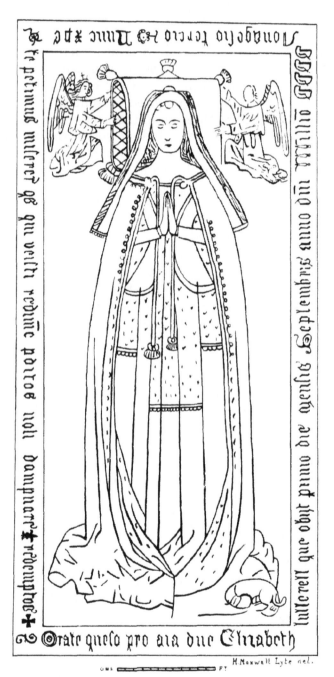

INCISED SLAB OF LADY ELIZABETH LUTTRELL.

A.D. 1493.

tons, belonging to the king's fleet.[1] Leland states positively that "Sir Hugh Luterell, in the time of Dame Margarete his wife, sister to the olde Lord Dalbeney made a fair tourre by north, cummyng into the castelle."[2] It has however been shewn already that the gatehouse was built in the reign of Henry V by the first Sir Hugh Luttrell, the Great Seneschal of Normandy.

The most important architectural work that is certainly known to have been done at Dunster in the time of the second Sir Hugh Luttrell was the formal division of the church of St. George into two separate parts. This church, like most of its neighbours, underwent considerable alteration during the period in which the Perpendicular style was in vogue, almost all traces of the Norman and Early English work being then destroyed or concealed. An aisle of four bays was first added on the north side of the nave, and then another of six bays on the south, the shortness of the north aisle and the absence of windows in the north wall of the nave being due to the plan of the conventual buildings which adjoined the church. A poor Perpendicular arch was about the same time inserted within the original round-headed doorway at the west end of the nave, and a large traceried window was placed above it. The eastern portion of the church was similarly altered and enlarged. The transepts appear to have been built or rebuilt in the early part of the fifteenth century, and the tower in 1443. Chapels were thrown out on the eastern side of the two transepts, and then converted into chancel aisles by the opening of low arches between them and the chancel. The northern of these chapels, which was probably dedicated to the Blessed Virgin, seems to be the older of the two, and is separated from the north transept by an ordinary Perpendicular arch. The arch between the corresponding chapel, which was probably the chantry of Holy Trinity, and the south transept has been very differently treated. Here the builders of the fifteenth century resorted to a most whimsical device for making a wide opening without any unnecessary waste of materials or money. Finding an Early English arch ready to

---

[1] Letters and Papers, Foreign and Domestic" (ed. Brewer), vol. i, p. 652,

[2] "Itinerary," vol. ii, p. 100.

hand and in good condition though somewhat too narrow for their requirements. they made use of the upper part by raising it on moulded jambs which were bent outward immediately under the capitals, thus giving more width below than above. The result is a shouldered arch whose marked peculiarity can hardly fail to arrest the attention of every visitor to the church. Inasmuch as the eastern wall of the southern chapel abutted against one of the lancet windows on the south side of the chancel, it was thought desirable to close them all, and then in order to get the light which had thus been lost, a large Perpendicular window was substituted for the three lancets in the east wall. The small chapel on the north side of the chancel was also rebuilt before or at the time of the erection of the monument of Sir Hugh Luttrell already described. Thus the church of St. George at Dunster

became a Perpendicular building of considerable dimensions, though of inferior workmanship. The high altar stood at the east end of the chancel, and there were other altars in the different chapels. The rood-loft stretched across the space under the western arch of the tower, and was approached by a staircase cut in the thickness of the north-western pier of the tower. The monks had their stalls and said their offices in the chancel, while the parishioners for the most part attended the ministrations of the vicar, a secular priest, who had the cure of their souls.

The Benedictine Order had by the end of the fifteenth

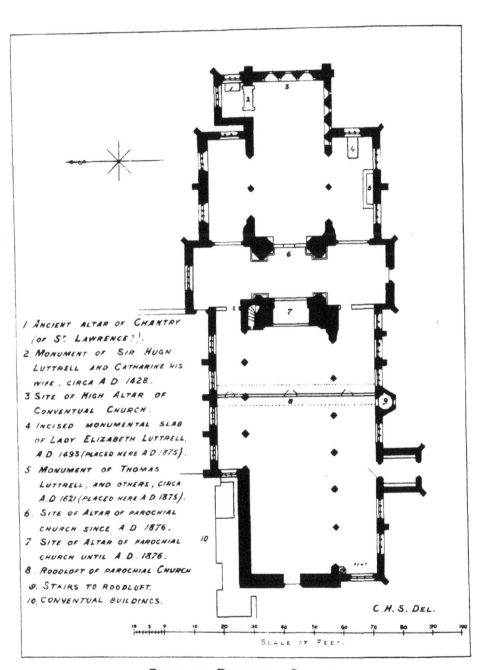

1. ANCIENT ALTAR OF CHANTRY
   (OF ST. LAWRENCE?).
2. MONUMENT OF SIR HUGH
   LUTTRELL AND CATHARINE HIS
   WIFE, CIRCA A.D. 1428.
3. SITE OF HIGH ALTAR OF
   CONVENTUAL CHURCH.
4. INCISED MONUMENTAL SLAB
   OF LADY ELIZABETH LUTTRELL,
   A.D. 1493 (PLACED HERE A.D. 1875).
5. MONUMENT OF THOMAS
   LUTTRELL, AND OTHERS, CIRCA
   A.D. 1621 (PLACED HERE A.D. 1875).
6. SITE OF ALTAR OF PAROCHIAL
   CHURCH SINCE A.D. 1876.
7. SITE OF ALTAR OF PAROCHIAL
   CHURCH UNTIL A.D. 1876.
8. ROODLOFT OF PAROCHIAL CHURCH
9. STAIRS TO ROODLOFT.
10. CONVENTUAL BUILDINGS.

C. H. S. DEL.

SCALE OF FEET.

PLAN OF DUNSTER CHURCH.

century lost the popularity which it formerly enjoyed in England, and its members were regarded with jealousy if not with suspicion. At Dunster a controversy arose in the reign of Henry VII between the monks and the parishioners at large about the rights and emoluments of the vicar. The Abbot of Glastonbury, Thomas Tremayle, one of the justices of the realm, and Thomas Gilbert, a Doctor of Canon Law, were chosen as arbitrators between the different parties concerned, Sir Hugh Luttrell appearing as the representative of the lay folk who were for the most part his own tenants. In the award which was formally delivered in April 1498, the arbitrators decreed that the eastern part of the church of St. George should belong exclusively to the monks, and that the parishioners should make a new chancel for their vicar in the eastern part of the nave at the altar of St. James which stood either between the western piers of the tower, or close against the south-western pier. This altar was thus converted into the main altar of the parochial church, and it was ordered that all offerings made there should be received by the vicar on behalf of the prior and brethren who had of old enjoyed the offerings made at the high altar of the undivided church. The eastern and western parts of the church became distinct and separate churches, the transepts and the tower being apparently treated as common to the monks and the parishioners alike. Inasmuch however as it was desirable that the regular and the secular clergy of Dunster should sometimes unite in solemn procession, it was decreed that on the thirteen principal festivals of the year the monks should walk down the middle of the old chancel, and so into the nave through a door on the north side of the parochial chancel. The order of procession was also strictly laid down by the arbitrators in order to prevent future dispute. First were to go the cross-bearer of the monks and the cross-bearer of the parishioners, then the vicar and his clerks, then the prior and brethren, and lastly the body of the parishioners. When the procession had made its accustomed circuit the monks were to return to their chancel and the vicar and his clerks to theirs.[1]

[1] Register of Bishop King at Wells.

The terms of this award explain the singular position of the external turret which contains the spiral staircase leading to the rood-loft. It will be seen by the view of Dunster Church from the south-west, as well as by the ground plan, that this turret instead of being attached to any part of the architectural chancel stands to the west of the transepts, and projects from the south aisle of the architectural nave. It was placed there in order to give access to the upper part of the beautiful rood-screen which the parishioners erected at the end of the fifteenth century to separate their new chancel from the nave. The south aisle of the architectural nave was at the same time either built from the ground or so altered as to allow the erection of the turret. The general design and the details of the rood-screen are almost exactly the same as those of the rood-screens in the adjoining parishes of Carhampton, Minehead and Timberscombe. The south porch dates from the reign of Henry VII or Henry VIII, its walls being in part made of fragments of older shafts. The rood-loft of the undivided church under the western arch of the tower was probably taken down when the new one was made to the west of it, and the monks appear to have put up an open screen at the western end of the old chancel and its aisles so as to separate them from the parochial church. At any rate the screen which now stands under the curious shouldered arch already described stood until lately under the eastern arch of the tower. The award of the Abbot of Glastonbury and his colleagues in 1498 has had a very lasting effect, for notwithstanding all the changes of nearly four hundred years there are still at Dunster two distinct churches under one roof.

The arrangement made about the emoluments of the vicar was that he and his successors should have the house in which he then dwelt, and a yearly stipend of £8, and also all the offerings that the devout parishioners might make for obits, trentals, anniversaries, private masses, together with the offerings known as "the Bederaele Penys."[1] Fresh disputes however arose before long, and in 1512 the Bishop of Bath and Wells, Cardinal Adrian de Castello, issued a new decree on the subject.

---

[1] Register of Bishop King.

PART OF THE ROODLOFT IN DUNSTER CHURCH.

By this he ordained that the Vicar of Dunster should receive a stipend of only £4 a year from the revenues of the Priory, together with the rent of a certain field, a rent of 2s. from some fulling mills, and another rent of 2s. from the house hitherto occupied by the vicar. He also restricted his other receipts to the payments made by the parishioners for the publication of the bede-roll after the gospel at high mass, and those made by them when they went to confession in Lent. On the other hand he ordained that the vicar should sit at table with the monks in their refectory, and partake of all their meals free of charge. He also assigned to him a chamber in a house adjoining the churchyard.[1] It is probable that the picturesque building at the south eastern corner of the churchyard near the south transept was the house formerly occupied by the vicars of Dunster for the time being. In a deed of the reign of Elizabeth, it is simply described as "the stone-healed house."[2]

Sir Hugh Luttrell's first wife was Margaret, daughter of Robert Hill by Alice his wife, daughter of John Stourton, and widow of William Daubeney.[3] There is among the family papers at Nettlecombe a letter from Giles, Lord Daubeney, to Sir John Trevelyan, thanking him for taking care of the king's game in the Forest of Exmoor. It proceeds :—

"Howe soo be it I am enformed that of late a litle grugge is fallen bitwene my brother Sr Hugh Luttrell and you, for that he hunted of late in the outewods of the same forest, and therupon a couple of hounds were taken up by servants of yours from his servants. After that, cousyn, inasmoche as my said brother Luttrell is a boderer of the said forest, and that ye knowe he hath maried my sister, and the man whom I doo love tenderly, my mynde is and desire unto you that you shuld have an yghe unto hym above all others in those parties. And that when it shall like hym to kyll a dere or to hunte for his disporte, that ye suffer nym soo to doe, I pray you as hertely as I can. Writen at Grenewich the xx daie of Feverer. And I pray you cousyn, let my said brother take his disporte, and if he list let hym kyll one dere in somer and a nother in wynter herafter."[4]

A contract of the year 1514 between Sir Thomas

[1] Register of Bishop Adrian at Wells, 104.

[2] Dunster Castle Muniments, Box xiv, No. 26. The existence of this deed was not known a few years ago when under

Mr. Street's directions the house in question was roofed with tiles.

[3] "Collectanea Topographica et Genealogica," vol. i, p. 313.

[4] "Trevelyan Papers" (Camden Soc.), vol. i, p. 120.

Wyndham and Sir Hugh Luttrell shows the way in which marriages were arranged in those days. The first clause runs :—

"Andrew sonn and heir apparent of the saied Sir Hugh by the grace of God shall marcy and take to his wief Margaret, one of the doughters of the saied Sir Thomas, or any other of the doughters of the said Sir Thomas suche as the saied Andrew shall best licke byfore Wonysdaie next after lowe Soundaie next comminge, after the cusdom and lawe of holye Churche, if the said Margaret or such of her sisters as the said Andrewe shall best licke therunto will agree, and the lawe of holy churche it wyll permytt and suffer."

The time specified was certainly not over-long, as there were only four weeks between the date of the contract and the last day allowed for the solemnization of the marriage. It was nevertheless stipulated that if Andrew Luttrell should die during that short interval his next brother John should in his stead marry one of the daughters of Sir Thomas Wyndham within forty days of the last day allowed for Andrew's wedding. Another clause runs :

"The said Sir Hugh at his proper costs and charges shall apparell the saied Andrewe or John that shall happen to marcy with one of the doughters of the said Sir Thomas at the saied daie of maryage as shalbe convenyent for his degree."

Sir Thomas Wyndham on his side undertook to "apparell" his daughter for the wedding, and to pay one half of all other expenses connected therewith. The lady's portion was seven hundred marks (£466 13s. 4d.), which were paid to Sir Hugh Luttrell in instalments, he giving a guarantee that his heir should eventually inherit all his real property.[1]

Andrew Luttrell was duly married to Margaret Wyndham, and on the death of his father, in February 1521, he became Lord of Dunster.[2] He had some trouble, however, with his stepmother Walthean, a lady who had survived three successive husbands, and who now claimed the manor of East Quantockshead as part of the jointure settled on her by Sir Hugh Luttrell. In her answer to a bill of complaints against her she stated that her stepson Andrew Luttrell, "of his wilful and cruel mind, without any cause reasonable," had on Sir Hugh's death taken away all her goods and chatels, not even leaving her

[1] Dunster Castle Muniments, Box ii, No. 3.   Henry VIII. The date is wrongly given on his monument as 1522.

[2] Inquisitiones post mortem, 12-13

dishes, pots, or pans, and that she and her children and servants "stood in daily peril of their lives." She accordingly removed· to London, leaving only a certain Lewis Griffyth and an "impotent poor man," eighty years of age, to keep possession of the manor of East Quantockshead in her name. She professed to have instructed her representative to offer no active resistance if Andrew Luttrell or any other person should attempt to eject him from the manor house. A serious fray, however, soon occurred in the deer-park known as Quantock Park. One of Andrew Luttrell's servants, John Gay by name, declared that on the 7th of June 1521, Lewis. Griffyth and several other evil disposed persons "with force and armys, that is to say araed in harnys with bowes and arrowes, swerds, bockelers and byllys," assaulted him "in ryottus wyse," shot eleven arrows at him and "grevously strake hym yn dyvers places of hys body, so that and yff socoure of trees hadde nott, byn they hadde kylled and murdered hym oute of hand." Griffyth's account of the affair was entirely different. He maintained that he had shot only one arrow, and that merely in order "to fere" Gay, who had unlawfully come with two other persons to cut sixty trees for posts in the Lady Walthean's park. According to his version, Gay and the two wood-cutters returned an hour later with "two idell men" from the town or village, assaulted and beat him and a child of sixteen, and took them nearly three miles to the house of Lord Fitz-Warren, who put them in fetters and locked them up for two hours in his porter's lodge. Gay's bill of complaint and Griffyth's answer were laid before the king, but it does not appear what course the Court of Star Chamber took in the matter.[1] The quarrel between Andrew Luttrell and his step-mother had probably been appeased before the marriage of his·sister Eleanor with Roger Yorke, Serjeant-at-Law, a son of Lady Walthean Luttrell by one of her former husbands.[2] John Luttrell of Dunster, Andrew's younger brother, became the ancestor of the Luttrells of Kentsbury and Spaxton.

---

[1] Star Chamber Proceedings, Henry VIII. (Record Office, Floor A, Press 3, Div. G, Shelf 3, No. 16, ff. 20-22).

[2] Dunster Castle Muniments, Box xxiii, No. 22.

Andrew Luttrell served the office of Sheriff of Dorset and Somerset in 1528, and soon afterward took knighthood.[1] Leland records that he re-built part of the wall of Dunster Castle on the east side.[2] Nevertheless he, like his father Sir Hugh, chose to live at East Quantockshead rather than at Dunster. It is probable that one or other of them built a great part of the manor-house at the former place, a tower at the south-western angle being the only part of the existing fabric that appears earlier than their time. The keep at Dunster had already fallen into decay, and the Luttrells may have found the buildings in the lower ward of the Castle ill suited to their mode of life in the peaceable reign of Henry VIII. Sir Andrew Luttrell described himself as "of East Quantocshead" in his will, and gave instructions that he should be buried in the chancel of that church.[3] A monument on the north side of the altar has the arms of Luttrell impaled with those of Hill and of Wyndham. The inscription which is cut in rude characters on the slab runs :—

"Here lupt hugh luttrell knpght tophe departpd 1522 the fprst dap of february, here lpt Andro luttrell knpght hps sone tophe departpd the pere of owr lord god mcccccxxrbiii the iiii dap of map on tophops soulps ihu habe m'cp."

Lady Margaret Luttrell survived her husband Sir Andrew by about forty years, and continued to occupy the manor-house at East Quantockshead.[4]

Sir Andrew Luttrell's son and successor, John Luttrell, spent very little of his time at Dunster, as he was generally engaged in the king's service. He fought with distinction in the Scotch wars, and in 1544 he was knighted at Leith by the Earl of Hertford, then Lieutenant of the English king.[5] Three years later he led three hundred men in the front of the battle of Pinkie, and by his skill and valour on this and other similar occasions he earned the reputation of "a noble captain."[6] He was afterwards sent to St. Coomes Ins on the Frith of Forth, in command of a hundred hakbutters, fifty pioneers, with two row-barks and seventy mariners.[7] In

---

[1] Fuller's "Worthies."
[2] "Itinerary," vol. ii, p. 101.
[3] Wills at Somerset House. "Dingeley," f. 20.
[4] East Quantockshead Register, 1580. July 7. "Died the right worshipful Dame Margaret Luttrell and was buried the 8th of August following."
[5] Stowe's "Annales" (1631), p. 586.
[6] "Machyn's Diary" (Camden Soc.).
[7] Holinshed's Chronicle, vol. iii, p. 990.

SIR JOHN LUTTRELL, A.D. 1550.
FROM AN ORIGINAL PAINTING AT DUNSTER CASTLE.
by Lucas de Heere.

February 1549 he borrowed the sum of £132 2s. "for the service of the King's Majestie in the northe parts of England."[1] A few months later, being in command of the fort of Bouticraig, he found himself attacked by the Scots and French, eight thousand strong, and although his troops made frequent sallies and captured the artillery of -the enemy, he was forced to yield himself a prisoner. The rest of the garrison was mercilessly put to the sword.[2] Sir John Luttrell was again at liberty and in England in 1550. Collinson says in his description of Dunster : —

"There is an ancient picture in the castle done by a tolerable hand, of a man swimming in the sea, and looking up to certain figures in the clouds ; to which is added, by a later and very indifferent painter, the figure of a lady floating by his side. This is traditionally said to have been the picture of Sir John Luttrell, and refers to his having saved a certain lady from drowning, whom he was then in love with, and afterwards married."[3]

Savage quotes this passage in his "History of the Hundred of Carhampton," and adds :—

"The lady is represented as being secured to his arm by a handkerchief, and he holds up the arm so that she may float on the surface of the sea, whilst he is swimming with the other. A figure of victory, accompanied by a numerous group, appears as if ready to crown him with laurel."

A careful examination of this interesting picture shows that these descriptions are grossly inaccurate. The man in the water is really represented in the act of wading ashore ; the handkerchief or scarf wound round his arm is not attached to any other person or thing, and the figure floating by his side is that of a young man with a well-defined moustache. The supposed crown of laurel is .a single sprig of olive or of bay. The chief figure is unquestionably that of Sir John Luttrell, but it is uncertain whether the picture is intended to commemorate a real event in his life, or whether it is wholly allegorical. The man-of-war in the background, struck by lightning and deserted by its affrighted crew, may be held either to represent a real wreck from which Sir John Luttrell made an adventurous escape, or, like the smaller boats and figures, to be a mere accessory illustrative of the violence

---

[1] Dunster Castle Muniments, Box iii, No. 3.
[2] Kennett's "Complete History," vol. ii, p. 291. Stowe's "Annales," p. 601.
[3] "History of Somerset," vol. ii, p. 12.

of the tempest.   The different inscriptions on the panel
seem rather to favour the latter view.   Sir John Luttrell
wears a bracelet on either arm inscribed respectively
"*Nec flexit lucrum,*" and "*Nec fregit discrimen.*"   A
rock in the foreground on the right bears the following
inscriptions :—

"MORE THE̅ THE THE ROCK AMYDYS THE RAGING SEAS

THE CONSTAT HERT NO DA̅GER DREDDYS NOR FEARYS.

S. I. L.

Effigiem renovare tuam fortissime miles
Ingens me meritum fecit amorque tui.
Nam nisi curasses hueredem scribere fratrem
Hei tua contigerant prædia nulla mihi.

1591.   G. L.

1550

HE."

The initials S. I. L. may be those of the author of the
English couplet, which evidently forms part of the picture
as originally painted in 1550.   The monogram HE is certainly that of Lucas de Heere, a Flemish artist who painted
in France and in England in the second half of the
sixteenth century.   This portrait must have been one of
his earliest works, as he was only sixteen years of age in
1550.   The head of Sir John Luttrell is done with some
spirit, but the drawing of the figures shows a very imperfect knowledge of anatomy.   As it is doubtful whether
de Heere visited England as early as the year 1550, it is
possible that he may have taken the portrait in France,
while Sir John Luttrell was a prisoner of war.   The Latin
lines were added by George Luttrell, Sir John's nephew,
when he had the picture "restored" in 1591.   The semi-
nude female figures above the clouds are evidently allegorical.   One of them holds Sir John Luttrell's war-horse,
another his breast-plate, another his sword, another his
money bag, another his helmet, and another his crest, a
peacock.   The principal female figure has in her right
hand a sprig of foliage, which, if intended to represent
olive, may be emblematical of the peace that was made
between England and Scotland in the very year in which
the picture was painted.   This is not the only picture in
which Lucas de Heere gave rein to his fancy, for in a

portrait of Queen Elizabeth at Kensington he introduced figures of Juno, Minerva, Venus, and Cupid.[1]

While Sir John Luttrell was in his teens, or absent serving in the king's wars, the great tide of religious innovation swept over the whole of England, and left its mark on Dunster, as on other places. At the dissolution of the monasteries the Priory of Dunster, which was then inhabited by three Benedictine monks of Bath, and which had a nett revenue of about £38 a year, was confiscated by Henry VIII.[2] The site was in 1539 let for twenty-one years to John Luttrell, the second son of Sir Hugh, at a yearly rent of £3 13s. 4d., with remainder to a certain Humphrey Colles, gentleman. The Luttrells were naturally unwilling that a building which adjoined and apparently included within its precinct the monastic chancel in which several of their ancestors lay buried should for ever pass into the hands of strangers. Accordingly in 1543 Lady Margaret Luttrell of East Quantockshead, widow of Sir Andrew and mother of Sir John, persuaded Humphry Colles to sell his remainder to her for the sum of £85 16s. 8d.[3] At her death, some forty years later, the priory with all its appurtenances passed to her nephew George Luttrell of Dunster Castle, and it is now the property of his descendant and representative.[4]

It should here be remarked that successive owners of Dunster Castle have for a long time past claimed as their own that part of Dunster Church which was assigned to the monks by the award of the Abbot of Glastonbury and his colleagues in 1498. They have claimed it, not in the sense in which a rector, whether clerical or lay, claims the chancel of an ordinary parochial church, but in the sense in which they have claimed their own castle. In other words, they have claimed the right to close it against the vicar, to secularize it, or even to pull it down. There are well-known instances of similar claims at Arundel and elsewhere, and in this case it is certain that the Luttrells were accounted responsible for the repair of "the old church" long before they acquired the Rectory and

[1] Walpole's "Anecdotes of Painting," vol. i.

[2] Dugdale's "Monasticon," vol. iv, pp. 200-203.

[3] Dunster Castle Muniments, Box xvi,

Nos. 14, 22. State Papers, 37 Hen. VIII Bundle iv, No. 60.

[4] Dunster Castle Muniments, Box xvi, No. 17.

advowson of the living in 1825. They kept it as their private mausoleum until a few years ago, and when a faculty was obtained for the restoration of the whole church under Mr. Street's direction, no mention was made in it of any part east of the transepts.

The dissolution of the monasteries was followed very shortly by the suppression of the colleges and chantries throughout the realm, and the property of the chantry of St. Laurence at Dunster became thereby vested in the Crown.[1]   Part of its revenue, which in the reign of Edward VI amounted to about £9 a year, was derived from a very picturesque weather-tiled house generally called "the Nunnery," on the north side of Middle Street in Dunster. This name, however, is of modern origin and quite misleading, the house in question having been known as "the High House," even in the present century. In former times it was described as "the Tenement of St. Laurence," and the street in which it stands as "Castle-bayly."[2]

There are two other old houses in Dunster which deserve a passing notice here. One of them known as "Lower Marsh," and standing near the railway station, has a rich Perpendicular oratory over the entrance porch, and traces of an open roofed hall. The other, now known as "the Luttrell Arms Hotel," stands at the north-eastern end of the principal street. Besides some curious plaster work of the time of James I, it has a stone porch pierced with openings for cross-bows, and a wing with a good open roof, and an elaborately carved façade of oak. Nothing is certainly known about the origin or history of this picturesque building, but there are some grounds for believing that it formerly belonged to the neighbouring Abbey of Cleeve.

There were in the early years of the Reformation at least three stone crosses in the parish of Dunster. Of the Early English cross which stood in the churchyard the steps and a short stump only remain in their old

[1] Certificates of Colleges and Chantries. (Augmentation Office), Somerset xlii, No. 42.

[2] Dunster Castle Muniments, Box viii, No. 2. (4 Henry VII.) "Totam illam shopam meam vocatam le Corner Shoppe situatam ad finem australem vici foralis de Dunster, inter vicum regium ex parte orientali, et tenementum Cantarie Sancti Laurentii ex parte occidentali, ac tenementum heredum Rogeri Ryvers ex parte boreali, et viam regiam ex parte australi." 30 Henry VI.

THE HIGH HOUSE

DUNSTER

position. The remains of the "Butter Cross" of the fifteenth century, which formerly stood at the southern end of the main street, were some years ago removed to a less frequented spot near the old road to Minehead. The Alcombe cross has entirely disappeared. An interesting little cross, bearing a figure of St. Michael, is still to be seen above the western gable of Dunster Church.

The rood or roods in the church and most of the side altars were probably taken down by the iconoclasts in the reign of Edward VI. In his second or third year a large Bible and a copy of the Paraphrases of Erasmus were bought for Dunster Church at a cost of £1 5s. and 13s. 4d. respectively.[1] There were about that time fifty "partakers of the Lordes holy sooper" resident in the parish. The vicar was still in receipt of daily food in kind and of a salary of £4 as allotted to him by the award of the Bishop in 1512.[2]

There is among the muniments at Dunster Castle the following small memorandum about swan-upping written on parchment in the time of Queen Elizabeth.

"Sr John Lutterell.

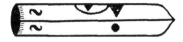

Sr Andrew Lutterell.

Theise were the markes wch theise men above writen had upon the beeles of their swanes belonginge unto the Castell of Dunster by inheritance and alwayes kepte at the Mere by Glastonberrye. Yt is good to renewe yt. S.L.".[3]

Soon after his escape or release from captivity in Scotland, Sir John Luttrell received from Edward VI a grant of a hundred marks a year for life in consideration of his faithful services.[4] Collinson says that in his desire to obtain glory Sir John Luttrell "greatly wasted the fair patrimony which descended to him from his ancestors: selling great part of his demesnes at Dunster, Kilton, and elsewhere; and at last mortgaging the plate and furni-

[1] Ministers' Accounts (Court of Augmentation), 1-2 Edward VI, Roll xliv. m. 16.
[2] Certificates of Colleges and Chantries.
Somerset xlii. No. 42.
[3] Box xxxvii. No. 24.
[4] Ibid. Box xxxvii. No. 27.

ture belonging to Dunster Castle and his other houses."[1] The chief foundation for this exaggerated statement lies in the fact that Minehead Park was in May 1551 mortgaged to Hugh Stewkeley for £230 13s 4d.[2]

Sir John Luttrell died at Greenwich, on the 10th of July 1551.[3] At the time of his death he was endeavouring to obtain a divorce from his wife, Mary, daughter of Sir Griffith Rys, K.B.[4] By her he had issue three daughters and co-heiresses, Catharine, Dorothy, and Mary. He was anxious, however, that his estates should be preserved in the Luttrell family, and he accordingly entailed them on the male issue of his brothers Thomas, Nicholas, and Andrew successively.[5] The property to which Thomas Luttrell succeeded on the death of Sir John was comparatively small. Lady Margaret Luttrell, his mother, was in possession for life of the manors of East Quantockshead, Vexford, Exton, Carhampton and Rodhuish, and Lady Mary Luttrell, the widow of Sir John, had received for her jointure the castle, lordship, and borough of Dunster, the manor of Chilton Luttrell and Kilton, and various other lands in the county of Somerset.[6] The arrangement by which this last widow received for her jointure the *caput* or head place of a feudal barony, was certainly unusual. She did not, however, care to inhabit the castle, and she let it and the demesne lands " of the parke of Dunster called Hanger," to a certain Robert Opy of Cornwall, for £47 a year.[7] She herself went to live at Kilton, and it was not very long before she married a second husband, James Godolphin. She was buried at East Quantockshead in 1588.[8] Lady Catherine Edgcombe of Cöthele, her mother, bequeathed to the eldest daughter of Sir John Luttrell " one cheque of gold with a flower set in two diamonds, and a rubie to the said cheque annexed," and to his other two daughters a great bowl apiece of silver gilt.[9] All these three ladies married, but there is no occasion to

[1] "History of Somerset," vol. ii, p. 12.
[2] Inquisitiones post mortem, 2-3 Philip and Mary.
[3] Machyn's "Diary" (Camden Soc.).
[4] Strype's "Ecclesiastical Memorials," book ii, c. 29.
[5] Dunster Castle Muniments, Box, ii, No. 12.
[6] Inquisitiones post mortem, 13 Eliz. Dunster Castle Muniments, Box ii, Nos. 14, 17.
[7] Ibid., Box ii, No. 13.
[8] Ibid. Box xiv, No. 6.
[9] Wills at Somerset House. "Tash," f. 22.

trace their history any further in this place, as they sold their third part of their father's lands to their uncle.[1]

Thomas Luttrell, like his elder brother Sir John, served in the wars against Scotland in the reign of Edward VI.[2] He, about that time, entered into a contract of marriage with Margaret, daughter and heiress of Christopher Hadley of Withycombe, a lady who brought him a considerable landed estate on the east of Dunster and Carhampton. It is not quite clear whether the marriage was solemnized in church with the accustomed rites, but however this may have been, it was pronounced invalid in the reactionary reign of Mary, on the score that the bridegroom's mother had stood godmother to the bride many years previously. The matter was referred to Pope Paul, and by his order the Cardinal of St. Angelo in November 1588, released the parties from the sentence of excommunication which they had incurred by marrying within the prohibited degrees, ordered them to go through a new marriage in the face of the church, and removed all taint of illegitimacy from their children.[3] It does not appear how much money it cost to obtain this concession from Rome. The re-marriage was solemnized at East Quantockshead in August 1560, the bride being described in the Register of that Church as Mrs. Margaret Hadley. The inscription on the monument of Thomas Luttrell, set up some sixty years later, mentions expressly that he was " lawfully married " to his wife.

He appears to have lived for the most part at Marshwood in the parish of Carhampton, which had been settled on him by his father Sir Andrew. He sold the manors of Stonehall and Woodhall in Suffolk and several outlying estates in Somersetshire, but on the other hand he bought land at Hopcot and Wootton Courtenay near his own home.[4] In 1556 he obtained from Robert Opy a surrender of his lease of Dunster Castle, though he at the same time re-let to him " the hall, parlor, kichyn, and every rome within the same pyle called the Inner pyle or lodginges of the said Castell, and the stables, the grist mill of

[1] Dunster Castle Muniments, Box xxix, No. 37.
[2] Ibid. Box iii, No. 3.
[3] Ibid. Box xxxvii, No. 26.
[4] Ibid. Box xxxviii, Nos. 81, 84. Box xxvi, No. 2.

Dunster aforesaid, and the fedinge and pasturinge of tenne rother beasts or kyne and three geldings in the hanger or park of Dunster" for two years if Lady Mary Luttrell should live so long.[1] In point of fact she survived her brother-in-law by several years, so that, though he seems to have lived at Dunster Castle in the later years of his life, he never held it and the Barony in fee. He died in January, 1571, being at that time Sheriff of Somerset.[2] It would appear that the monument to his memory in Dunster Church was not erected until about fifty years after his death.

Nicholas Luttrell, a younger brother of Sir John and Thomas, lived at Honibere, and was buried at Lillstock in 1592. His son Andrew married Prudence, daughter of William Abbot of Hartland Abbey in Devonshire, and became ancestor of the Luttrells of that place, and of Saunton Court. Narcissus Luttrell of Chelsea, the author of the well-known political Diary, was a great-grandson of this Andrew Luttrell.

George Luttrell, the eldest son of Thomas and Margaret, was under eleven years of age at the time of his father's death. During the later part of his minority he was in ward to his cousin Hugh Stewkeley of Marsh in the parish of Dunster, a London lawyer. When he was little more than fifteen years old he was induced to plight his troth to his guardian's daughter Joan, who was a year or two younger than himself. Thenceforth he styled himself her husband, and addressed her parents as "father" and "mother" respectively. His own family, however, opposed the match strenuously, declaring that he would be "utterlie cast away in mariing with such a miserees daughter," and saying that "she was a slutt and that she had no good qualities." They wished him to go over to Wales "to be matched to some other which they would appoynt." His grandmother Lady Margaret Luttrell of East Quantockshead threatened that if he should marry in defiance of her wishes she would leave away from him the Priory of Dunster, and so make him "a poore gentleman."[3] The marriage was nevertheless

[1] Dunster Castle Muniments, Box xiv, No. 5.

[2] Inquisitiones post mortem, 13 Eliz.

[3] Dunster Castle Muniments.

duly celebrated at Dunster in September, 1580, when he had finished his studies at Cambridge, and Lady Margaret Luttrell so far relented as to bequeath to her grandson George "the hanging of arras that was made for the Parlor at Dunster, and two bolles of sylver guilt, and a drinking cup of sylver guilt that was his father's, and two spoons and a salt," and, what was more valuable, "the Priorie of Dunster with all the landes and other revenues and other profitts belonging to the same."[1]

Hugh Stewkeley was evidently unpopular in Somerset-shire. In 1566 the inhabitants of Dunster made formal complaint that though he had bought the great tithes, which were worth more than a hundred marks a year, he allowed only £8 a year to the curate, and that as no clergyman would undertake the duty for this low stipend, the cure of Dunster, which was the head church of the Deanery, was "altogether unserved," to the infringement of the Queen's orders and to the "great disquiet" of the parishioners.[2] At another time we find him claiming of his son-in-law George Luttrell a shoulder of every deer killed in his park, on the score that in the reign of Edward VI the South Lawn was in tillage and consequently subject to tithe[3] The Hanger Park began to be called Dunster Park in the middle of the sixteenth century, although the greater part of it lay in the parish of Carhampton. Two men who one night in the month of June, 1595, went to Dunster Park "weaponed with diverse unlawfull weapones and did together with others in most riotouse and unlawfull manner hunt, hurte, and kille some of George Luttrell's deer," were committed to the Fleet Prison for three months by the Court of Star Chamber, and subjected to a fine of no less than £100 apiece to the Queen, a very large sum in those days.[4] George Luttrell had a deer-park at East Quantockshead as well as at Dunster, and in 1584 he undertook to give yearly to his mother, Margaret Strode, "one fee bucke of season in the summer, and one fee doe in the winter," from one or other of these parks at her choice.[5]

On the successive deaths of his mother, his grand-

---

[1] Wills at Somerset House. "Butts," f. 8.
[2] Dunster Castle Muniments, Box xiv, No. 14.
[3] Ibid. No. 6.
[4] Ibid. No. 39.
[5] Ibid. No. 24.

mother, and his uncle's widow, George Luttrell became possessed of the different estates that they held for their jointures. In the course of his long and prosperous life he greatly improved the chief houses on his property. At Dunster he transformed the building at the north-eastern end of the lower ward of the old fortress into a comfortable Elizabethan residence. It is not always easy to distinguish his walls from those of an earlier date, but the whole of the principal façade appears to have been rebuilt by him. The plaster ceiling of the hall, and many of the existing doors and windows may safely be ascribed to him. There only remain two Edwardian windows, those of a garderobe, in the whole castle, and except in the gatehouse there are very few Perpendicular windows or doors left. The alterations must have been in hand some time, as a coat of arms in the hall is dated 1589, and a fireplace in one of the rooms upstairs is dated 1620. The graceful cornice of the gallery is probably of this later date. Nothing unfortunately is known about the history of the interesting *corami*, or leather hangings, with which the walls of this gallery are decorated. They are certainly of Italian, and probably of Venetian origin, and they must date from the seventeenth century. The skins are covered with silver leaf, which in some parts is glazed over with a warm transparent colour, giving the effect of gold, and there are a number of small patterns stamped on them with bookbinders' tools. On this uneven surface there are depicted in oil colours, several incidents from the history of Antony and Cleopatra. As the original series of *corami* did not exactly fit the wall spaces in the gallery at Dunster, they were supplemented by upright strips of the same work representing female figures. Some leather hangings similar in execution, though not in design, were presented to the Duke of Marlborough by Victor Amadeus II of Savoy about the year 1708. There was also another set in the old palace at Turin.[1]

The very picturesque octagonal market house in the main street of Dunster was built by George Luttrell, who was Sheriff of Somerset in 1593 and 1609. The initials G. L., however, pierced on its vane are those of

---

[1] Ex inf. P.C. Hardwick. See also "Archæological Journal," vol. xvi, p. 178.

LUTTRELL ARMS HOTEL.
DUNSTER.

MARSHWOOD HOUSE.

F F Lyte del

OVER – MANTELS.
IN PLASTER
Circa A.D. 1621.

his grandson of the same name, who repaired it in 1647, a year after the siege of Dunster Castle by the Parliamentary forces under Blake. This market house was erected for the sale of yarns, for which the neighbourhood was formerly famous. Leland, writing in the reign of Henry VIII, says, "The town of Dunestorre makith cloth," and an Act of Parliament of the reign of James I specifies the exact width and weight of the "broadcloth commonly called Tauntons, Bridgewaters, and Dunsters." Deeds of the latter reign mention " two tuckinge milles or fullars mylles under one rough" near the grist mills, and the terraces may still be seen on Grabbist, on which the fullers had their racks for drying the new cloth.[1]

The broad street leading from the Yarn Market and the Luttrell Arms Hotel towards "the Castle Tor" was, until about sixty years ago, two streets, the space between them being occupied by shambles. At the southern end of it formerly stood the Butter Cross already mentioned.

There is in one of the upstair rooms at the Luttrell Arms Hotel a curious mantel-piece, on which are represented in plaster three figures in costume of the seventeenth century, a group of dogs devouring a man, presumably Actæon, and shields of the arms of England and France. This and other mantel-pieces in the same material at Dunster Castle, at Marshwood, at East Quantockshead, and at other places in the neighbourhood are evidently the work of one man, as they have a distinctive character of their own. The arabesques and other ornaments on them are bold and spirited, though the figures, and especially the faces, are somewhat grotesque. The earliest of these mantel-pieces at East Quantockshead is dated 1614, that in Dunster Castle 1620. George Luttrell rebuilt the house at Marshwood about the time of the marriage of his eldest son Thomas with Jane daughter of Sir Francis Popham, a lady who brought £3000 to her husband.[2] He also built the quay at Minehead, at a cost of £5000. On the death of his wife Joan Stewkeley in 1621 he erected a large monument on the south side of the old chancel of Dunster Church to her memory and to the memory of his own father and

[1] Dunster Castle Muniments, Box xv, Nos. 10, 29, 52.

[2] Ibid. Box iii, No. 6. Inquisitiones post mortem, 6 Charles I.

mother. These three persons being all dead are represented in a recumbent position, facing eastwards, as if expecting the general resurrection, while George Luttrell, being alive, is represented kneeling westwards. There is also a portrait of George Luttrell in the hall at Dunster Castle painted in oils in 1594 when he was 34 years of age. Soon after the death of his first wife he married Silvestra Capps a person of humble extraction.[1] His own children were not too well pleased at the liberal scale on which he provided for her and her children in the closing years of his life. For her benefit he greatly altered and enlarged the old manor-house at East Quantockshead. The whole of the eastern front, except the south-eastern angle, was added by him, as he built a spacious hall, with a large wing and a porch tower projecting from it against the former outer wall, which is easily recognized by its great thickness. The head of a

leaden water pipe has the initials of George and Silvestra Luttrell and the date 1628. A stately staircase, square on plan, was about the same time substituted for the old winding stairs. George Luttrell died on the 1st of April 1629 and was buried at Dunster. Nine months later his widow was married at East Quantockshead, to Sir Edmund Scory, and in 1634 she was married at the same place to a certain Giles Penny.[2]

Thomas Luttrell, son and heir of George, found it very difficult to steer a safe course through the political troubles of the reign of Charles I. His sympathies were on the Parliamentary side : his interests made him for a time appear a Royalist.[3] Clarendon relates that in the middle of June, 1643, the Marquis of Hertford obtained in three days Taunton and Bridgewater, and that

[1] Dunster Castle Muniments, Box iii, No. 5.
[2] Register of East Quantockshead.
[3] "Trevelyan Papers" (Camden Soc.),

vol. iii, pp. 234, 251, 252. "Domestic State Papers," Charles I, vol. cclv, No. 39. "Lords' Journals," vol. v, p. 189.

"Dunstar castle, so much stronger than both the other, that it could not have been forced; yet by the dexterity of Francis Windham, who wrought upon the fears of the owner and master of it, Mr. Luttrel was, with as little bloodshed as the other, delivered up to the king; into which the marquis put in him that took it as governor; as he well deserved."[1]

On the 23rd of that month Thomas Luttrell paid down £500 as part of the sum of £1000 which he undertook to contribute towards the expenses of the King's army in the west.[2] Two years later, after the battle of Naseby, Charles I gave orders that the Prince of Wales should take up his residence at Dunster Castle in order to "encourage the new levies," it being "not known at Court that the plague, which had driven him from Bristol, was as hot in Dunster town, just under the walls of the castle."[3] An account-book, formerly belonging to Minehead Church, records payments amounting to 14s "given to the ringers in beer at severall times when the prince and other great men came to the town," and a payment of 5s 6d "to the prince's footman which he claymed as due to him to his fee."[4] A room leading out of the gallery is still known as King Charles's room. There is a secret door in one of its walls giving access to a very narrow chamber, which has no window and only contains a stone bench. Prince Charles, however, can hardly have required a place of concealment when he was at Dunster surrounded by loyal soldiers. "The King's chamber" is mentioned in an inventory of the year 1705, and it was certainly situated near the gallery, though some descriptions of it do not quite suit King Charles's room. The plague of 1645 was deemed so terrible that the inhabitants of a long street in Dunster are said to have established communication along it by opening doors internally between the different houses, "so as to avoid all necessity of going into the open street."[5]

In order to understand clearly how it was that Dunster Castle was held successively for the Parliament, for the king, and then again for the Parliament, it may be desirable to revert to the year 1642, which witnessed the outbreak of the civil war.

[1] "History of the Rebellion" (1826), vol. iv, p. 110.
[2] Dunster Castle Muniments.
[3] Clarendon, vol. v, p. 189.
[4] Savage's "History of Carhampton," p. 591.
[5] "Archæological Journal," vol. xv, p. 388.

PART IV.

THE SIEGE AND SURRENDER

OF

DUNSTER CASTLE.

Communicated by

EMANUEL GREEN.

When the Marquis of Hertford, came into Somerset in August, 1642, to raise the militia for the king, the county rose against him and drove him from Wells to Sherborne. This place in turn he soon found to be untenable, and while negotiating or pretending to negotiate for a surrender, he suddenly escaped, on the 19th of September, with about four hundred followers,[1] and directed his course to Minehead. The Earl of Bedford, commanding for the Parliament, at once issued warrants for the apprehension of any of the party, and sent off posts to "Master" Luttrell at Dunster bidding him strengthen and make good his castle there.[2] Thomas Luttrell obeyed quickly and readily, increased his garrison by one hundred men, and, supposing the Royalists would endeavour to cross over to Wales, caused the rudders to be removed from all the ships in Minehead harbour.[3] On arriving at Minehead the Marquis fortified himself in a "strong inn," and then, as had been anticipated, attempted to get possession of Dunster Castle. For this purpose sixty of Sir Ralph Hopton's men were sent thither to demand an entrance, a demand which was immediately and peremptorily refused. After some parley, as the party declined to leave, "Mistresse" Luttrell commanded the men within to "give fire," a command which the Royalist officer without ordered them to disregard ; but "Mistresse" Luttrell again commanded them "upon their lives to do it," "which accordingly they did."[4] To be fired at from

---

[1] "England's Memorable Accidents." Most of the publications quoted in this Part are to be found among the Newspapers and the King's Pamphlets in the British Museum

[2] "Special Passages"

[3] "England's Memorable Accidents, No. 25."

[4] "Special Passages."

behind a rampart was more than these cavaliers expected, and so they forthwith beat a hasty retreat. Eventually the Royalists escaped in some coal-ships to Wales, but there arose a great anxiety lest they should return suddenly, and by surprise get possession of the castle, from which it was believed that ten thousand men could not dislodge them. Proposals for raising horse and foot to guard it were promptly made, but the " very thoughts " that such a thing might occur caused the Minehead people to forget to entertain the Earl of Bedford when he arrived in pursuit.[1] By Lord Hertford the unexpected mishap at Dunster was greatly regretted, as the place was at this time considered impregnable. In his vexation he charged Sir Ralph Hopton's men with cowardice in the business.

" I have acquainted His Majesty [he wrote] of our disastrous fortune at Minicard and Dunstar occasioned by the multitude of your Countrymen's evill dispositions and cowardly behaviour in them, upon which I remembred a reverent speech of that worthy Souldier, Swinden, who was Generall of Ostend in the time of the Infanta, Arch-Duchesse of Flanders, who said that our English nation stood too much upon their owne conceipt and valour, and that he would with a considerable Army runne through our whole Kingdome, knowing the vulgar sort of our Nation to be fainthearted and unexperienced in Martiall discipline. This relation of the Generall's happened to be true, for in our best actions and in the middest of our hopefull successe, Captaine Digbie's, Sir John Stowel's and your owne Souldiers ran cowardly away from us, insomuch that had it not been for that small number of my owne Horse and Foot we had lost our Ordnances, hazarded our persons, and lost the honour of that daye's work."

To this Sir Ralph Hopton replied :—

" May it please your Lordship, with humble pardon, according to my weake ability I have considered your worthy advertisements, and vindicate myselfe and Country of your Lordship's mistake, I shall make it appeare that my actions and those under my Command have bin concurrent to your Lordship's Command and I have in briefe devoted myselfe to answere to every particuler of your Lordship's letter. First, whereas your Lordship condemned our endevours cowardly behaviour at Minicard and Dunster, your Lordship may well remember and saw, three to one of the Earle of Bedford's forces forsaken him then those of our County under your Lordship might see that his Majesties forces under your Lordship's command had good successe considering the great oddes five to one. Secondly, that whereas your Lordship remembred of the Generall his speech of Ostend, that our Nation stood too much upon our owne strength and valour and that he

[1] "Special Passages," Nos. 8-9.

would with a few experienced soldiers run through our Kingdom. My Lord the question herein is not disputable, for nature at home bindeth filiall affection, and one brother or one nation to fight against another is not warrantable by God's lawes, and in that respect there might be faint-heartednes in our Nation, but my Lord, let the Generall of Ostend or any other forraine Princes, invade this our land. I know that your Lordship beleeves that our Nation will not runne or give one foot of ground to such an Enemy, for we are all sencible with whom we quarrell, the Father against the Sonne, and the Sonne against the Father, and if Alexander the Great or the Emperour of Persia were now alive, whose armies dranke Rivers of water, yet my Lord it would daunt the hearts of these gallants to destroy their owne blood."[1]

Early in January, 1643, the Welshmen gave trouble on the Somerset coast. Some blockaded Minehead, and by preventing the entry of all boats or barques, kept back the supplies of provisions and coal. Others, about five hundred in number, under Captain Paulet landed there, " invaded " the county, and "constrained the inhabitants to yeeld to any taxation, and to submit themselves servants and slaves to every poore base companion, to save their throats from being cut," an operation daily threatened. This party attacked Dunster Castle, but Mr. Luttrell being prepared, was able to defeat them and secure the town from plunder. In the attack, a shot from the castle killed some of Captain Paulet's men, which " moved him to wroth," and he vowed he would quarter the " murderer " limb from limb and hang his quarters on the castle as food for ravens. Being thus unsuccessful here, he went on to Barnstaple with two hundred of his musketeers and forty horse,[2] and Dunster Castle continued to be held for the Parliament until after the fall of Bridgwater in this year. The successes of the royalists then added so much to their prestige that many began to think that victory was a certainty for the king. Mr. Luttrell, amongst others, seems to have been of this opinion and to have trimmed his conduct accordingly, for Mr. Francis Windham, "found that he had good inclinations in him" to deliver up the castle; inclinations, however, in which he was much "distracted and disturbed" by some persons near him, that is to say by his wife. The eventual surrender of the Castle to the king in June 1643, and the visit of the Prince of Wales two years

[1] " New plots discovered against the Parliament and the peace of the King-dome in two Letters."

[2] " Special Passages."

later, have already been noticed. It may, however, be remarked that Thomas Luttrell died in 1644, in the middle of the civil war.

After the reverses of the royalist party at Langport, Taunton, and Bridgwater, in the summer of 1645, Dunster Castle remained the only place held for the king in Somerset, but, isolated as it was, it was harmless except as a means of annoyance to the district immediately around it. As it was desirable to stop even this power, Colonel Blake and Colonel Sydenham, taking a small party from Taunton, laid siege to it early in November, and by the sixth had so completely blocked it that its surrender seemed certain, if it were not taken by surprise. Neither of these expectations were realised, for the besieged held out, although by the end of the month they were said to be straitened for provisions and suffering sadly from want of water. It was reported that Colonel Francis Windham, the Governor, about the 20th of November wrote to Lord Goring, then commanding the king's forces in Devon, that he could hold out but a fortnight or three weeks longer, and that he was only enabled to do that from having secured a good supply of water from some late heavy rains.[1] He at least wrote for aid, as in response, Goring sent some foot to Bideford, to be forwarded to Dunster by sea, and a party of horse was got in readiness to march by land to protect them on arrival.[2] But, possibly not knowing their destination until they arrived at Bideford, and then not getting their promised pay, and finding they were to be out for more than the twenty days agreed for with Lord Hopton, they deserted and ran away. Sir Richard Grenville went after them at once to bring them back, but the plan for this time resulted in failure.[3] The design becoming known, Sir Thomas Fairfax stationed some men to command the road and prevent or check the repetition of any similar attempt. Thus when another party endeavoured to pass early in December, the troops who were guarding the roads about Tiverton and Crediton, encountered them and compelled them to return.[4]

Meanwhile Colonel Blake had repeatedly summoned

[1] "Perfect Passages," No. 56.   [3] "Moderate Intelligencer," No. 38.
[2] "Perfect Diurnal," No. 125,   [4] "Weekly Account."

the Governor to surrender, but always receiving a curt refusal, he had pushed forward his approaches and batteries and worked busily at his mines, as these were "next to determine the business."[1] A summons was again sent in, this time accompanied by a threat that the Castle would be stormed if it were not surrendered. Colonel Windham replied as before, that as he had formerly announced his intention to keep his charge to his utmost, so he was still and would continue *semper idem*—always the same.

At the very end of December, 1645, or about the 1st of January, 1646, a story was circulated by the royalist party at Oxford, on the reported authority of two men supposed to have come from Dunster, that the castle was relieved and the siege raised.   The story was, that the besiegers, having taken prisoner the Governor's mother, sent in their last summons thus—" If you will yet deliver up the Castle, you shall have faire Quarter, if not, expect no mercy, your mother shall be in the Front, to receive the first fury of your Canon: we expect your answer." The Governor is supposed to reply, "If you doe what you threaten you do the most barbarous and villanous Act [that] was ever done; my mother I honour: but the cause I fight for and the maisters I serve, God and the King, I honour more; Mother, do you forgive me and give me your blessing, and let the Rebells answer for spilling that blood of yours, which I would save with the losse of mine owne, if I had enough for both my master and yourselfe."   To this the mother is supposed to answer, "Sonne, I forgive thee, and pray God to blesse thee for this brave resolution; if I live I shall love thee the better for it; God's will be done."   The story then adds that just at this moment there suddenly appeared Lord Wentworth, Sir Richard Grenville, and Colonel Webb, who attacking the besiegers, killed many, took a thousand prisoners, rescued the mother, and relieved the castle.[2]

This report is here quoted from its original source; it has been often repeated since, but it was not true.   The siege was not raised, the castle was not relieved at this time, and the supposed chief actors in the affair were then in Cornwall or on the western borders of Devon.[3]   The

[1] "Perfect Occurrences."   [3] "Mercurius Civicus," No. 136.
[2] "Mercurius Academicus," No. 3.

Parliamentary party soon denounced the report as "ale-house intelligence" and a "feeble lie."[1]

About the 6th of January, 1646, Blake received a reinforcement of fifteen hundred horse, and these he quartered some five or six miles from the castle, to keep a sharp watch on the Exeter road.[2] As relief was constantly attempted and as often prevented, these troopers had a very harassing and hard duty to perform, and this, with the continuance of the siege and the frequent marches and countermarches drew general attention towards Dunster.

As the Governor seemed determined not to surrender, Fairfax wrote to order Colonel Blake to proceed with the siege and spring his mines.[3] This he did on the 3rd of January, fully expecting to blow up the castle. But the garrison, aware of what had been going on, had discovered one mine, and had spoilt it by countermining. Another was not fired or did not spring, whilst the third, although it exploded fairly, only destroyed a part of the wall, causing a considerable breach, but yet making more noise than execution.[4] The road opened by it was altogether too steep for approach, and proved so inaccessible that the intended attack could not be made. Thus the hoped for opportunity was lost. For the defenders, however, now very short of necessaries, the breach proved a great annoyance, as they were put to double duty to keep their guards. In this emergency Sir Richard Grenville wrote to Colonel Windham exhorting him to hold out yet a little longer and promising that help should certainly be sent.[5] Two regiments accordingly set out on the 8th of January, ostensibly to relieve Exeter, but really destined for Dunster. Their plan was either betrayed or discovered by their opponents, for some horse and foot were called from their winter quarters to watch them, and if necessary to go and strengthen Colonel Blake. Seeing that their enemy was thus prepared, and that relief was impossible, the Royalists once more retired, and the blockade of Dunster was continued without interruption until the end of January.

1 "Mercurius Britannicus," No. 114.   4 "Moderate Intelligencer," No. 44.
2 "Moderate Intelligencer," No. 44.   5 "Weekly Account," No.2.
3 "Perfect Passages," No. 63.

Towards the end of 1645 the king's army being cooped up in Devon, the Parliamentary forces that were gathering in Somerset and along the line of its retreat, concluded that at last the country had some chance of peace and that the royal troops were securely and certainly trapped. A report however now came that Goring intended to break through the ring and get his whole force away. Orders were at once sent for the reserves in the rear to be ready to meet such a movement, and Major-General Massey busied himself with making preparations near Crewkerne.[1] Taking advantage of the attention of the Parliamentary force in Devon being given to this matter, a party of fifteen hundred horse and three hundred foot, sent by Lord Hopton under the command of Colonel Finch, managed to reach Dunster, and on the 5th of February relieved the Castle with four barrels of powder, thirty cows and fifty sheep. Having done this they spoilt the mines and destroyed the works thrown up by the besiegers, and then returned to Barnstaple. Finding the relieving party too strong for him, Colonel Blake on their arrival retired for protection into "a strong house" and remained there unmolested. As they left, however, he sallied out on their rear and took fifty-three prisoners, but in turn got himself into an awkward position, from which he had some difficulty in making an honourable retreat without great loss.[2] A report was now circulated to the effect that the owner of the castle, and others had offered to raise a thousand men to help the Parliamentary army in the west,[3] but Blake determined simply to renew and continue the blockade, until he could be strongly reinforced from the main army. From his better information he may have judged that this would soon be possible, as not long afterwards Exeter fell. Sir Thomas Fairfax then, with his usual energy, quickly moved off for fresh work, and on the 8th of April his army was camped around Chard, from whence he sent Colonel Lambert's regiment to strengthen the force before Dunster.[4]

[1] "Perfect Passages," No. 65.
[2] "Perfect Passages," No. 68. "A Diary," No. 3. "Mod. Intell.," No. 49.
"The Citties Weekly Post," No. 9.
[3] "Mod. Intell.," No. 50.
[4] "Mod. Intell.," No. 59.

Colonel Blake had gone to meet the general, when, on Thursday night, the 16th of April, those in the castle called to Captain Burridge, who was left in command, to know if it were true, as some of his soldiers had stated, that Exeter and Barnstaple had both fallen. Captain Burridge "hearkening" to what was said, they asked to be allowed to send to Barnstaple for confirmation of the news, promising that if it were true they would capitulate. The captain answered "that he would not by any false way of smooth language goe about to begge their castle," and offered himself as a hostage if they would give one of like rank whilst they sent for intelligence. He declared himself willing to forfeit his life if what he had said was not true, provided they would agree to surrender on a day named if all the news were confirmed. Weak and reduced as the garrison now was, and barely able to defend more than the keep, this conversation "wrought so much upon them" that on Friday morning it was re-opened and a request was again made for leave to send for intelligence. Notice having meantime arrived that Blake was returning, Captain Burridge desired them to have a little patience, inasmuch as they should get an answer from the colonel himself. About noon Blake arrived, having with him Major-General Skippon's regiment and the remainder of his own. This force he drew up in two bodies on a hill facing the Castle, and, in accordance with orders given by Sir Thomas Fairfax, he sent in another summons for surrender.[1] Deprived of all hope of relief, Colonel Windham, in reply, demanded a parley, the result of which was that after having sustained a close siege of about a hundred and sixty days, with a loss of twenty men, he surrendered on the 19th of April on the following conditions :—

"1. That the Castle, together with the Armes, ammunition, and other furniture of War (except what is hereunder excepted), be delivered up into the hands of the said Colonel Blake for his Excellency Sir Thomas Fairfax, to the use of the King and Parliament.

2. That all Commissioners Officers in the Castle shall march away with horses and Armes and all other necessary accouterments appertaining.

3. That common Officers and Souldiers, both Horse and Foot, shall march away with their armes and either horse or foot souldier shall have

---

[1] "Sir Thomas Fairfax's further proceedings in the west."

three Charges of Powder and Bullet, with three yards of Match, for those that have match locks, together with Colours and Drums.

4. That the said Colonell Windham shall carry with him all that is properly his, and that which doth properly belong to the Lady Windham shall be sent to her.

5. That all Officers and Souldiers with all particular persons of the castle shall march forth secure, as many as will, to Oxford without delay, and those who are otherwise minded shall lay down their armes and have Let passes to their homes, or to any other places they shall desire with protection against the violence of the soldiers.

6. That prisoners to either party be released.

7. That the said Colonell Francis Windham and his Souldiers march to Oxford in twelve daies."[1]

Under this agreement the castle was delivered up on the 22nd of April. Six pieces of ordnance and two hundred stand of arms were all the booty found within it. Colonel Blake, writing from Taunton, 21st of April, to report the event to the Parliament, remarked that, at the price of time and blood, he could no doubt have obtained very different terms, but that he was induced to accept these, by his wish to follow the exemplary clemency of his general. "The place," he said, was "strong and of importance for the passage into Ireland."[2] A public thanksgiving was now ordered for the many and continued successes of the Parliamentary forces, Dunster being named n the list of places whose capture deserved especial emphasis.[3] Minehead, too, rejoiced that her disagreeable neighbour had fallen, and "gave the ringers when Dunster was yielded" four shillings and eight pence.[4]

With this surrender of Dunster the fighting ceased in Somerset. The "trumpet left off his summons, the cannon forbode his chiding," and all the county was hushed into obedience to the Parliament. The war was now virtually over. The royal army, defeated everywhere, was soon disbanded, and the king, a captive, bought and sold, was destined to remain a prisoner till the bitter end.

---

[1] "Mercurius Civicus," No. 152. "Four Strong Castles Taken," &c.
[2] "Mercurius Civicus," No. 152.
[3] "Perfect Diurnal," No. 144.
[4] Savage's "History of Carhampton."

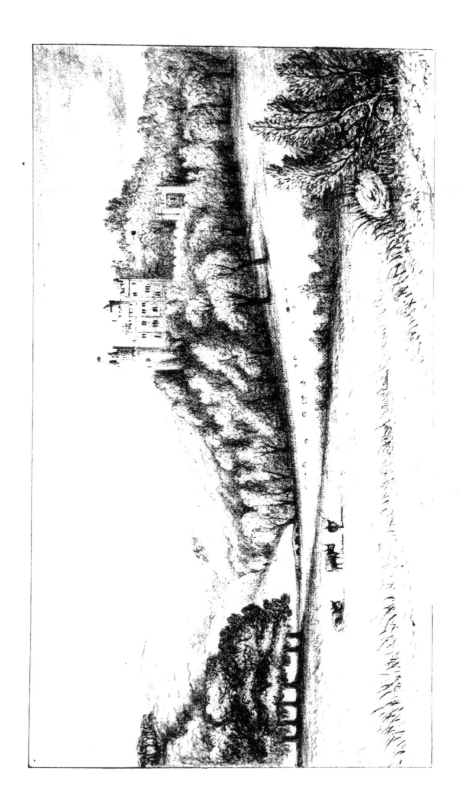

Part V.

A garrison was maintained in Dunster Castle for more than five years after its surrender to the Parliamentary forces under Blake. George Luttrell, though apparently allowed to live in his own house, was made to feel that he was not master there. On the 26th of March, 1650, the Council of State resolved:—

"That it be referred to the Committee which confers with the Officers of the Armie to consider whether or noe Dunster Castle and Taunton Castle or either of them are fitt to be demolished and to report to the Councell their opinions therein."[1]

On the 6th of May twelve barrels of gunpowder were issued "for the supply of Taunton and Dunster Castle," and on the 25th of the same month, a further demand of the Governor of Dunster Castle for arms and ammunition was referred to the Committee of the Ordinance.[2] The following resolutions relating to Dunster Castle are entered in the order-books of the Council of State for the year 1650 :—

6th June. "That a letter bee written to Colonell Desbrow, to let him know that this Councell leaves it to him to put in such number of men into Dunster and Taunton Castles as hee shall thinke fit to secure them."

5th August. "That it bee referred to the Committee which meets with the Officers of the Armie to take into consideration the present condition of Dunster Castle and to report to the Councell their opinions what they thinke fitt to bee done therein, either as to the makeing it untenable or repairing of it."[4]

10th August. "At the Committee for Marshall affaires. Ordered: That the Committee haveing seriously considered the present state of the Guarrison at Dunster Castle and finding that the makeing of it every way

[1] Domestic State Papers, I, 64, f. 120.
[2] Ibid., ff. 312, 389.
[3] Ibid., f. 426.
[4] Domestic State Papers, I, 8, f. 49.

teneable against an Enemy will require a great summe of money, which they conceive the Councell at present cannot well spare, conceive it necessary that the said Guarrison be drawne to Taunton, And that the Castle be soe farre slighted as that it may not be made suddainely teneable by an Enemy, and that it be referred to Major Generall Debrow to the Commissioners of the Militia for the County to see this done and to send an Account thereof to the Councell."[1]

The work of destruction was set in hand without delay, and a rate was levied in Somersetshire "for pulling downe Dunster Castle."[2] A communication from Dunster Castle, dated the 27th of August, states :—

" Here hath been above two hundred men working at this Castle these twelve daies about sleighting the same, which is almost finished except the dwelling house of Mr. Lutterell and the Gatehouse, according to Order of the Councel of State."[3]

The preservation of such parts of the fabric as still remain is due to a resolution passed by the Council of State on the 20th of August:—

" To write to Major Robinson that Dunster Castle be continued in the condition it is till further order of the Councell, and that there bee twenty or thertie chozen men there for the defence thereof, and that letters be written to him for that purpose."[4]

In a very brief notice of his cousin George Luttrell, Narcissus Luttrell writes :—

" At his father's death his Castle of Dunster & estate was in the Enemies hands, he enjoyed little thereof till reduced ; the walls of Dunster Castle, the Mount Stephens & a fair new building were totally demolished, & his Gatehouse much defaced by orders from Whitehal under Bradshaw's hand, and from the Militia of the County in August 1650, to about £3000 damages, without any recompence, & to save the charge of a garrison the very mansion house was advised to be pulled down by the militia but afterwards countermanded."[5]

The " Mount Stephens " here mentioned was the lofty keep, which, as far back as the year 1254, contained a chapel dedicated to the proto-martyr. The summit of the tor, now occupied by a bowling-green, was known as "St. Stevens" until 1719, if not later.[6] The foundations of some old buildings were discovered there a few years ago, but they did not afford any indication of the size or shape of the Norman keep of the Mohuns.

[1] Domestic State Papers, I, 8, f. 70.

[2] Savage's " History of Carhampton," p. 436.

[3] " A Perfect Diurnall," No. 38 (Brit. Mus. Newspapers, vol. xxxiv.)

[4] Domestic State Papers, I, 9, f. 13.

[5] MS. at Dunster Castle.

[6] " Paid for a roop to draw the stons out of the winke at St Stevens 5s 6d." "Disbursements of William Withycombe," 1719. Dunster Manor Office, Box xxi.

During part of the time that Dunster Castle was in the hands of the Government, it served as the prison of William Prynne, whose political writings were as offensive to Cromwell and the other ruling powers as they had been to Charles I and Laud. The warrant for his arrest and confinement at Dunster "for seditiously writing and practising against the Commonwealth" was issued on the 25th of June 1650, and orders were given that no one should be allowed to confer with him alone.[1] Finding that the muniments of George Luttrell were in " a confused chaos," he employed part of his enforced leisure in making the existing arrangement of them according to their subjects and dates. He also compiled a general calendar of them at the end of which there is a characteristic note, stating that it was made " by William Prynne of Swainswick, Esq., in the eight months of his illegall, causeless, close Imprisonment in Dunster Castle, by Mr. Bradshaw and his Companions at Whitehall, Feb. 18, Anno Dom. 1650, 2 Car. II." From Dunster Prynne was, in 1651, removed to Taunton, and thence to Pendennis Castle.[2]

The following letters show the subsequent decisions of the Council of State with respect to Dunster Castle :—

"To the Commissioners of the Militia of the County of Somersett.
"Gentlemen,
"Although there appeare not much at present of any stirring of the Enemy, yet Wee have sure information that they have designes on foot at present of great danger to the Commonwealth and particularly in those parts, to prevent which Wee thinke it necessary that such places as are not yet made untenable should have some strength put into them to prevent the Enemyes surprize. And Wee being informed that Dunster Castle, the house of Mr. Lutterell, is yet in a Condition that if it be seized by the Enemy might proove dangerous, Wee therefore desire you to appoint some militia forces to prevent the surprize of it till there may be some course taken to make it untenable or that the state of affaires may not be subject to the like danger as now they are.
    "Whitehall, 25 March 1651."[3]

    "To Major Generall Desborowe.
    " Wee are informed from Major Robinson Governour of Taunton and Dunster Castle that the Forces remayning in those Garrisons are not sufficient to enable Him to preserve the same for the Service of the State. Wee therefore desire you to consider those Places and the Forces in them, and in what you find those Forces defective to make supply thereof that

---

[1] Calendar of Domestic State Papers.   [3] Ibid., f. 73.
[2] Domestic State Papers, I, 96, f. 253.

the Governor may bee able to give a good Accompt thereof to the Comon Wealth. "Whitehall, 20° Maij 1651."[1]

"To George Lutterell Esq[re] of Dunster Castle.

"Wee conceive it hath beene some prejudice to you that your house hath beene still continued a Garrison, which Wee are willing you should be freed from, soe as the Comon Wealth may be assured from danger by it. And Wee doubt not but you will bee carefull to keepe the Place from the Enemies surprise, in respect of your Interest in it; But that Wee may be able to give the Comon Wealth a good Accompt of that Place upon the remove of that Garrison, Wee hold fit that you enter Recognizance before two Justices of the Peace with two Suretyes to the Keepers of the Liberty of the Comon Wealth of England, your selfe in £6000 and £3000 each of your Suretyes. The Condition to bee, that you shall not suffer any use to bee made of your said House of Dunster Castle to the prejudice of the Comon Wealth and present Government, which being done Wee have given Order to Major Generall Desborow to draw off the Men that are in the same Castle and dispose of them as Wee have given Order. Wee have had Informations of Designes upon that your Castle, the prevention of the operation whereof hath occasioned our putting of a Guard there; and haveing now put it into this Way wherein Wee have had (sic) of your Conveniency; Wee expect you to be carefull of what besides your particular herein concernes the Interest of the Publique.

"Whitehall, 27° Maij 1651."[2]

On the same day Major-General Desborow was ordered to draw off the twenty men who were quartered at Dunster, as soon as George Luttrell had entered into the necessary recognizances.[3]

The Government afterwards became so well satisfied of George Luttrell's loyalty to the commonwealth that he was appointed Sheriff of Somerset in November, 1652. There is in the hall of Dunster Castle a fine half-length portrait of Oliver Cromwell, which has been ascribed to Vandyke. When the times became quieter George Luttrell set himself to repairing the damage done to his property during the recent siege, some of the wooden buildings in the middle of the High Street having been riddled with shot. The hole made by a cannon ball fired from the castle through one of the rafters of the octagonal Yarn-Market is still visible, though the roof above it was substantially repaired in 1647. Some traces of earthworks still remain in the park behind the Luttrell Arms Hotel, and tradition says that it was there that Blake planted some of his cannons for bombarding the castle.

[1] Domestic State Papers, I, 96, f. 193.   [3] Ibid., f. 203.
[2] Ibid., f. 202.

George Luttrell's first wife, Elizabeth Prideaux, died on the 22nd of May, 1652, and was buried at Dunster the same evening. A few weeks later, in the early part of July, he was married at Buckland Filleigh to her cousin Honora, daughter of John Fortescue of that place.[1] His two sons by his first wife died in infancy, and his second wife proved childless. On his death, therefore, at the age of thirty in 1655, his estates passed to his brother Francis, who enjoyed them for about eleven years. In the first Parliament of Charles II. Francis Luttrell sat as member for the neighbouring borough of Minehead, which had on five previous occasions returned other members of his family. From the time of the Restoration until the disfranchisement of the borough by the Reform Act of 1832, the owners of Dunster Castle exercised a preponderating influence in all Parliamentary elections at Minehead, being always able to return one of the members and sometimes both.

Francis Luttrell died in 1666, leaving three sons, all of whom eventually inherited the property. Thomas the eldest died a minor in 1670, and was succeeded by his brother Francis, who was then about eleven years of age. There was some question of buying a peerage for this Francis Luttrell while he was still an undergraduate at Oxford. Anthony à Wood records in his autobiography under the date of October 26, 1678 :—

"I was told from Sir Thomas Spencer's house that the King had given Dr. Fell, bishop of Oxford, a patent for an EARLL (which comes to about 1000*l.*) towards the finishing of the great gate of Christ Church next to Pembroke College. He intends to bestow it on Mr. Lutterell, a gentleman commoner of Christ Church, of Somersetshire, having 4000*l.* per annum at present."[2]

On attaining his majority in 1680 Francis Luttrell married Mary, daughter and heiress of John Tregonwell of Milton Abbas. To him are due the elaborate plaster ceilings of the great staircase, and of the parlour and of the small adjoining room at Dunster Castle. That of the parlour bears the arms of Luttrell impaled with Tregonwell, the Tregonwell crest, and the date, "ANNO

[1] Dunster Parish Register.
[2] "Life of Anthony à Wood" (1848), p. 205. A few years after this, Alexander Luttrell, a younger brother of Francis, and like him a gentleman commoner of Christ Church, got into trouble at Oxford for dragging old Lady Lovelace out of her coach at night and breaking windows in the town, after a carouse at the Crown tavern. Ibid., p. 230.

DOMMINI *(sic)* CHRISTI MDCLXXXI." Francis Luttrell was
in command of the Somerset militia at Taunton in June,
1685, but was compelled to evacuate the town on the
approach of the Duke of Monmouth's army.[1] He was
one of the first men of importance to join the standard of
the Prince of Orange at Exeter in November, 1688.[2] He
died at Plymouth in July, 1690, being at that time in
command of one of the king's regiments.[3] Mary his widow
had a considerable fortune, and under the terms of his
will had the use of his furniture and jewels for life.[4] She
accordingly went to live in London, taking with her many
valuable things from Dunster Castle. Narcissus Luttrell
records the sequel in his Diary under the date of November 19, 1696 :—

"Yesterday morning a sudden fire hapned in Mrs. Luttrells house in
St. James's street, being newly and richly furnished, which burnt it to
the ground, the lady herself narrowly escaping, and 'tis said she lost in
plate, jewells, &c. to the value of 10,000*l.*[5]

A tradition in the family relates that nothing was
saved but one diamond ring. A few weeks after this
catastrophe Mrs. Luttrell married Jacob Bancks, a Swede
by birth, who held a commission as captain in the English
navy.[6] He is said to have laid a considerable wager that
he would make the rich widow his wife. He was knighted
in 1699, and through the Luttrell influence was elected
member for Minehead in nine successive Parliaments.[7]

Tregonwell Luttrell of Dunster Castle, the only son of
Colonel Francis Luttrell, died in 1703 before attaining
his majority, and the estates passed to his uncle, Colonel
Alexander Luttrell, who, however, only enjoyed them for
about eight years.[8] From 1711 until her own death in
1723 Dorothy, widow of Colonel Alexander Luttrell, had
the management of them on behalf of her eldest boy
Alexander. During her time two changes were made on the
Tor of Dunster. Up to the beginning of the eighteenth
century there had been but one approach to the castle.

[1] Narcissus Luttrell's Diary, vol. i,
p. 347.

[2] Ibid., p. 478. "Report of Historical
Manuscripts Commission," vol. vii, pp.
226, 416. "Hatton Correspondence"
(Camden Society), vol. ii, pp. 106, 108,
110.

[3] Narcissus Luttrell's Diary, vol. ii,

[4] Wills at Somerset House, "Coker,"
f. 40.

[5] Vol. iv, p. 142.

[6] Narcissus Luttrell's Diary, vol. iv,
p. 150.

[7] Savage's "History of Carhampton."

[8] Dunster Parish Register.

Northwest front of
Dunster Castle. 1868
F.F. Lyte del.

After ascending the slope to Sir Hugh Luttrell's gate-house and passing under its vaulted archway, carriages had to turn abruptly to the right through the older gateway between the Edwardian towers. Thence they had to describe a long curve to the left to reach the porch on the north-western façade of the Elizabethan mansion. From first to last the road from the town was extremely steep, and the angle between the two gateways was so sharp that in descending the hill some skill was required to drive a carriage safely through them. Mrs. Luttrell, therefore, in 1716, made an alternative road, which branched off to the left of the other some way below the gatehouse, and then wound round the eastern and southern sides of the Tor, ascending gradually until it reached the level of the south-eastern angle of the castle, towards which it then turned rather sharply. It ended ✳ on a small gravel platform outside the offices.[1] The trees lining "the new way" are very properly represented as quite young in the engraved view of Dunster Castle, which was published by Buck in 1733. Under the advice of Sir James Thornhill a florid chapel was built on the south-eastern side of the castle in 1722 and 1723, at a cost of about £1300.[2]

Alexander, son and successor of Colonel Alexander Luttrell, lived very extravagantly in London and elsewhere, and died in 1737 deeply in debt.[3] In him the male line of the Luttrells of Dunster came to an end. For the fifth time in less than a century the estates passed to a minor. Margaret, daughter of Sir John Trevelyan and widow of the last Alexander Luttrell, had the charge for many years of the two Luttrell heiresses, her own daughter Margaret, and her husband's niece Ann, who had lost both her parents while still an infant.[4] The former of these ladies was in 1747 married to Henry Fownes of Nethway in the county of Devon, who accordingly assumed the name and arms of Luttrell.

Further structural changes were made at Dunster in the second half of the eighteenth century. The piece of

---

[1] Dunster Manor Office, Box xxi.
[2] Ibid.
[3] After his death it was even found desirable to sell the family plate. Sir John Trevelyan appears to have bought most of it at a sale that took place at Taunton during the assize week. Dunster Manor Office, Box i.
[4] Dunster Manor Office, Box xxii. Epitaph in Dunster Church.

the curtain wall that connected the Elizabethan mansion with the Edwardian gateway was partially rebuilt in 1761. Two years later it was resolved to make a new carriage road, to supersede entirely the dangerous old one, which passed through that gateway. The "new way" of 1719, it must be remembered, did not lead up to the front door, the southern end of the residence being built against the solid rock of the Tor, which at that point was almost precipitous. There was thus no means of external access from the gravelled platform at the upper end of the "new way," except by some steep flights of steps. A surveyor named Hull suggested two different plans for a road, which should ascend from the town to the castle by zigzags, but eventually recommended that the road made in 1719 should be prolonged round the western and northern sides of the Tor until it reached the front door. This last scheme was adopted, and the work was carried out in 1763 and 1764. It involved the destruction of the wall against the hill which formed the southern boundary of the lower ward of the ancient castle, and of the western wall, which extended northwards from it and joined the curtain wall at an angle of 110 degrees at a point about forty-five feet to the west of an old bastion, which still remains. All the buildings in the northern part of the lower ward, near the gatehouse, were demolished, and the whole surface of the lower ward, which had hitherto sloped down towards the north, was made absolutely level, by lowering it a little on the south side and raising it considerably on the north. The massive wooden doors of the Edwardian gateway were closed and a wall was built close to them, to protect them from the pressure of the earth that was being piled up behind. The course of the old road that used to lead up to the front door of the residence was at the same time entirely obliterated under a lawn of smooth turf.[1] The artificial platform thus created in 1764, and retained ever since, came up to the level of the floor of the upper storey of Sir Hugh Luttrell's gatehouse, which had hitherto been approached only from below, by means of winding steps. It was therefore

---

[1] Plans, etc. by Thomas Hull. Dunster Manor Office.

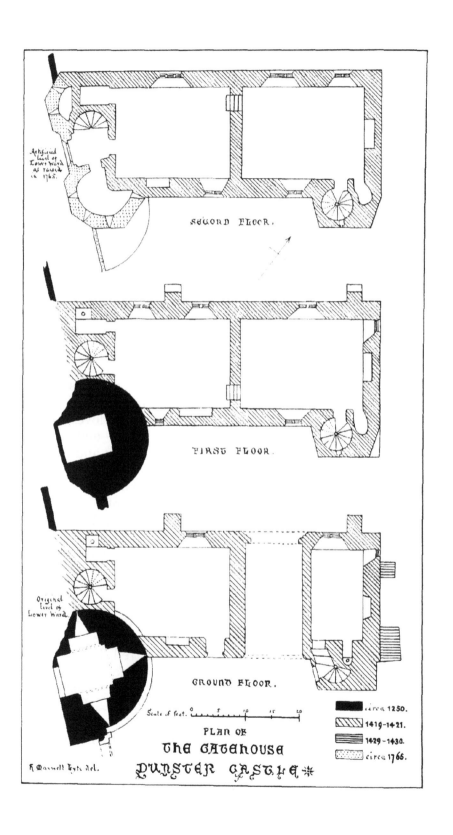

SECOND FLOOR.

Artificial
Level of
Lower Ward
as raised
in 1765.

FIRST FLOOR.

Original
Level of
Lower Ward

GROUND FLOOR.

Scale of feet. 0   5   10   15   20

◼   circa 1250.

▨   1419–1421.

▤   1429–1430.

▨   circa 1765.

PLAN OF
THE GATEHOUSE
DUNSTER CASTLE ✳

R. Maxwell Lyte del.

resolved soon afterwards to make an entrance from it into the highest landing of the southern staircase of the gatehouse. A late Perpendicular doorway, removed from one of the demolished buildings of the old castle, was set up parallel with the line of the curtain wall, and a polygonal turret was built on either side of it, battlemented above and pierced below with narrow apertures, that were intended to represent loopholes. So boldly was this southern front of the gatehouse designed, and so venerable does it now look under its thick mantle of ivy, that it has generally been considered a genuine work of the sixteenth century. It was most probably in the time of Henry Fownes Luttrell that doorways were made between the northern and southern chambers of the two upper storeys of the gatehouse, so as to give easy access to the former from the inhabited portion of the castle. The gatehouse, as built in the reign of Henry V, appears to have been divided into two parts by a solid stone wall, which ran right across it and supported two distinct roofs. Each part had its own staircase and its own series of garderobes, the floors and windows of the northern part being, moreover, on a higher level than those in the southern part. A hollow tower and other artificial ruins were built on Conygar Hill in and about the year 1775.[1]

Henry Fownes Luttrell survived his wife, the heiress of Dunster, by several years, and died in 1780. His son and successor, John Fownes Luttrell, died in 1816, and was succeeded by his son of the same name.

All the timber houses and shambles in the middle of the main street, except the octagonal Yarn-market, were pulled down in 1825, a new market house having been built on the east side of the street. The advowson of the church and the great tithes of Dunster were about the same time purchased of Lord Sherborne by the owner of the castle. John Fownes Luttrell, the second of that name, died in 1857, and was succeeded by his brother Henry, on whose death, ten years later, the property passed to his nephew George Fownes Luttrell, the present possessor.

Great changes and improvements have been effected at

[1] Dunster Manor Office, Box iv.

Dunster since 1867. A suitable residence for the vicar of the parish, who had hitherto had no house of his own, was built from the designs of Mr. St. Aubyn near the dovecot of the former Benedictine priory. This was soon followed by the erection of some commodious parochial schools, a little to the west of the churchyard. The castle was next taken in hand, the Elizabethan mansion proving utterly inadequate to modern requirements. By the advice of Mr. Salvin, the northern tower of the principal façade was pulled down and replaced by a much larger one, with a projecting turret staircase attached to it. The porch was at the same time rebuilt on a larger scale, and an additional storey added to a great part of the residence. The hall was greatly enlarged by the addition to it of the space formerly occupied by two small rooms and a passage. Solid stone mullioned windows were in several places substituted for spurious Gothic windows of the eighteenth century, and the incongruous chapel of 1722 was utterly demolished. On its site was built a lofty tower, containing a drawing-room on the ground floor and bedrooms above. The kitchen and other offices that formerly occupied the southern part of the building were converted into sitting rooms, and a new range of offices was constructed along the line of the curtain wall between the basement under the parlour and the old Edwardian gateway. The massive doors of this gateway were once more thrown open, and a staircase was made behind it to give access to the lawn in front of the house. A covered passage was at the same time made between the offices and the gatehouse, and the upper stories of the gatehouse have since been converted into one room more than forty-six feet long. A new carriage road has also been carried round the Tor on an easy gradient, that made a hundred years previously being turned into a footpath.

The alterations at Dunster Castle were scarcely completed before the difficult task of restoring the parish church was entrusted to Mr. Street. A Norman doorway discovered in the west wall was re-opened, and the whole of the nave was substantially repaired and fitted with carved oak benches. A raised platform separated from the transepts by open screens was constructed under the

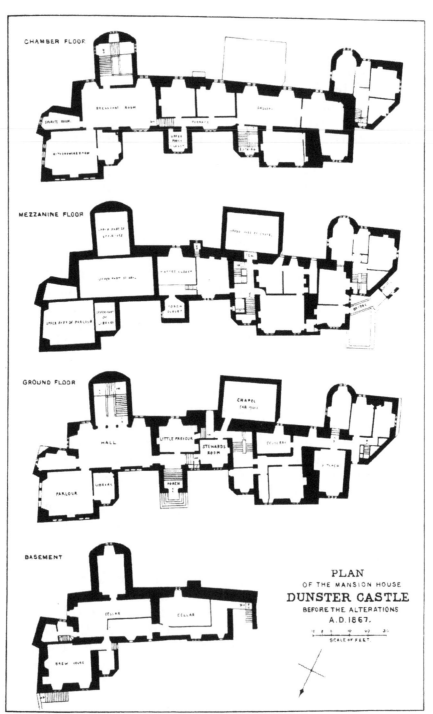

CHAMBER FLOOR

MEZZANINE FLOOR

GROUND FLOOR

BASEMENT

PLAN
OF THE MANSION HOUSE
DUNSTER CASTLE
BEFORE THE ALTERATIONS
A.D. 1867.

SCALE OF FEET.

tower, and the altar, which had stood under the western arch of the tower, was placed on it about sixteen feet to the east of its former position, the division of the building into two distinct parts being still maintained. The eastern or monastic part of the old church, claimed by Mr. Luttrell as his private property, was at the same time restored at his sole expense without any faculty. The fragments of Early English mouldings found in the walls afforded a certain clue for the reconstruction of the original lancet windows in the east wall and of the piscina and sedilia on the south side. Other Early English windows were also re-opened. All the old encaustic tiles found in the building were collected together, and relaid in the small outlying chapel on the north, and the rest of the choir and its aisles was paved with heraldic tiles copied from these old ones, the only new shield added to the series being that of the Luttrell family. An old altar-slab found in the pavement was set up tablewise against the eastern wall on five alabaster pillars, and the monastic church being thus once more made available for divine worship, was licensed by the Bishop of the Diocese in 1881.

The present owner of Dunster Castle has lately added to his property another place of high archæological and artistic interest by his purchase of the site of the Cistercian Abbey of Cleeve, where he has arrested the decay of the conventual buildings and has laid bare the fine encaustic pavements of the church and of the original refectory.

Dunster Castle has in the course of the last three centuries been shorn of much of its military character, and its lords have lost many of their ancient rights by the dissolution of the monasteries, and by the abolition of feudal tenures. The estate around it however still corresponds very closely with that which the Luttrells bought of the Mohuns in the reign of Edward III, augmented by the lands which they inherited through the Paganels of Quantockshead, and the Hadleys of Withycombe.

FINES.

APPENDIX F.

THE ARMS AND SEALS OF THE LUTTRELL FAMILY.

The heraldry of the Luttrell family presents several points of interest, and the series of seals of the Somersetshire branch preserved among the muniments at Dunster Castle is remarkably perfect.

Nothing is known as to the arms that Geoffrey Luttrell, the original founder of the family, may have borne. His son, Sir Andrew Luttrell, who died in 1265, granted East Quantockshead to his second son Alexander, and ratified the deed with a seal bearing three bars on a pointed shield, and the inscription :—SIGILL ANDRE LUTEREL.[1] There are no means of ascertaining what the tinctures of the shield may have been. The woodcut (No. 8) is copied from a finer impression of the same seal in the British Museum.[2]

The bearing of the three bars must have been soon abandoned, for a deed of the year 1261, by which "Geoffrey Luterel, son of Sir Andrew Luterel," granted common of pasture at Hoton Pagnell to the Prior and Brethren of St. John of Jerusalem in England, is attested by a green seal (No. 9) bearing the device of six martlets, and the inscription— SIGILL GALFRIDI LUTEREL.[3] Another deed, by which the same Geoffrey conveyed the manor of East Quantockshead to his younger brother Alexander, is attested by a white seal (No. 10) which shows four martlets on a shield divided quarterly.[4] Here, again, there is no trace of the tinctures, and the legend round the seal has unfortunately disappeared. The date of the deed cannot be later than 1266.

The grandson of Geoffery Luttrell, of the same name, bore for his arms :—*Azure a bend between six martlets argent.*[5] This coat was certainly borne by his descendants the Luttrells of Irnham, co. Lincoln, though some modern books erroneously assign to them the arms of the Luttrells of Somersetshire.[6] It is, or was, to be seen in the church of Hawton, co. Nottingham,[7] and it occurs several times in the Luttrell Psalter. In

[1] Dunster Castle Muniments. Box xxii, No. 1.
[2] Additional Charter 21268.
[3] Topham Charter 16.
[4] Dunster Castle Muniments. Box xxii, No 1.
[5] Guillim's Roll of Arms of the time of Edward I., printed in "The Genealogist," vol. i, p. 325.
[6] Nicolas's "Roll of Arms of the reign of Edward II.," and "Roll of Arms of the reign of Edward III."
[7] Thoroton's "History of Nottinghamshire," vol. i, p. 357.

SEALS.

8.
Sir Andrew Luttrell.
d. 1265.

9.
Sir Geoffrey Luttrell.
d. 1269 or 1270.

10.
Sir Geoffrey Luttrell.
d. 1269 or 1270.

SEALS.

11.
Sir Geoffrey Luttrell.
d. 1419.

12.
Sir Alexander
Luttrell.
d. 1318— 1354.

13.
Sir John Luttrell,
K.B.
d. 1403.

14.
Lady Elizabeth Luttrell.
d. 1395.

that beautiful manuscript the Lady Agnes Luttrell is represented as attired in a dress on which her husband's arms are impaled with those of Sutton—*Or* a lion rampant *vert.* Her daughter-in-law the Lady Beatrix Luttrell appears in the same illumination in a dress on which the arms of Sir Andrew Luttrell are impaled with *Azure* a bend *or,* a label *argent,* for Scrope of Masham.[1] The arms of another Sir Andrew are duly blazoned in a roll of the time of Richard II, as *Azure* a bend between six martlets *argent.*[2] His son, Sir Geoffrey, the last of the Luttrells of Irnham had a beautiful seal (No. 11) on which his arms are shown under a richly mantled helmet crowned with an orle and surmounted by his crest, a fish's tail. The trees on either side of the helmet appear to have been introduced merely as ornaments. The inscription runs :—Sigillum Galfridi Louterell.[3]

Like their cousins in Lincolnshire the Luttrells of East Quantockshead bore for arms a bend between six martlets, but with this important difference that the field was blazoned *or* instead of *azure,* and the charges on it *sable* instead of *argent.* Thus, in a Roll of Arms of the reign of Edward II, we read :—

" *Sire Andreu Loterel, de or, a une bende e vj merelos de sable.*

Sire Geffrey Loterel, de azure, a une bende e vj merelos de argent."[4]

Sir Andrew Luttrell of East Quantockshead is there placed among the knights of the county of Lincoln, because his estates, though in Somersetshire, were held under his cousin Sir Geoffrey, as part of the Barony of Irnham.

Sir Alexander Luttrell, the son and successor of this Sir Andrew, used a small seal (No. 12) showing his coat of arms within a decorated quatrefoil. The inscription runs :—Sigillu Alexandri Loterell.[5]

Sir John Luttrell, K.B., in whom the main line of the Luttrells of East Quantockshead became extinct in 1403, used a small seal (No. 13) bearing his arms and the legend—Sigill Johis Loterel.[6]

The Luttrells of Chilton, co. Devon, a cadet branch of the Luttrells of East Quantockshead, differenced their shield by the addition of a bordure engrailed *sable.* The seal of the Lady Elizabeth Luttrell, the purchaser of Dunster (No. 14), shows the Luttrell arms within this bordure, impaled with those of Courtenay. It should be remarked that the shield is mounted on a double rose. The inscription round this beautiful seal is :—Sigillum Elizabeth Luterel.[7] The arms of Lady Elizabeth Luttrell are, or were, to be seen at Canterbury, her brother having been Archbishop of that see.[8]

In the month of September, 1403, six standards bearing the arms of Sir Hugh Luttrell were delivered to some ships that were to convey provisions to him in Wales from the port of Minehead.[9] When this worthy knight served under Henry V. at the siege of Rouen a few years later, his shield was blazoned—*Or,* a bend between six martlets *sable* within a border engrailed of the same.[10] These arms appear on the seal (No. 15) which he used during the greater part of his life for legal and

---

[1] " Vetusta Monumenta," vol. vi.

[2] Willement's "Roll of Arms."

[3] British Museum. Additional Charters, 21037, 21038.

[4] Nicolas's " Roll of Arms of the reign of Edward II."

[5] Dunster Castle Muniments, Box xxii.

[6] *Ibid.* Box xxii. No. 4.

[7] Dunster Castle Muniments. Box xxxvii. No. 41.

[8] Willement's " Heraldic Notices of Canterbury," p. 160.

[9] See Appendix H.

[10] Harleian MS., 1586, f. 85.

official purposes in England and in Normandy alike. Proud of the Bohun blood that ran in his veins, he placed over his shield a swan, the well-known badge of the Bohun family. The inscription on the seal is—Sigillum Hugonis Lutrell militis.[1] In attesting private letters, warrants to his receiver-general, and other papers of an informal character, Sir Hugh Luttrell always used a small signet (No. 16) bearing a single martlet and two sprigs of foliage, instead of his large heraldic seal.[2] Some impressions of this signet, preserved among the muniments at Dunster Castle, are attached to documents written on parchment by a little strip of that material as shown in the woodcut opposite; others are affixed to the manuscripts themselves on a foundation made of a twist of straw. Lady Catherine Luttrell, Sir Hugh's wife, used a signet (No. 17) bearing a Catherine-wheel in allusion to her christian name.[3]

There is in a volume at the College of Arms a transcript of a very interesting French deed by which Hugh Courtenay, Earl of Devon, granted his badges to his cousin Sir Hugh Luttrell, in 1421.[4] It runs as follows :—

"A tous y ceux que cestes nos lettres verront ou orront Hugh Courtnay Count de Devon et Sᵣ d'Ockhampton feiz et hair a Monsᵣ l'honorable (?)[5] et tresnoble Sᵣ Edward Courtney Count de Devon et Sᵣ d'Okhampton que Dieu assoile saluz en Dieu, Sachez nous avon don et grantée et par y cestes nos lettres confirme a nostre tres chere et bon ame coscyn Hugh Lutrel Chᵣ et Sᵣ Donstarre nos Bages cest a savoire un Sengler Blanc armé d'or portans come nous portons avecque un diffrence dun doble rose dor sur lespald en dit sengler a avoir et tenoir le dites Bages de nostre don al dit Sᵣ Hugh de Luttrell et ses hoires a tous jours En testmonance de quel chose a y cestes nos presentz lettres nous avons mis nostre seale de nous Armes Donne a Plimmouth le 13 jour de Juell a temps que nous avons[6] priz nostre voyage[7] par Grace de Deux envers nostre tresouveraigne Roy en Normandie l'an du Raigne le dit nostre Sᵣ le Roy Sᵣ le Henri quint puis le Conquest 9º."[8]

On the strength of this the Luttrell crest is given as a boar passant *argent*, armed *or*, charged on the shoulder with a double rose of the second, a notable example of one metal being placed on another. In point of fact the boar was never used as a crest or as a badge by the Luttrells of Dunster. It is possible that the double rose on the seal of Lady Elizabeth Luttrell, already described, may have been derived from the Courtenays, though of course not in consequence of the grant to Sir Hugh Luttrell, which was not made until some years after her death. Sir Hugh Luttrell seems to have placed a peculiar interpretation of his own on the grant of his noble kinsman, for while practically rejecting the badge of the white boar proffered in it, he did adopt the crest and the supporters of the head of the Courtenay family. The fine heraldic seal

---

[1] Dunster Castle Muniments, and Brit. Mus. Additional Charter, 1397.

[2] Dunster Castle Muniments. Box xi., No. 1.

[3] *Ibid.* Box xxii.

[4] C. 22. f. 391.

[5] "*Thome*" in transcript, the spelling of which seems to be incorrect in several other places.

[6] "*a nome*" in transcript.

[7] "*Brage*" in transcript.

[8] The year is given as 7 Henry V, instead of 9 Henry V, in a translation of this document in Cleaveland's "History of the Family of Courtenay," p. 211, but only on the authority of Sampson Leonard, the very herald who compiled the MS. at the College of Arms. He is said to have seen the original deed with the Earl of Devon's seal attached, but Prynne does not mention it in the Calendar of the Muniments at Dunster Castle which he made in 1650.

SEALS.

15.
Sir Hugh Luttrell.
d. 1428.

16.
Sir Hugh Luttrell.
d. 1428.

17.
Lady Catharine
Luttrell.
d. 1435.

18.
Sir Hugh Luttrell.
d. 1428.

P. H. DELAMOTTE & F. F. LYTE, del.   W. M. R. QUICK, sc.

SEALS.

19.
Sir John Luttrell.
d. 1430.

20.
Sir John Luttrell.
d. 1430.

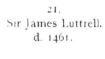

21.
Sir James Luttrell.
d. 1461.

22.
Sir James Luttrell.
d. 1461.

F. W. DELAMOTTE & F. F. LYTE. del.   W. M. P. CLR.

(No. 18) which he used during the last few years of his life, is a free copy of that which the Earl of Devon affixed to the French deed just quoted.[1] On both of them the crest is a large panache or plume of feathers, rising out of a coronet which encircles the helmet; on both of them the supporters are a pair of swans collared and chained, as borne by the Bohuns. The shield on Sir Hugh Luttrell's second seal shows the bend and the six martlets, without the engrailed bordure which appears on his first seal. By the successive deaths of Sir John Luttrell, K.B., of East Quantockshead, in 1403, and of Sir Geoffrey Luttrell, of Irnham, in 1419, Sir Hugh Luttrell had become the chief male representative of his family, and there was no longer any occasion for him to exhibit a mark of cadency on his coat of arms. The inscription on his second seal is S. Hugonis [Luttrell] militis dni de Dunsterre.[2]

For many years after attaining his majority John Luttrell was in the habit of using a seal (No. 19) closely resembling the first seal of his father Sir Hugh. It will be observed, however, that the swan above the shield is represented with closed wings, and that the shield is charged with a label as a mark of cadency. The inscription is:—Sigillum Johannis Luttrell armigeri.[3] John Luttrell also had a signet (No. 20) bearing the device of an otter with some water and a letter "L" below and the letters "trell" above, which was evidently intended as a pun on his surname, as the French for an otter, Loutre, when followed by the syllable "trell" made up "Loutretrell," or shortly "Loutrell."[4] Such a signet, though good enough for an heir apparent, was not deemed worthy of the Lord of Dunster, and the lawyers of the day seem to have raised objections to it. The result was that when John Luttrell affixed it to a release shortly after his father's death a memorandum was drawn up to the effect that he had sealed the deed with his signet in the presence of certain credible witnesses, but that he would seal it again with a seal bearing his coat of arms after his next visit to London where he intended to order a suitable seal.[5] He had probably abandoned his heraldic seal at the time when his father resolved to omit the engrailed bordure from the arms of the Luttrells of Dunster, and it does not appear that he lived long enough to carry out his intention of having another one engraved. It is recorded in the Heralds' Visitation for the County of Devon, that "This Sir John tooke the Queen of Scotts Prisoner in the fielde, after which hee bare a Coronett for his Crest, and after he took an Earle of France prisoner & may bere a swan for his Creast collered and chained."[6] The

---

[1] There are several impressions of the seal of Hugh, Earl of Devon, in the British Museum.

[2] Dunster Castle Muniments. Box xxiv. No. 6.

[3] Ibid. Box xxxvii. Nos. 46, 52.

[4] Ibid. Box xxxvi. No. 2.

[5] "Memorandum quod Johannes Lutrell filius et heres Hugonis Lutrell sigillavit istam relaxacionem cum signeto suo apud Glastoniam in Comitatu Somersetensi tercio die Septembris anno regni Regis Henrici Sexti post conquestum septimo in presentia Thome Stawell militis, Hugonis Cary senescalli Abbatis Glastonie, Thome Levesham de Scaccario domini Regis, Willelmi Corner et Thome Colbroke armigerorum et plurimorum aliorum. Et predictus Johannes Lutrell concessit prefato Hugoni Cary ad sigillandam predictam relaxacionem cum sigillo armorum suorum quando sigillum suum erit factum, quia in veritate sigillum suum non est adhuc factum, sed erit, quando predictus Johannes Lutrell, proxime venerit ad Londoniam, quod erit infra breve tempus." Transcript of Surrenden Charters made by the late Rev. Lambert B. Larking.

[6] Harleian MS. 1080, f. 156, and 1163, f. 116. It may be remarked that the early part of the Luttrell pedigree there given is not entitled to credit.

story, however, is not supported by any contemporary evidence and it may safely be dismissed as mythical, inasmuch as the crest-coronet and the chained swan were borne by Sir John Luttrell's father and derived from the Courtenays.   Lady Margaret Luttrell, the widow of Sir John, did not use a signet, her receipts being simply attested by her signature.

James Luttrell, Sir John's son and successor, bore on his signet (No. 21) a single martlet.[1]   His larger seal (No. 22) shows the Luttrell shield supported by swans.   Here first appears the crest of a fox which was used by several of his descendants.   The inscription is simply :—James Luttrell, and the character of the engraving shows the decadence in art.[2]

Sir Hugh Luttrell, K.B., the eventual successor to Sir James, used a very similar seal. (No. 23.)   The inscription is :—Hugh Luttrell, Knyght.[3] His signet (No. 24) which is square in form bears a martlet reversed and a sprig of foliage.[4]   This Sir Hugh Luttrell appears to have put up the heraldic tablet which is to be seen over the western arch of the gatehouse at Dunster Castle.   The Luttrell shield is there represented in the upper compartment as supported on the backs of two swans collared and chained as usual.   Over this is a richly mantled helm affrontee and in high relief, carrying as a crest some animal of which the body and the forelegs alone now remain, while above all a second crest, a fox courant, is shown on the same plane as the shield.   In the lower compartment there are eight shields :—1. Luttrell (without any bordure) impaling Courtenay ; 2. Luttrell impaling Beaumont ; 3. Luttrell impaling Audley ; 4. Luttrell impaling Courtenay of Powderham ; 5. Luttrell impaling Hill ; 6. Luttrell impaling a blank.   The seventh and eighth shields are blank.   The arms of Sir Hugh Luttrell impaling a saltire *vair* between four mullets pierced, the arms of his first wife Margaret Hill, are also on his monument in the church of East Quantockshead.

Sir Andrew Luttrell did not fill up the shield prepared for him on the Gatehouse at Dunster, but his arms impaled with those of Wyndham, a chevron between three lions' heads are carved on the monument at East Quantockshead.   It does not appear whether he ever had a heraldic seal. His signet (No. 25) bears his badge the swan collared and a French motto which may be read either TOUS SUR, or SUR TOUS.[5]

Sir John Luttrell, the "noble captain," used a signet (No. 26) which bears a swan collared and chained, without any motto.[6]   After his death this signet was successively used by his brother Thomas, and his nephew George Luttrell.[7]   It is not certain whether the peacock in the curious portrait of Sir John Luttrell by Lucas de Heere is intended as an allusion to the panache crest of the Luttrell family or as an emblem of Juno.

Nicholas Luttrell of Honibere, a younger brother of Sir John, bore on his signet (No. 27) a bird which somewhat resembles a crow, but which was doubtless intended to represent a martlet.[8]   His descendants, the Luttrells of Hartland, differenced the arms of the Luttrells of Dunster by the addition of a crescent.   According to the Heralds' Visitation for

---

[1] Dunster Castle Muniments, Box xxxv, No. 4.

[2] Ibid. Box xxxvii. No. 15.

[3] Ibid. Box i. No. 30 ; and Box ii. No. 4.

[4] Dunster Castle Muniments.

[5] Dunster Castle Muniments, Box v, No. 18.

[6] Ibid. Box xix. No. 25. This deed is also signed, "By me John Luttrel, Squyar."

[7] Dunster Castle Muniments.

[8] Ibid. Box xiv. No. 12.

SEALS.

24.
Sir Hugh Luttrell, K.B.
d. 1521.

25.
Sir Andrew Luttrell.
d. 1538.

23.
Sir Hugh Luttrell, K.B.
d. 1521.

26.
Sir John Luttrell.
d. 1551.

27.
Nicholas Luttrell.
d. 1592.

SEALS.

30.
Honora Luttrell.
fl. 1652—1656.

28.
George Luttrell.
d. 1629.

33.
Col. Alex. Luttrell.
d. 1711.

31.
Lucy Luttrell.
d. 1718.

34.
Alexander Luttrell.
d. 1737.

29.
Thomas Luttrell.
d. 1644.

32.
Col. Francis Luttrell.
d. 1690.

35.
Alexander Luttrell.
d. 1737.

Devonshire they bore as a crest the Courtenay badge granted to Sir Hugh Luttrell by the Earl of Devon, a boar *argent*, armed and crined *or*, charged on the shoulder with a double rose of the second.[1]

On a brass of the year 1566, which was once to be seen in the church of Bryanston, co. Dorset, there were engraved the arms of Rogers impaled with those of Luttrell, charged with a mullet for difference, recording the alliance between Sir Richard Rogers of that place and Cicely daughter of Sir Andrew Luttrell of Dunster.[2]

As has already been stated, Thomas Luttrell of Dunster, and his son "old George Luttrell," the re-builder of the castle, used the signet of Sir John Luttrell (No. 26). The latter of these two, however, found it convenient to have a distinctive seal of his own, and reverted to the panache crest, which had not been used by his ancestors since the time of the first Sir Hugh Luttrell. His seal (No. 28) shows a plume of twelve feathers arranged in two rows rising out of a crest-coronet.[3] The fox, however, still appears as the crest over the coat of arms which George Luttrell set up in the hall at Dunster Castle in 1589. The shield there, supported by two swans collared and chained *proper*, is divided quarterly 1 and 4 Luttrell, 2 and 3 quarterly, 1 and 2 *gules* on a chevron *or* three cross-crosslets *sable* for Hadley, 2 and 3 *or* on a bend cotised *sable* three horses' heads *argent*, bridled *gules*, for Durborough. The motto beneath is:—QUÆSITA MARTE TUENDA ARTE. These arms appear again on the pompous monument which George Luttrell set up in Dunster Church in 1621, surmounted in this case with two helmets carrying his crests, the panache and the fox. The arms of George Luttrell with the panache crest occur at the Luttrell Arms Hotel, at Dunster, and at the Manor House, East Quantockshead. In a room on the first floor in the former of these houses the arms of Luttrell are impaled with a chevron between three trefoils slipped, which were probably the arms of Silvestra Capps, the second wife of George Luttrell.

Thomas Luttrell, eldest son and successor of George, used a seal of which the woodcut (No. 29) is to some extent a conjectural restoration, the original impression of it being very much defaced.[4] The arms of this Thomas Luttrell impaled with those of his wife Jane Popham, *argent* on a chief *gules*, two bucks' heads cabossed *or* with a crescent for difference, may be seen on a monument in Dunster Church and at the old house at Marshwood. The arms of his younger brother Hugh, impaled with those of his wife Jane Lyte, *gules* a chevron between three swans *argent*, were set up in the domestic chapel of the old manor-house of Lytes Cary, co. Somerset, in 1631.

Honora Luttrell, the daughter-in-law of Thomas Luttrell, used a small seal (No. 30) which had doubtless belonged to her husband, George Luttrell. It bears the Luttrell arms with a fox as crest.

Lucy Luttrell, the widow of Francis Luttrell, the next owner of Dunster Castle, used a very similar seal (No. 31).

Francis Luttrell, of Dunster Castle, her son, also used a similar seal (No. 32) rather larger in size. His arms impaled with those of Tregonwell, *argent* three pellets in fesse cotised *sable* between three Cornish choughs *proper*, are introduced into the ornamental frieze of the parlour at

---

[1] Harleian MS. 108, f. 156.

[2] "Diary of Richard Symonds," Camden Society, p. 128.

[3] Dunster Castle Muniments. Box vii.

No. 17.

[4] Dunster Castle Muniments. Box vii. No. 17.

Dunster Castle, supported by chained swans and surmounted by a plume of feathers.   The Tregonwell crest is there given on a separate medallion.

Colonel Alexander Luttrell, of Dunster Castle, used a seal (No. 33) bearing the Luttrell arms differenced with a crescent, as he had been for many years a younger son.   The crest is a fox.

Alexander Luttrell, his eldest son and successor, sometimes used this seal, but had another (No. 34) engraved for himself, on which his arms are impaled with those of Trevelyan *gules* a demi-horse *argent*, hoofed and maned *or*, issuing out of water in base *proper*.   He had yet another seal (No. 35), which shows the Luttrell arms supported by chained swans, and surmounted by a well-shaped panache.   The motto is—QUÆSITA MARTE TUENDA ARTE.

Since the marriage of the heiress, Margaret Luttrell with Henry Fownes in 1747, their descendants have borne a quarterly shield—1 and 4 Luttrell ; 2 and 3 Fownes :—*Azure* two eagles displayed, and in base a mullet *argent*.   The crest of the fox has been quietly abandoned, and the fine panache crest has dwindled down into a plume of five stiff feathers issuing out of a coronet.   The motto " Quæsita marte tuenda arte " has become practically hereditary, and the successive heads of the family have maintained the claim—so rare among English Commoners, of using supporters.   The noble swans of the Bohuns and Courtenays are conspicuous on the new porch of Dunster Castle.

Glass Quarry in Dunster Church.

APPENDIX G.

PEDIGREE OF THE PAGANEL FAMILY.[1]

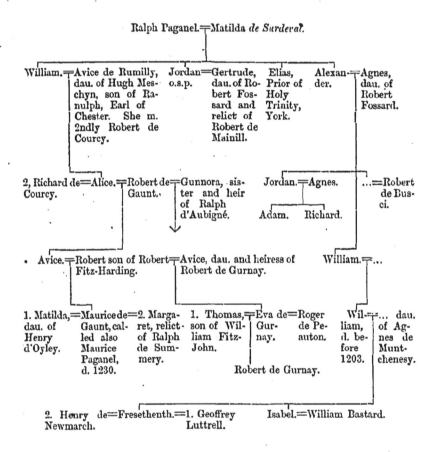

[1] Tabulated from the Paper on Holy Trinity, York, by Mr. Stapleton, in the York volume of the Archæological Institute.

DUNSTER HOUSEHOLD ACCOUNTS OF THE REIGNS OF HENRY IV, HENRY V, AND HENRY VI.

In addition to many Court-rolls, Rentals, and Bailiffs' Accounts, there are in the Muniment Room at Dunster Castle several rolls which show the general receipts and expenses of the Lords of Dunster in the first half of the fifteenth century. Sir Hugh Luttrell was so often absent on state affairs in Normandy and elsewhere that he found it necessary to have a Receiver-General in the West of England, and the system which he established was continued for some few years after his death. The accounts of the Receiver-General were from time to time subjected to audit, when a summary of them was drawn up on parchment for future reference, the vouchers and the detailed statements being for the most part cancelled or destroyed. Thus there now remains only one of the paper rolls on which the different items of daily expenditure were recorded. Most of the following extracts are taken from the parchment rolls, the omission of the less interesting entries being in every case marked by asterisks. In preparing them for press all contractions that occur in the original manuscripts have been extended, but the old spelling has, as far as possible, been retained. For the sake of convenience all numerals have been given in Arabic figures.

Accounts of John Dennyng, Receiver, Michaelmas 2 Henry IV, to Michaelmas 4 Henry IV, 1401-1403.

" Computat solvisse domino per manus Johannis Lutrell filii Ricardi Lutrell apud London in adventu suo de Calec ad festum natalis beati Johannis anno quarto 22 marcas (£14 6s. 8d.) Item eodem domino apud Gillyngham £4. . . . Et computat solvisse Thomæ Kyng pro pensione sua per literam dicti Johannis in ecclesia Sancti Pauli Londonie 5s. Et eidem Thome in Aula Westmonasterii alia vice 4s. Et computat solvisse Radulfo Swayn pro vino empto apud Calec ex prece domini 60s. Et computat solvisse Ricardo Rectori de Cantokeshede ad solvendum executoribus domini Johannis Lutrell pro diversis rebus emptis ad usum domini £10 13s. 4d. Et computat solvisse eisdem executoribus per manus Ricardi Popham per indenturam 6 marcas (£4.) . . . . In expensis Ricardi Lutrell et ipsius computantis anno secundo hujus compoti equitancium diversis vicibus apud Cantok, Bruggewater et Puriton, ad loquendum cum domino Petro de Courtenay pro consilio petendo, ac etiam ipsius computantis pro curiis tenendis et redditis querendis ut supra, 18s."

Accounts of John Bacwell, Steward, from 27 June 6 Henry IV, to 27 June 7 Henry IV, 1405-1406.

This very interesting roll on paper gives the daily expenses of the household for a whole year. Those for the first week are as follows :—

" In primis in die dominica 28° die Junii, In carnibus bovinis emptis 5s., In carnibus ovinis emptis 2s. 10d., In carnibus vitulinis emptis 5s. 7d., In 14 pullis 16d., Item die Mercurii primo die Julii in piscibus recentibus emptis 4s. 6d., In 4 lagenis[1] lactis 4d., In butiro 7d., In diversis speciebus 8d., In 12 congros 4s. ex conserva [or consuetudine] manerii de Minhede, In 12 milwelles[2] 3s. ex eadem conserva, [or consuetudine] Item die Jovis 2° die Julii, In 2 quarteriis unius vituli emptis 10d., Item die Veneris 3° die Julii, In piscibus salsis et recentibus emptis 2s. 11d., In 8 quarteriis avenarum emptis pro prebenda equorum domini et servientium ejus, pretium cujuslibet quarterii 16d., 10s. 8d., In feno empto pro eisdem equis 2s., In ferrura eorundem equorum 2s. 0½d., In stipendio 1 garcionis cariantis boscum per 2 dies 6d. ; Summa 46s. 9½d."

The following entries occur in different subsequent weeks :—
July 8, "In 1 lagena vini empta causa domini de Penbroke 8d. ;" July 15, "In 2 quarteriis frumenti emptis, pretium quarterii 6s. 8d., 13s. 4d. ;" July 17, "In turbut 5d., In 1 milwell 6d., In 1 anguilla 3d., In bremis et aliis piscibus recentibus emptis 14d., . . In 2 bussellis salis 2s. 4d., In 3 potellis mustarde 7½d., . . In 22 trusses de vrissen [or brissen] 3s. 4d. ;" July 19, "In saffron 3d., In ovis 13½d. " . . . In pulvere 2d. ;" July 26, "In 1 capriola 8d ;" July 29, "In 1 potello vini causa Archidiaconi de Taunton 4d. ;" August 2, "In 3 maulardes 6d. ;" August 6, "In carne porcina 1s. ;" August 7, "In 100 allec[3] 16d. ;" August 9, "In 2 porcellis emptis 12d. ;" August 16, "In 4 aucis emptis 10d. ;" August 21, "In 12 libris candelarum Parisiensium[4] 2s. ;" August 28, In 2 raics emptis ad Minhede 6d., . . In 4½ lagenis vini rubei emptis causa extraneorum 3s. ;" September 3, "In 1 quarterio multonis empto 6d. ;" September 6, "In 8 dosinis aucarum emptis in Alliremore per Henricum Baker 22s. ;" September 11, "In 5 currubus cariantibus boscum de Mersshwode ad Castrum, currus ad 4d., 20d., In 1 curru per 2 vices carianti victualia de Castro ad portum versus dominum existentem in Wallia 6d ;" September 30, "In 1 salmone 7d. ;" October 2, "In allec albis 17d. . . . In pane et cervisia emptis pro certis marinariis in batella Howell existentibus et missis ad partes Wallie ad scienda nova de domino ibidem existenti in comitiva Regis 12d. ;" October 9, "In soluto pro 1 panello pro cella equi cariagii hospicii 10d., In 88 panibus frumenti emptis et ad dominum missis in partes Wallie, quolibet pane ad obolum 3s. 8d. ;" October 11, "In pulvere zinziberis et piperis 4d ;" October 14, "In sepo recenti empto pro pedibus equorum domini 2d. ;" October 16, "In 4 capistris[5] emptis pro equis chariette 2d. ;" October 21, "In 1 haque[6] empta 5d. ;" October 22, "In 3 wodecokes emptis 3d. ;" October 23, "In 2 salmonibus emptis apud le Merssh 12d., In pane equino empto pro equis domini existentis apud Dunstre 22d., In soluto in 3 parvis barellis ad imponendum vertjus 2s., . . . In 15 porcis vivis emptis in grosso 42s. de quibus vendebantur 6 pro 20s. 4d., Et novem fiebant bacon." October 28, "In 200 ostreis 6d ;" October 29, "In carne multonis et bovis recenti pro hawkes domini 17d., In 4 pullis pro eisdem emptis 6d. ;" October 30, "In 2 ollis terreis pro coquina 2d. ;" November 1, "In 5 widec[okes] 4d. ;" November 6, "In 1 olla terrea

[1] Lagen = gallon.
[2] Milwell = mulvel = green fish, cf. "Munimenta Gildhallæ Londiniensis," ed. Riley, vol. ii, p. 816.
[3] Allec = herring, cf. Wright's "Volume of Vocabularies," p. 189.
[4] Periscandelle, Wardrobe Accounts, Edward IV, p. 121, quoted by Halliwell.
[5] Capistrum = halter. Wright, pp. 234, 108, and "Promptorium Parvulorum," p. 235.
[6] Haque = hake.

ad imponendum salem album 1½d., . . . In 2 bobus emptis pro hospicio 11s. 8d., . . . In 2 shakelles ad ligandos boves ne forte abeant 2d;" November 13, "In 2 bobus emptis in grosso pro hospicio 23s. 8d.;" November 20, "In comine empto 2d., . . In incausto empto 1d., In 1 pecia panni saccei de quo fiunt 5 sacci in pistrina, precium 3s. 8d., In 1 bundello de macchernes[1] pro candelis Parisiensibus conficiendis 3s. 4d.;" November 25, "In 22 multonibus vivis in Wallia emptis 11s., In 8 bobus et vaccis ibidem emptis ad diversas vices precium 46s. 8d.;" December 11, "In 10 canibus marinis emptis[2] 10d.;" December 13, "In parvis volucribus emptis 2d.;" December 16, "In 3 bollis pro coquina emptis 10d., In 12 ciphis pro butteria emptis 12d. In una lanterna empta pro gradubus aule 9d;" December 18, "In 1 gournard empto 2d., . . In melle empto 4d., . . In 4 dosinis vasorum stanneorum emptis apud Brigewater 72s. In costis 1 hominis eadem vasa versus Dunster conducentis 7d, In 20 libris de rosin emptis 20d., In 100 libris cere emptis 55s., In 12 libris de almondes emptis 3s., In 12 libris de dates emptis 3s., In 6 ulnis de cannevas emptis pro coquina 2s. 6d., In 11½ ronnes fili lichenii[3] pro torticibus emptis 6s. 1d., In custis 1 hominis prædicta conducentis de Brigewater ad Dunsterre 2s. 2d.;" December 25, "In lacte et creme emptis 12d.;" December 27, "In vino empto et de Taunton adducto causa festi per dominum tenti 7s., In volatilibus emptis 10d."

January 14, "In 1 Corlue empta 3d., In 3 maulardes emptis 9d.;" January 15, "In 1 potello mellis empto 8d.;" January 22, "In 4 discis ligneis pro coquina emptis 4d.;" February 5, "In olla lignea pro panetria 1d.;" February 12, "In coklis emptis 1d., . . . In 130 haques achatez a Bristuyt le haque a 2½d. et 120 pro 100, 31s. 3d. In 500 Scalpines[4] emptis 100 ad 2s. 6d., 12s. 6d. In 15 lagenis olei olive, lagena ad 12d., 15s., In 1 parvo barello pro oleo et 1 pipa pro piscibus predictis imponendis 2s. 9d., In stowagio et cariagio predictorum usque Dunsterre 16d., In 2 copulis[5] fructus ficuum et racinorum 12s., In expensis J. Bacwell super emptione predictorum et aliorum negociorum domini equitantis per 8 dies 13s. 4d., In 2 cadis allec rubii emptis, cadus ad 6s. 8d., 13s. 4d., In 3 dosinis de Countours emptis pro scaccario 9d., Et in cariagio allec et 1 pipe de piscibus Bristollie emptis de Minehede ad Dunsterre 10d.;" February 19, "In casio empto 4d.;" February 21, "In 1 hirco empto 6d., . . In 1 Teel empta 1d.;" February 28, "In lacte empto pro filio domini infra etatem existenti 4d. . . . In 5 lagenis vini albi emptis apud Brigewater ad perimplendam 1 pipam vini aliqualiter attenuatam 3s. 4d.;" March 7, "In melet recente empta 1d. In lavacione et portagio piscium predictorum 4d.;" March 10, "In 4 tancardes ligneis emptis ad parcendum ollis factis ex corio 12d. . . In musculis emptis 1d."

The expenses amounted to only 4s. 11½d in the following week, salt fish being almost the only kind of food consumed by the members of the household. The following entries occur after Easter :—

---

[1] Macchernes = matches = wicks.

[2] Canes marini = sea dogs; chiens-de-mer were an article of food in France also, cf. Wright's "Volume of Vocabularies," p. 98.

[3] Filum lichinum = wick thread.

[4] Scalpin = "scalyn fyshe," cf. "Promptorium Parvulorum," p. 442.

[5] Copulus = copellus = a measure.

May 14, " In canibus marinis, melet, barces et aliis piscibus emptis 14d., In 140 ovis emptis 7d. ;" June 11, " In ferrura equorum cariagii et aliorum serviencium hospicii tam apud Wachet quam apud Pottesham equis domini existentibus apud Cantok 4s. 2d., In factura 6 barelles pro cervisia imponenda 2s, Et pro 1 corda et 2 citulis[1] prope novum fontem factum emptis 2s."

Beer cost 1½d. per gallon from Midsummer to Michaëlmas, 1¼d. from Michaelmas to Christmas, and 1d. from Christmas to Midsummer. Thirteen gallons were reckoned as twelve. At these prices the bill for beer for a twelvemonth came to £34 1s. 2¼d.

The following entries occur among the miscellaneous payments :— " 3º die Julii in soluto de mandato domini pro expensis unius varletti domine Comitisse de la Marche cum literis suis domino missis, ut in equo suo in villa existenti 15½d. Item 8º die Julii in soluto de mandato domini pro expensis equorum Comitis de Penbroke versus regem equitantis 20d., Item eodem die In dono domini diversis pissionariis[2] de la Marssh melet et alios pisces sibi presentantibus 12d., Item 10º die Julii in soluto in expensis factis per ipsum dominum et extraneos sibi confluentes apud Yevelchestre, eo quod adversarii sui proponebant eodem die arraineasse assisam contra ipsum 67s. 11d., Item 17º die Julii in soluto pro cirpis in aula et camera struendis 4d., In 1 libra cere ad candelas in capella conficiendas 7d. In furrura et filo pro toga domini reparanda 6d. Et in sotularibus, caligis, camisis et braccis Willelmo Russell domini henxteman[3] liberatis 20d., . . . Item ultimo die Julii in solutis de mandato domini Willelmo Godwyn pro tantis de se mutuatis die quo bestie in Exmore existentes fuerunt insimul congregate 3s. 4d., Item 24º die Augusti in dono domini uni piscatori 1 porpes sibi presentanti 12d. . . . Item 25º die Augusti In dono domini uni nuncio Regis sibi literas suas afferenti per quas Rex ipsum jussit versus partes Wallie festinare 3s. 4d., Item eodem die in soluto de mandato domini pro expensis equorum Comitis de Penbroke de Rege revertentis et aliorum extraneorum 3s. 5½d., Item eodem die in soluto pro factura 2 dowbletes pro Willelmo Russell et Roberto equorum domini custode, una cum braccis et calcaribus eisdem emptis per manus Johannis Hunt 2s. 6d., Item 28º die Augusti in soluto de mandato domini pro expensis equorum Johannis Cobleston per unam noctem 18d. . . . Item 11º die Septembris in 1 corda empta pro campana supra aulam 2d, Et in sotularibus pro garcione pistrine 4d., Item eodem die in soluto pro 6 estandardes armorum domini liberatis diversis navibus de Minhede domino in partibus Wallie victualia adducentibus 2s., Item solutum in expensis domini et familie sue versus Regem Leicestre existentem equitantis et per quatuor septimanas integras absentis £4 15s. 8d., Item solutum Johanni Cotes in hospicio suo apud Henyngham domino ibidem existenti, prout in indenturis inter dominum et ipsum confectis plenius continetur £4 13s 4d., Item 12º die Septembris In soluto 2 armarariis armaturam domini purgantibus per 14½ dies ad 14d. per diem, tam pro eis quam pro 1 famulo eisdem servienti per idem tempus 16s. 11d., Item le 12me jor d' Octobre In soluto 1 plumbario super emendacione turrium operantis per 16 dies ad 2d. pe

---

[1] Citulæ = situlæ = buckets.
[2] Pissionarii = piscenarii = fishmongers,

[3] Henxteman = henchman = page, cf. " Promptorium Parvulorum," p. 233.

diem 2s 8d Et in 16 libris stanni emptis ad conficiendam solduram, libra ad 3s. 4d., 6s. 8d., Item eodem die In soluto Hugoni Taillor pro camisis et caligis per ipsum emptis pro 3 garcionibus stabuli 17d., In parvis clavis pro fenestris scaccarii 2d., In olio pro herness domini 1d., In panno lineo, et filo, empto pro 2 paribus caligarum domini 12d. . . . Item eodem die in soluto pro emendacione besagiorum[1] domini 2d., In 1 clave empta pro hostio turris supra portam 2d., In jemeux[2] staples, haspes et 1 bolte ferreis pro sappis[3] in porta positis 12d., In 1 cera, 1 clave, 1 haspe et 1 stapulo emptis pro turri versus Occidentem in le Dongeon 8d., In 1 cera, et 1 clave emptis pro hostio latrine in fine aule 6d., Item 26º die Octobris, In liberato domino eunti peregre ad capellam Sancte Trinitatis de Bircombe 12d., Item eodem die, In liberato Johanni Hunt, camerario domini pro calcaribus et aliis necessariis garcionibus stabuli emendis de mandato suo 16d. . . . Item eodem die In soluto pro 2 bussellis calcis emptis 2d. In 100 lathmailles emptis 4d., In 1 operario cooperienti penticium turris super angulum de dongeon versus occidentem per 2 dies 4d., In 1 carpentario idem penticium facienti per 3 dies 6d. ad mensam domini 16d. . . . In soluto pro 3 bordes de pipler[4] emptis pro garderoba domini 2s, . . . Item 13º die Novembris In soluto 2 armarariis armaturam domini purgantibus per 11 dies, quolibet ad 4d. per diem 7s. 4d., In recenti sepo porci pro eisdem 7d. . . . In dono domine Thome Kynge versus Saunton[5] in negocio suo equitanti 8d. . . . In dono domini Johanni Charettier dominam conducenti de London usque Dunsterre 20s., et pro certis expensis per ipsum factis et solutis ut asseruit 15d. . . . Item 20º die Decembris. . . . In dono domini de mandato suo duobus servientibus Prioris de Dunsterre 12 capones, duas parvas bacones, et 4 bussellos viridum pisarum domine presentantibus 16d., Item eodem die In soluto pro caligis et sotularibus Willelmo Russell et Roberto equorum custodi necessariis causa festi Natalis domini sequentis 20d. In soluto pro furrura 6 togarum domine et filiarum suarum erga idem festum 4s. 10d., Item eodem die, In dono domini uni varletto Johannis Clifdon 2 damos apportanti de Gill[ingham] 20d. Item in vigilia Natalis domini in cirpis emptis ad sternendum in aula et cameris 6d., Item in festo Natalis domini In oblacionibus servient . hospicii in ecclesia distributis de mandato domini 2s, Item 26º die Decembris In dono domini tribus tenentibus Johannis Cobleston ludentibus coram eo 3s. 4d., In dono ejusdem 6 tenentibus de Dunsterre ludentibus coram eo 3s. 4d. In dono ejusdem pluribus parvulis de Minhede coram eo trepidiantibus[6] 20d, Item 3º die Januarii In soluto pro 2 pellu[briis][7] de laton ad mingendum emptis 2s. 7d., In soluto pro 4 quarternis[8] papiri emptis 2s., In soluto pro 12 pellibus pergameni ad superscribendum evidencias domini apud Briggewater 2s. 8d. In expensis Johannis Bacwell super scriptura earundem evidenciarum et alia negocia domini ibidem existentis per 6 dies 12s, Item in 5º die Januarii videlicet in vigilia Epiphanie domini In expensis domini ad Brigewater venientis certis de causis placitum suum tangentibus

---

[1] Besacia = wallet.
[2] Jemeux = gemela = hinges, cf. "Promptorium Parvulorum," p. 235 ; Halliwell, p. 396.
[3] Sappi = firs, or pieces of fir.

co. Devon, the residence of the mother of Lady Katharine Luttrell.
[6] Trepidiare = to dance, cf. Wright, p. 216.
[7] Pellubrium = a vessel for water.
[8] Quaternum = a quire.

Braunton,

3s. 1d., Et in dono suo uni juridico cognato Ricardi Popham 6s. 8d., et in expensis Johannis Leget de Harleston missi cum literis ad Dunsterre 13d. . . . Item eodem die In soluto in dono domini duobus servientibus domine de Pawlet apportantibus unum carcasium bovis et unum aprum cum 1 grue vivo et domine presentantibus 6s. 8d., et in expensis equorum suorum in villa existencium per unam noctem 17d., Item eodem die In dono domini 1 servienti Willelmi Godwyn apportanti unum aprum et domine presentanti erga natale domini 20d., Item eodem die In soluto pro emendacione de 1 grant firepan et in 1 dressyng knyfe empto 20d., Item in dono domini Clericis Sancti Nicholai 12d., Et in 3 virgis de russet emptis per Bacwell pro caligis garcionibus coquine, pistrine et butlerie necessariis 2s., Et in sotularibus pro eisdem 11d. . . . In 1 acu et pakthreed ad suendum saccos pistrine 1d. . . . Item eodem die In soluto duobus masones operantibus supra capellam in le dongeon per 9½ dies, quolibet ad 2d. per diem 3s. 2d., In soluto 3 operariis cariantibus terram pro eisdem, quolibet ad 3d. per diem, per unum diem 9d., In soluto pro 2 quarteriis Calcis apud Wachet emptis, una cum 2d. de cariagio eorundem 18d., Item eodem die In soluto 1 carpentario per 14 dies et 2 carpentariis per 2 dies, quolibet ad 2d. per diem, operantibus cippes, bordes, tresteles et fenestras et hostia in castro superiori et inferiori 3s., Item eodem die in 200 clavis ad 4d., In 150 clavis ad 6d., In 100 clavis ad 6d., 16d., In 22 libris ferri operati in twystes, hokes et aliis necesariis, libra ad 1½d., 2s. 9d., In emendacione chariette et diversorum operum in portis 20d., In 1 nova cera cum 2 clavibus et emendacione cerarum, hostiorum panetrie, coquine, et avenarum 10d., Item eodem die In soluto pro mundacione domus intra portas fimo implete 4d., Item 11° die Februarii In soluto Johanni Corbet, Fabro, pro 1 wexpan, 2 wexirens, 1 wexknyfe, 1 iren rake, 1 pikeys, 1 matok, 36 hoques pro bacones pendendis in coquina, 2 twistez pro hostio in turri super angulum de dongeon et parvis barris pro fenestris vitreis in aula 6s. 8d., Item eodem die in soluto 1 vitriario facienti fenestras vitreas in aula et cameris domini existentes, ad 2d. per diem, per 21 dies 3s. 6d., Item eodem die In soluto pro 2 hoques et 2 jemeux pro foliis fenestrarum vitrearum in capite aule 2d., Item eodem die In soluto 2 carpentariis operantibus cistas de mandato domine, ac etiam lez rakkes in porta per 6 dies, quolibet ad 2d. per diem, 2s., Et in 200 clavis pro eisdem cistis 1s., In 3 jemeux pro eisdem 4d., In 2 hamis et 3 magnis clavis pro dictis rakkis 2d., In una nova cera pendenti et alterius emendacione 4d., Item eodem die In soluto pro factura unius muri terrei infra turrim supra portam 20d., Et pro factura unius hostii cum lacche in eodem 3d. Item in 2 slipes fili linci per dominam empti 3s. 6d. Et in textura ejusdem 4d., Item in soluto 10° die Aprilis pro caligis, sotularibus, camisis, et braccis garcionibus pistrine, coquine et stabuli necessariis et emptis 3s. 8d. . . . Et in 2 virgis panni linei et fili emptis per manus Michaelis Strecche pro doublettes domini 18d., Item eodem die In soluto Willelmo Wardrobier de Wellis pro 1 magna dragge matrasz pro lecto domini empta 20s, Item eodem die In soluto fratri Gilberto Ley pro emendacione illuminacione, coopertura, et ligatura unius missalis unius portat[orii][1] et unius libri Gallici de mandato domine 6s. 8d., Item eodem die In factura 1 loggei pro capones ad finem pistrine, videlicet in carpentaria et territoria (?)

---

[1] Portiforium = breviary.

20d., Item in die Pasche in oblacionibus domine et filiarum suarum 4d., Et in dono domini J. fratri Carmelite de Bristollia mendicanti 12d., Et in oblacionibus domine die Pentecostes 2d., Item in vigilia Sancti Marci In soluto pro expensis Johannis Bacwell ex precepto domine missi ad Brigewater propter Johannem Sonier fratrem Dunsterre veniendum causa mariagii inter filiam domini et Willelmum Harleston faciendi 2s., Item primo die Junii In soluto pro expensis equorum domini Hugonis Courteney de Baunton et domini Hugonis filii Comitis factis par duas noctes et unum diem, et in expensis 1 varletti sui ante ipsos missi cum veneison 4s. 9d., Item 7º die Junii In liberatis Willelmo Brit de London missi et London revertenti pro expensis suis revertendo 10s., Item 11º die Junii in soluto domine peregre proficiscentis versus Clivam 6d."

Accounts of Thomas Hody, Receiver General, Michaelmas 12 Henry IV, to Michaelmas 13 Henry IV, 1411-1412.

" In certis ponderibus emptis pro pane ponderando in Dunstre 3s. 6d. . . In soluto Thome Pacchehole carpentario pro factura unius domus apud Gillynghame 13s. 4d." "Solutio debitorum domini—In soluto Abbati de Clyve de debito domini £50. In soluto Hayne Cokes servienti domini £6 13s. 4d. In soluto Thome Beaumond de debito domini £15 3s. In soluto Johanni Slugge pro 1 equo ab eo empto per dominum £4."

Accounts of Thomas Hody, Receiver General, Michaelmas 2 Henry V, to Michaelmas 3 Henry V, 1414-1415.

" In libris petris emptis juxta Bristolliam cum cariagio eorundem cum plaustris ad portum Bristollie, et eisdem cariandis per mare versus Dunster 42s. 5d. . . In liberato eidem domino (Sir Hugh Luttrell) ut in vasis argenteis ad usum suum emptis de executoribus Ivonis Fitz Waryn Militis, ex precepto et assignacione domini £54 "

Accounts of Thomas Hody, Receiver General, Michaelmas 3 Henry V, to Michaelmas 4 Henry V, 1415-1416.

" In soluto Willelmo filio domini de mandato domini 10s. In 4000 libris plumbi emptis, per 100, 5s. 6d., £11. In cariagio ejusdem plumbi de Wellys usque Dunsterr 8s. In expensis pro dicto plumbo emendo 2s. . . . In expensis Thome Hody laborantis versus London de assignacione domini transeuntis versus mare 6s. 8d. . . . . In expensis diversorum serviencium domini transeuncium versus Warwykshyre cum Margareta filia domini de assignacione domini 28s. 9d. . . In expensis Thome Hody et Johannis Bakwell cum 3 famulis et 6 equis de Hampton versus Dunsterr 9s. 9½d."
" Expense hospicii domini in castro de Dunsterr. In expensis Johannis Bakwell capellani ibidem existentis a vigilia Sancti Laurencii usque festum Omnium Sanctorum tunc proximum per 12 septimanas unde 5 septimane post tempus compoti, per septimanam 20d., 20s. Item 4 valettorum per idem tempus pro quolibet per septimanam 14d., 56s. Item Willelmi Lutrell filii domini per 2 septimanas 3s. 4d. Item 1 fratris de Normannia per 1 septimanam 20d. Item 1 garcionis predicti Johannis capellani per 12 septimanas predictas per septimanam 12d., 12s.

Item Johannis Hunte venatoris, Willelmi Bayllyf et Johannis Bogby per 9 septimanas cuilibet per septimanam 12d., 27s.   Item Roberti Hylwen garcionis domini per 1 septimanam pro equis domini querendis 12d., Item 1 garcionis Johannis Lutrell filii domini per 5 septimanas et 1 garcionis Willelmi filii domini per 5 septimanas 10s.   Item 1 plumpmarii per 4 septimanas per septimanam 14d., 4s. 8d.   Item Thome Hody et 1 garcionis sui per 13 septimanas ad ratam 10 librarum per annum 50s. Summa £9 5s. 8d."

"In expensis 1 garcionis laborantis de Dunsterr versus Taunton 3 vicibus pro curacione 1 equi domini ibidem infirmi 15½d.   In bordes et nailles emptis pro coopertura turrium in castro 23d. In 9½ libris de sawdura [1] emptis 14½d., In salario 1 plumpmarii per 4 septimanas 10s.   In soluto Roberto Hylwen garcioni domini pro expensis suis cum aliis 2 garcionibus et pro 7 equis domini de Dunsterr usque London 13s. 4d.   In 17 solutaribus equinis emptis in equis domini imponendis 2s. 10d.   In 14 revets pro eisdem 7d.   In 1 sadelhousse empta pro cella domini et aliis necessariis emptis pro aliis cellis et equis 3s.   In soluto Thome Skynner pro 1 domo pro canibus domini ab eo conducto pro hoc anno 3s. 4d."

"Johanni Hunte magistro currum domini pro expensis circa equos et currus domini per 1 talliam cujus contrafolium non exhibetur £6 13s 4d."

Accounts of Thomas Hody, Receiver General, Michaelmas 4 Henry V, to Michaelmas 5 Henry V, 1416-1417.

"In primis soluto uni carpentario super reparacione portarum Castri inferioris per 7 dies ad 3d. per diem 21d.   Item in operibus ferreis pro eisdem portis, ut patet, viz. 87 libris, libra ad 1¼d. in clavis, platis, et vinculis 9s. 0¾d."   Item in parvis clavis emptis cum 1 clavi pro hostio camere J. Bacwell, 4d.   Item in 1 clavi pro camera garderobe et in 1 clavi pro hostio horrei in bertona de Donnsterr 4d. . . . . Item in 4 hamis pro hostio capelle in aula 2d.   Item in reparacione 2 vinculorum ferreorum cum clavis eisdem necessariis pro porta principali in le dongeon 4d.   Item in secacione 1 valve in eadem porta 1d., Item in 2 geminis [2] ferreis pro eadem valva cum clavis necessariis 4d.   Item in 1 hagodeday [3] cum 1 lacche pro eadem valva 3d.   Item in 1 muratore facienti 1 caminum in domo janitoris per 5½ dies 11d.   Item in vectura 1 petre pro clavi dicti camini per Priorem de Dunsterre date 1d.   Item in reparacione 2 cerarum super cameram porte exterioris castri, cum 1 clavi pro domo pistrine 5¼d.   Item in platis, clavis, cum 1 martella super portam castri interiorem ponderis 104 librarum, libra ad 1¼d., 10s. 10d. Item in expensis 1 mason venientis de Brigewater ad videndum aulam domini in castro reedificandam 3s. 8d.   Item in 16° die Januarii liberato Ricardo Meryman lathamo in partem majoris summe super 1 logge fiendo 20s. Item Philippo carpentario et socio suo super paludes findendos pro stagnis claudendis in le Hanger in parte solucionis 18s. 4d.   Item in prebenda equorum domini et domine per 3 septimanas infra tempus predictum 19s. 4d. . .   Item in transitu domini in soluto pro carne sumpta pro falcone domini et expensis usque idem tempus 16d.   Item

---

[1] Sawdara = solder.
[2] Gemini = hinges.
[3] Halliwell defines "haggaday" as "a

kind of wooden latch for the door;" but the context here seems to show that this definition is not quite accurate.

post transitum domini in 2 capistris emptis pro equis domini exeuntis de Mersshwode et in custodia positis 2d. Item in unguento empto pro pedibus eorundem 2d. . . . Item in 2 pipis vini de Gasconia emptis ad usum domini £4 13 4d. Item in cariagio ejusdem vini in castrum 5d. Item in expensis factis super captione 4 copulorum cuniculorum et volucrum missorum Johanni Merchaunt de Taunton in purificatione uxoris sue 2d. Item in 1 horscombe empto 3d. . . . Item in canevass pro panellis[1] cellarum et collarium 3s. 4½d. Item in 9 cingulis[2] duplicibus pro equis domini 16d. Item in lignis 7 cellarum pro cariagio 2s. 10d. Item in 20 libris flokkis pro stuffura earundem 18d. Item in cordis vocatis Teugropis[3] 8d. Item in diversis cordis emptis pro charetta domini 14d. . . . Item in cordis pro flagello 2d. Item in cordis pro equis charette regendis 2d. Item in 2 paribus de steroppis pro cellis cariagii et 7 polys et 3 reynes et 8 contre-single boucles pro supradictis cellis cariagii 4s. Item in takkys et clavis pro charetta 1s. 5d. . . . Item in emendacione 2 Ronges pro charetta 2d. Item in Teughookys 7d. Item in 7 Teugys 12d. Item in 7 panelles pro 7 semesadils, pecia ad 8d., 3s. 4d. Item in 1 strake[4] et dowlys pro rotis charette ponderis 12 librarum ferri 16d. Item in vertgrese pro 1 equo domini infirmo ½d. Item in albo vino pro eodem 1d. . . Item in cariagio musculorum usque portum de Donnsterre 40s 8d. . . Item liberatum 3 Britonibus prisonariis euntibus in Britanniam pro redempcione sua et sociorum suorum pro expensis suis 10s. . . . In expensis unius fratris Gallici per 6 septimanas pro septimana 20d., 10s. . . Item 6 Britonum et 1 Pagetti[5] captivorum quorum 3 pro 13 septimanis per septimanam 10d. et 3 per 4 septimanas et Pagetti per 10 septimanas 50s. 10d. Item 1 hominis Portigalensis per 7 septimanas 8s. 2d., unius alterius de Portigallia per 2 septimanas 2s. 4d. . . . Thome Hody pro expensis domini transeuntis ad mare 8° die Julii £7 11s. 4d. Willelmo Waryner de la Poole pro vino £7. Diversis piscatoribus de Mynhede pro piscibus et cariagio ad Gillyngham 42s. Ricardo Arnold de Glastonia pro casio 8s. 3½d."

———

" Bargia vocata Leonardus de Donnstere. Compotus Philippi Clopton, Magistri Bargie nobilis domini domini Hugonis Lutrell militis, Domini de Donnstre, ut pro uno viagio per ipsum facto de portu de Mynhede versus Bordegaliam et retro anno regni regis Henrici quinti quinto.

Idem recepit de £40 10s. receptis de fretta vini diversorum mercatorum pro viagio predicto.

In soluto pro cibis, potibus, tabulis, clavis, stipendiis operariorum et aliis necessariis emptis et expensis, ut in reparacione dicte Bargie in parte per supervisum prepositi de Minhede ut patet per unam cedulam . . . £4 10s. 10d. Et in 6 peciis de Tielde pro coopertura navis emptis 13s. 4d. In 2 rotulis de Oleyn pro velo reparando emptis 42s. In ancoris antiquis reparatis 6s. 8d. In canevas empto pro velo predicto reparando 7s. In pipis vacuis et barelles emptis pro farina imponenda una cum cepo pro eadem bargia fricanda 11s. In 7 tabulis largis emptis pro alcassing ejusdem 6s. 8d. In 5 bobus vivis emptis pecia ad 12s., deductis 5s. pro coriis venditis 55s. In 2 pipis cervisie et aliis barelles

[1] Panel = pad, cf. Halliwell, p. 602, and Wright, p. 99.

[2] Cingula = horse-girth, Wright, p. 234.

[3] Tug = trace.

[4] Strake = the rim of a wheel, cf. Halliwell, p. 815.

[5] Pagettus = pagius = page.

emptis 36s. In 2 pipis cezare emptis cum cariagio 19s. 4d. . . Summa expense £42 3s. 1d." ·

Accounts of Thomas Hody, Receiver General, from Michaelmas 5 Henry V, to Michaelmas 6 Henry V, 1417-1418.

In expensis Johannis Bacwell diversis vicibus laborantis pro negociis domini de vicaria sua de Pilton versus Dounsterre et ad alia loca eundo et redeundo, ut patet per unam billam super compotum examinatam 20s. In expensis Hugonis Cary una vice venientis pro negociis domini 15d. In baselardo et cultello domini mundatis 4½d. Item in uno coopertore per duos dies ad mensam domini pro domo pistrine 4d. In 1 lathamo per 5 dies ad mensam domini pro certis cameris emendatis in castro 10d. In 1 cerrura exterioris porte castri reparata 3d. . . In expensis domine ibidem existentis ut in parte in fine Junii et in parte mensis Julii ut per quinque septimanas in toto ut patet per papirum super compotum exhibitum 33s. 5d. In diversis victualibus emptis pro domino et sibi missis apud Harflete per manus Ricardi Arnolde ut in denariis eidem Ricardo liberatis per talliam £104 13½d. In 1 pipa vini empta ad usum domine et matris sue ex precepto domini ut de dono suo 49s. 4d." "In expensis . 2 pressonariorum, utroque ad 10d per septimanam ut per 12 septimanas 20s, 1 incarcerati per septimanam ad 10d. ut per 19 septimanas 15s 10d." ·

Accounts of Thomas Hody, Receiver General, from Michaelmas 6 Henry V, to Michaelmas 7 Henry V, 1418-1419.

"In soluto diversis sementariis carpentariis et laborariis conductis, ac calce, petris, tegulis, clavis et omnibus aliis pertinentibus pro una domo vocata Logge in cunacuculario[1] de novo facienda ut patet per 1 billam inde factam et super compotum examinatam £8 6s. 10½d. . . In expensis hospicii domini apud Dunster a die mercurii in crastino festi Assumpcionis beate Marie usque festum Sancti Michaelis et ulterius a dicto festo usque dominicam in crastino festi Apostolorum Simonis et Jude ut per 10 septimanas et 4 dies per 1 talliam contra Ricardum Arnol £28 13s. 9½d. In 25 quarteriis fabarum emptis et missis apud Arflue prout continetur in litera domini de data 23 die Januarii hoc anno per bussellum 3½d., 58s. 4d. In 1 pipa salmonis empta et missa ibidem £4. . . . . In 5 quarteriis 2 bussellis fabarum emptis et missis ibidem pro bussello 3½d, 12s. 3d. In 47 quarteriis 4 bussellis avenarum emptis et ibidem missis, pro quarterio 2s. 4d., 110s. 10d. In 1 quarterio 6 bussellis pisidum viridum emptis et ibidem missis pro 12d, 14s. . . In 4 cadis de allec emptis et ibidem missis 60s. . . In soluto pro fretto 25 quarteriorum fabarum, 1 pipe salmonis, 1 pipe skalpyn, 1 pipe pisidum viridum versus Arflue 63s. In 13 dosenis dimidia de leynges et melewell emptis pro dosina 3s., 40s. 6d. In eisdem cariandis de Mynheade usque Dunster et tunc usque Hampton 46s. 2d. In 100 hakys emptis et apud Arflue domino missis 30s. . . . In 400 multones emptis pro stauro apud Est Kantok cum custuma soluta in Wallia et cum cariagio abinde simul computatis £23 9s. 2d. . . . In expensis factis in familia domini ibidem a dominica proxima ante festum Omnium Sanctorum anno regis Henrici quinti 6° usque festum Assumpcionis beate Marie tunc proximum sequens ut per 41 septimanas 3 dies, et tunc dominus fuit ad hospicium suum . . £14 3s. 6d."

[1] Cunacularium = Conygar, a hill at Dunster.

Accounts of Richard Arnold Receiver from Michaelmas 7 Henry V, to Michaelmas 8 Henry V, 1419-1420.

" Dompno Johanni Buryngton monacho 69s. 4d.　Cuidam capellano celebranti apud Byrcomb[1] hoc anno de assignacione domini £1 16s. 6d., Johanni Blounche parcario de Mersshewode 20s. . . . In expensis Ricardi Arnold laborantis de Hampton versus Dunster et secum ducentis 2 equos domini 5s. . . . In soluto de rewardo facto Willelmo Franceys armigero domini pro expensis suis per Johannem filium domini, Thomam Beaumont et alios de consilio domini 2° die Septembris existentes apud Dunster et ibidem existentes pro negociis domini 20s., In 1 homine conducto ad laborandum versus Hampton ad faciendum predictum Willelmum Franceys veniendum usque Dunster pro negociis domini faciendis, 3s. . . . In soluto Nicholao Furbour pro harnesio domini purgando 4s. 5d. In 3 bussellis avenarum emptis pro cignis domini sustentandis 10½d. In 1 homine conducto ad cariandos pisces de Magistro de Bruggewater ad stagnum domini in Dunster 3s. 9d. In soluto cuidam servienti Rectoris de Aller simili modo pisces carianti de dono domini 20d., In 1 libra cere empta pro capella domini cum factura 7d., In expensis Johannis filii domini, Thome Beaumont, Hugonis Cary et aliorum de consilio domini existencium apud Dunster mense Augusti pro negociis domini 9s. 5½d., In expensis equorum Thome Beaumont eadem vice 2s. 4d., In expensis equorum Hugonis Cary eadem vice 2s 9d., In 1 clave empta pro ostio lardarii 3d., In certis rebus domini existentibus apud Mynheade provenientibus de Arflu in custodia Rogeri Kyng cariandis versus Dunster 3d., In expensis Johannis filii domini et Willelmi Godwyn laborancium versus London pro patentis domini tangentibus Bristoll et pro aliis negociis domini eundo et redeundo ut per 16 dies in toto 40s., In soluto clerico de pipis[2] pro supervidendo evidentias et recordum de receptis Constabilis Bristollie de et consuetis sibi accedentibus 3s. 4d. . . . Item solutum Rogero Kyng shipman pro diversis victualibus domini cariandis de Pole usque Harfleu hoc anno £11."

" Novum edificium in castro domini.　In diversis hominibus laborariis conductis pro veteribus muris deponendis tam pro parte murorum aule quam pro parte muri Castri deponendis, et pro fundamento novi edificii prope dictam aulam faciendo, et pro veteri meremio aule cum depositum fuerit longeis removendo ac etiam pro grossis petris tractandis, ac pro dictis petris simul cum zabulone et meremio cariandis, simul cum empcione librarum petrarum apud Bristolliam, et cum cariagio earundem per mare et ultimo per terram, et cum cariagio aque, ac pro hurdelles faciendis, simul cum empcione roparum, cordularum, et aliarum diversarum rerum pro opere pertinencium, et similiter in hominibus conductis pro calce juxta Castrum in puteo cremanda, cum factura ejusdem putei, et carbonibus ac focalibus emptis ad idem, cum ferraturis equorum et boum domini pro cariagio faciendo, et in diversis ferramentis, videlicet, crowes, mattokkes, pycoyses, wegges, spades et schovylles ac sleigges, faciendis et reparandis, omnibus simul computatis, ut patet in papiro inde facto et super compotum examinato, £45 15s. 10d. In 2379 libris

---

[1] Bircombe seems to have been near Minehead.　　[2] De pipis=of the Pipe.

ferri empti et operati, videlicet pro gumphis[1] kacchers pro lacchis ut pro hostiis et fenestris, et eciam pro ferramentis illuminaribus fenestrarum imponendis £14 17s. 4½d., In 141 quarteriis 4 bussellis calcis emptis pro quarterio 8d., £4 14s. 4d., Item soluto Thome Hydon latamo pro factura murorum in parte solucionis majoris summe £11, Item soluto Willelmo Boulond sementario librarum petrarum ultra 100s. anno preterito per ipsum receptis de Thoma Hody, ut patet in compoto ipsius Thome Hody in parte solucionis majoris summe £20. Item in soluto Thome Pacchehole carpentario ultra 60s. anno preterito receptis de Thoma Hody in parte solucionis majoris summe 20s. In 13 quarteriis carbonum emptis in grosso pro calce cremanda 15s. 4d.

Summa £98 2s. 10½d."

" In expensis domini apud Dunster a festo Omnium Sanctorum anno 7°. usque festum Sancti Andree tunc proxime sequens ut patet per billam sub signeto domini £14 8s. 3d. In diversis victualibus emptis et missis versus Arflu pro domino ibidem existenti 20° die Julii hoc anno, per indenturam eidem domino missam per Rogerum Kyng de Mynheade shepman omnibus computatis cum £16 17s., superius oneratis de victualibus emptis per Willelmum Godwyn et in predicta indentura contentis £42 6s. 4d., In expensis domini existentis apud Domerham, Hampton et Portysmouth, ut patet per billam sub signeto domini de data 10° die Februarii hoc anno regis Henrici quinti 7°., £64 8s. In soluto preposito de Domerham pro expensis domini existentis, ut patet in billa sub signeto domini 55s. 8d. In certis victualibus emptis per Robertum Ponyngys chivaler ad usum domini et missis apud Arflu ut patet per indenturam de data 7° die Aprilis anno 8°, sub signeto domini et signeto predicti Roberti £10 4s. In 12 dosenis myllewell et leyngys emptis et missis apud Arflu ad precem domini apud Mynheade, et misse fuerunt domino per Rogerum Kyng per indenturam 36s. In 12 coungerys emptis et missis ibidem per eundem Rogerum 8s., In expensis domini venientis de Hampton die Jovis proxima ante festum Natalis Domini, et existentis apud Dunsterr per certum tempus, et tunc laborando versus Saunton, omnibus computatis per Willelmum Person 12s. 11½d. In expensis ejusdem domini in suo tunc proximo adventu de Saunton et apud Dunstere existentis per certum tempus in Prioratu ibidem 6s. 1d. In 1 pipa cerevisie empta pro domino 6d. . In diversis victualibus cariandis, videlicet, carnes, farinam, avenas, candelas et alia diversa victualia de Sheftysbery usque Pole 10s. In piscibus domini cariandis de Mynheade versus Dunstere 4d."

" In liberato domine sue de assignacione domini sui per talliam £13 6s. 8d. In soluto eidem domine ex mutuo domini ad dandum operariis domine de Saunton de assignacione ejusdem 6s. 8d. In liberato eidem domine pro vino empto ad usum suum et domine matris sue contra solucionem factam per dominum pro eodem 6s. 8d. Summa £14."

" This beth the parcel of the of the (sic) costages that beth makid by Williham Godewyn and Richard Arnolde of Bruton a boghte diverse vitaills the wheche the forsaide Richard hath delyvered to Rogger Kyng of Mynheade shipman at the harbor of Pole to the use and the profitez

---

[1] Gumphus = a door-band or hinge. Wright, pp. 237, 261.

of my lorde Sir Hugh Lutrell, as hit is specyfyed in endenters bytwixt hem therof maked ; Forst in 18 quarteres of whete boght by Godewyn, price the bushelez 10d., £6. Item in 23 quarteres 2 bushelez whete price the bushelez 8d. Summa £6 4s. Item paied for cariage of the same from the contre to the ship 5s. . . Item in 10 quarteres of Barly malt boght by Godewyn price the bushelez 10d., 66s. 8d. Item in 54 quarteres of Barly malt price the bushelez 3s. 9d., £16 4s. Item in 6 bobus price of 103s. In 30 motons price of 45s. Item in 2 quarters 3 bushelez salt for the same flessh 7s. 6d. Item in 3 pipes for the same flessh 1 hoiggeshede for otemele and 1 barell for candelles price in al 4s. Item in 6 bushelez of otemele price the bushelez 16d., 8s. Item in 9 dosyn poudez of candelles 10s. 6d. In reward of the lardyner for syltyng and dyghtyng of al the flessh 20d. . . In 1 quarter 3 bushelez of cole price the bushelez 3½d., 3s. 3d. In 1 pipe for the same 10d. Item payed for beryng of whete from the hous of W. Waryner in to the ship 16d. Item in mattys and nailles boght for to make a caban in the ship for savyng of the corne and of the malt 3s. Item in caryng of 13 dosyns of fyssh from Dunsterre to the Pole, 12s. . . . This was write at Pole Pole *(sic)* in Ingelonde the 20 day of July the 8 yere of the reignyng of Henry our Kyng the 5th."

Accounts of Richard Arnold, Receiver, Michaelmas 8 Henry V, to Michaelmas 9 Henry V, 1420-1421.

" De £20 receptis de Willelmo Godewyn de feodo domini ut de Castro de Bristollia hoc anno receptis."

" In soluto Johanni filio domini £10. Johanni Byriton monacho 69s. 4d., Capellano domini celebranti in capella de Byrcomb £6 13s. 4d. Willelmo Gosse senescallo terrarum domini 100s., Ricardo Arnold receptori denariorum domini 60s., Henrico Crosse auditori compotorum ministrorum domini 26s. 8d., Johanni Muskeham attornato domini 20s., Henrico Stone, ballivo de Dunster 40s., Roberto Drapere clerico domini 20s., Johanni Blouche, parcario de Mersshwode 20s., Willelmo Person a festo Sancti Michaelis usque festum Pasche 13s. 4d., Philippo Wylly per annum 26s. 8d., Willelmo Tylly, coco, 20s. . . . . In liberato Willelmo vocato lytelwille servienti domini pro expensis suis apud Pole et alibi in negociis domini hoc anno mense Decembris 10s. . . . Item in soluto Thome Pacchehole pro factura de reckis et mangers in stabulo domini factis per preceptum domini 13s. 4d. . . . In 4 virgis panni russeti emptis et deliberatis Thome Pury preposito de Estkantok, precium virge 18d. 6s. . . . . In 1 bagga empta pro rotulo compotorum imponendo, 3d. . . . . In 54 quarteriis frumenti emptis apud Blancforde et Wymborne precium bussellez 10d., £18. Item in 5 quarteriis frumenti emptis apud Ruysshton, pretium bussellez 8d., 26s. 8d. Item in 51 quarteriis avenarum emptis apud Blanford, Wymborne, et Ruysshton precium bussellez, 4d., £6 16s. Item soluto Willelmo Warnere pro una domo ab eo conducta pro bladis domini imponendis apud Pole 6s. 8d. In expensis Ricardi Arnold laborantis in diversis locis ut patet supra pro predictis bladis emendis 10s. In tabulis, clavis, mattis, et stramine emptis pro granario inde faciendo in nave pro dictis granis imponendis et salvandis 4s. In portagio dictorum granorum 15d. Item in soluto Gervasio Knyte de Pole shipman pro omnibus

predictis bladis versus Harefleu ad usum domini cariandis £6. . . .
Item in salmone 3s. In 61 mullewell et lynggys 31s. 9d. In 64
hakys 11s. 8d. In 49 couples de Pullockes 5s., emptis et missis domino
apud Harefleu, summa empcionis 51s. 5d., In dictis piscibus de
Mynheade versus Hampton cariandis 14s., In 1 sarpler[1] empta predictis piscibus involvenda 6d., In maylyngcordes emptis pro eisdem
4d."

"Item in una pipa vini pro domina existente apud Saunton empta de
Rogero Kyng de Mynheade ad hospicium domine hoc anno 46s. 8d.
Item in soluto Johanni Taunton custodi equorum domini pro avenis
et pane equino emptis pro equis domini ante festum Sancti Dionisii anno
nono 17s. 9½d. . . . In soluto Georgio capellano domini apud
Gyllyngham pro expensis domini ibidem in suo redeundo de London
15d. . . . . In soluto Laurentio Taillor, Londonie, pro factura
2 juparum domini de Felewet[2] 13s. 4d. . . . Liberato domine de
assignacione domini per 4 tallias hoc anno £13 6s. 6d."

"Dere frende y charge ȝow þt ȝe take litill Will oure servant 20s. for
his fee of þe last ȝer and ȝif hit so be þat he compleine to ȝow of his
manoir yat y take him be spendid in my servise þat ȝe take him
whanne he departith fro ȝow to come to me resonable despenses and þis
cedule signed wyth my signet sall be ȝour warant. And in al manere
wyse þenkyth on my stuf of fich ageyns lentin. Writt at Harfleu þe
xviij⁴ daie of Octobre [anno viijᵒ Henrici quinti.]
        Hugh Lutrel Knight, Lord of Dunsterr and Senescall
                of Normandie.
Unto Richard Arnold oure resseviour at Dunsterr."

"In primis a coppe with a park, a coppe with a sterr, a coppe with
oute pomell, a coppe with a perle in the pomel, a coppe with an egle y
gylt in þe pomell, 2 coppis with eglis of silvyr in þe pomelles, 3 hie
coppis with þe coverclis, 2 coppis with 2 okurlis of silvyr in þe pomell,
2 flatte pecis with coverclis, a vat y coveryd, an hie coppe y coveryd
with feþeris y plomyd, a coppe y namyd Bath, a coppe y namyd
Courtenay, 6 flatte pecis with oute coverclis, a note,[3] a spice dissch,
3 eweris, 2 sponis and all þs ys gylt, a peyr doble baceynys,
3 single bacynys with 3 eweris þerto, a galon potte, 2 potell pottis,
4 quart pottis, an ewer with 10 coppis withynne hym and 3 coverclis, a
round coppe y coveryd and 8 withynne hym, 3 grete pecis y coveryd,
and 17 rounde coppis, and a tastour, and an ewer for water, a ... spone
and a verke fore grene gyngyn and 15 flatte pecis and 3 coverclis,
4 chargeris, 2 doseyn disschis and 23 sauceris, 22 sponis of on sort and
17 sponis of a lasse sort, and 3 grete saucerys with 2 coverclis, and
5 flatte saleris,[4] and an ymage of Synd Jon of silver and gylt and an
horne y gylt, and 4 candilstikkis of silver. Item por le Chapell, In
primis a litil chaleis y gylt, a pax bred y gylt, 2 cructis of silver, a
corperas, a peir of vestymentis, 2 towelles, a lytil masboke, 2 parelles for
the auter and a superaltar.
    Of þe whiche somme above saide my lord hathe with hym to Harflu

---

[1] Sarpelere=canvas for wrapping up wares. Halliwell.

[2] Felwet=velvet.

[3] Probably a cocoa-nut mounted in silver.

[4] Salere=salt cellar.

2 chargeris, 12 disschis, 12 sauceris of silver, 2 coppis and a ewer y gylt, an hie coppe and 8 with ynne, a gret flat pece with a covercle, 7 flatte peces and on covercle, a basyn and an ewer, 11 sponis, 2 salers with a covercle and þe chapelles hole, 2 quarte pottys and an hie coppe with a covercle y gylt and 6 littel sponys, and 2 candelstykys of silver."

"Visus compoti Henrici Stone de receptis et expensis per ipsum factis in novo edificio in Castro domini simul cum aliis expensis forinsecis ibidem solutis a festo Sancti. Michaelis anno regis Henrici Quinti 7° usque idem festum Sancti Michaelis anno 9° .. . In petris libris emptis de Willelmo Boulond mason £3 6s. 8d." . . . "Custus latamorum . . summa £15 15s. 2d. . . Custus operariorum . . . summa £16 3s. 5d. . . Viagium per mare . . summa £6 16s. 4d. Opera de limekyll . . summa £7 5s. 10d."

Accounts of Robert Draper from All Saints 1 Henry VI, to Sunday after Michaelmas 2 Henry VI, 1422-1423.

"In certo panno sanguineo et viridi empto pro liberatura familie hospicii domini hoc anno . . £4 15s. 4d. . . Et tanto magis hoc anno quod Elizabeth Harleston filia domini fuit in supradicto hospicio cum 5 hominibus et 7 equis ad custus et expensas dicti hospicii per 17 septimanas &c. Item Jak Stone Schephurd fuit in hospicio per totum annum nihil solvendo."

Accounts of Robert Draper, clerk of the household of Sir Hugh Luttrell, from Sunday after Michaelmas 2 Henry VI, to 1 October 3 Henry VI, 1423-1424.

"Receptio . . de £10 4s. 4½d. receptis de Elizabetha domina de Haryngton pro mensa sua et familie sue ac omnium extraneorum eidem domine superveniencium ad dictum hospicium per indenturam cujus data est apud Dunsterr die Lune proxima ante festum Conversionis Sancti Pauli anno supradicti Regis secundo. Et de £11 11s. ¼d. receptis de eadem domina per manus Johannis Coplestone junioris, ut pro prandio predicte domine, familie sue et extraneorum veniencium ad dictum hospicium a die lune proxima ante festum Conversionis Sancti Pauli anno supradicti Regis 2° usque 23 diem Aprilis anno predicto per eandem indenturam. Et de £9 18s. 4d. receptis de eadem domina ut pro prandio dicte domine, familie sue, et extraneorum veniencium ad dictum hospicium a 23° die Aprilis usque primum diem mensis Octobris extunc proxime sequentem."

"In 1 apro empto pro expensis dicti hospicii hoc anno apud Bronton, cum cariagio ejusdem ab inde 8s. 4d. . . In 5 duodenis panni blodii emptis apud Benehangre pro liberatura familie hospicii domini hoc anno cum expensis emptorum cariandorum . . 103s. 4d. . . In 5 paribus manticarum brandred pro 5 generosis domini pro eorum liberatura . . 16s. Et in 7 paribus manticarum brandred pro 7 valentis *(sic)* domini pro eorum liberatura . . . 15s. Et in 2 manticis brand pro 2 garcionibus hoc anno pro eorum liberatura . . 2s. 2d. . . Et postea oneratur de 5s. pro mensa Margarete uxoris Johannis Lutrell et unius generose sue per

1 septimanam existencium in hospicio domini. . . . Nota. Et isto
anno fuit in hospicio domini Magister Johannes Odelond per 18 septimanas diversis vicibus nichil solvendo.   Johannes Scolemaystre consimili
modo per 10 septimanas ut per vices.   Thomas Pacchole carpenter aliquando cum 1 carpentario et aliquando cum 2 carpentariis in hospicio per
19 septimanas hoc anno nichil solvendo.   Thomas Hydon, mason cum 1
famulo existens in hospicio per 11 septimanas hoc anno nichil solvendo.
Jak Stone, schephurd fuit in hospicio hoc anno per totum annum nichil
solvendo."

---

*Accounts of Robert Draper, clerk of the household, from Michaelmas
4 Henry VI, to Michaelmas 5 Henry VI, 1425-1426.*

"In 25 lagenis vini rubei, 18 lagenis vini vocati Bastard emptis . . .
cum cariagio et expensis earundem £25 7s. . . . In panno viridi et
rubeo videlicet 66 virgis utriusque coloris emptis pro liberatura 4 genero-
sorum 11 valettorum, et 4 garcionum in hospicio existencium. . . .
£7 11s. 6½d., cum expensis et cariagio eorundem." "Et de 1 pipa vini
de rein."

---

*Accounts of Robert Ryvers, Bailiff at Dunster from Michaelmas
4 Henry VI to Michaelmas 5 Henry VI, 1425-1426.*

"Pro twystys yemeaux et clavis emptis de Hugone Lokyer pro le spere[1]
et novo hostio in aula domini 3s. 10d.   Et Johanni Burgh pro 2
cariagiis meremii de le lymkyll usque Castrum pro le dit Spere in aula
domini 2d.   . .   In 1000 pynnys tegulinys emptis 3d. . .   In 2000
petris tegulinis emptis de Henrico Helyer 20d.   In cariagio dictarum
petrarum tegulinarum de Treburgh usque Castrum de Dunsterr 3s. 4d.
. . . .   In soluto Johanni Eylysworthi tegulatori ibidem conducto
ad reparandam cameram domini et cameram constabularii, per 3
dies ad repastum domini 9d. . . . In 1 magna clave empta de Hugone
Lokyer et in emendacione 1 sere pro damhawys towre[2] 4d. . . . In
Johanne Bolkinam conducto per 1 diem ad purgandam damhawys toure
ad sibum domini 2d. . . .   Item Thome Pacheholl cum famulo
suo ibidem conducto per 1 diem et dimidiam ad faciendum 3 gestys de
novo in Castello juxta le Portcoleys ad cibum domini 7½d. In clavis
emptis ad emendandum le store hous in castello quo armature domini
posite sunt 1d. . . . Pro 2 cariagiis meremii de le Fysspole in le hanger
versus predictum stabulum sine sibo 2d. . . . In 10,000 de petris
tegulinis emptis pro stauro domini venientibus de Cornubia ad portum
de Dunsterre, precium de 1000, 2s. 7d., summa in toto 25s. 10d., In
predictis lapidibus portandis de navi versus le slymvat 4d."

---

*Accounts of Robert Ryvers, Bailiff at Dunster, Michaelmas 5 Henry VI,
to Michaelmas 6 Henry VI, 1426-1427.*

"Thomas [Pacheholl] ibidem fuit conductus ad faciendum le enterclos
et hachys inter aulam domini et capellam ibidem per 2 septimanas

---

[1] Spere=screen. "Promptorium Parvulorum."

[2] For "damhawys towre," see Part 1.

ad cibum domini capiendo per septimanam 18d. 3s. . . . In soluto Thome Smyth pro 6 paribus de yemeaux pro lez hacchys in capella ibidem 2s. Et Thomas Pacheholl ibidem fuit conductus ad faciendum 1 Copbord de novo per 5 dies ad cibum domini, capiendo per diem 3d. 15d. . . . Item soluto Johanni Myryman de Wylyton pro 2 lapidibus clavell[1] ab eo emptis pro 2 caminis in castello de novo faciendis 3s. . . . Thomas Pacheholl conductus fuit ad ordinacionem Thome Bemont ad castellum ad decadendam veterem coquinam in le donyon per 1 septimanam ad repastum domini 18d. . . . Et Thomas Pachehole ibidem fuit conductus ad faciendum 1 whelberve[2] per 1 diem ad repastum domini 3d."

Accounts of Robert Ryvers, Receiver-General of Sir John Luttrell, from Maundy Thursday 6 Henry VI to the morrow of Michaelmas 7 Henry VI, 1428.

" Soluto Johanni Riever (?) de Shafton per manus Willelmi Godewyn pro speciebus ab eodem emptis pro interemento dicti Hugonis [Luttrell] 19° die Augusti 44s. 1d. . . . Item Thome Wylhamo pro panno albo ab eodem empto ad interementum dicti Hugonis £6 4s., Item soluto Johanni Slug pro avenis providendis contra interementum dicti Hugonis 11s., Item soluto Willelmo Stone pro panno albo et nigro ab eodem empto uno cum factura 16 juparum et totidem capiciorum pro 16 pauperibus tempore interementi dicti Hugonis 74s. . . . Item solutum Thome Tonker de Waysshford pro 1 bargia empta de Johanne Foughler de Hibernia ad opus domini ut de 4ª parte ejusdem Bargie £20. . . . Item liberatum Roberto Draper per manus Thome Kynggestum pro convivio domine Johanne Lutrell monialis de Shafton 27° die Julii precepto domini £10, Item solutum Johanni Mathu pro 1 burthyn et dimidio piscium salsarum ab eo emptarum pro Johanne de Stourton juniore et Willelmo Carent, precepto domini 16s., Item solutum Johanni Foughler de Mynhede per manus vicarii de Mynhede pro vino empto ad hospicium domini apud Karampton anno precedenti precepto domini 66s. 8d. . . . Item Johanni Eylesworthe tegulatori conducto per 3½ dies ad tegulandam cameram supra portam juxta stabulum domini ad mensam domini capiendo per diem 3d. 10½d. . . . Item in 4 paribus sotularum emptis pro Johanue Fitz-James 3 vicibus 12d., Item in 2 paribus caligarum emptarum pro eodem Johanne 10d. . . . Item stipendio Johannis Eylesworth tegulatoris conducti pro domo juxta portam exteriorem castri sementanda pro sale in eadem ponenda per 1½ diem ad mensam domini capiendo per diem 3d., 4½d. Item solutum Johanni Yevan pro ferruris unius affri cariagii de Carampton 6d."

Accounts of Robert Ryvers, Receiver-General of Sir John Luttrell, Michaelmas 8 Henry VI to Michaelmas 9 Henry VI, 1429-1430.

" Solutum domine Katharine nuper uxori Hugonis Lutrell militis de parte dotis sue ut pro termino Natalis Domini per acquietanciam cujus data est 27° die Februarii anno supradicti Regis 8°· £25. Et eidem domine pro dote sua predicta per acquietanciam cujus data est 22° die

---

[1] Clavell=mantel-piece.   [2] Whelberve=wheelbarrow.

Julii anno supradicto ut pro termino Natalis Sancti Johannis Baptiste £10. Et eidem domine pro dote sua predicta per acquientanciam cujus data est 28° die Julii eodem anno £10. Et eidem domine pro consimili ut pro termino Sancti Michaelis in fine istius anni per acquietanciam cujus data est die Sabbati proxima post festum Sancti Luce Evangeliste anno supradicti Regis nono £16 13s. 4d.   Et eidem domine per manus Willelmi Person ut pro eodem termino per 1 talliam 60s. Et eidem domine pro consimili ut pro eodem termino per manus Roberti Draper 4° die Decembris post datam hujus compoti 106s. 8d. . . .   Et liberatum Roberto Couke pro serico emendo apud London pro domina Margareta Lutrell 13° die Februarii 6s. 8d. . . Et soluto Johanni Joce conducto ad colligendos lapides super Croudon[1] pro les Botreaux juxta portam Castri de Dunsterre per 1 diem ad cibum domini 2d. Et soluto domino Roberto Kent capellano precepto domini ad distribuendum inter capellanos hic existentes die anniversarii Hugonis Lutrell militis, ultimo die Martii 2s. 9d. Et soluto Thome Marchaunt pro victualibus emendis pro bargia domini precepto domini 20s. . . . Et soluto Johanni Stourton militi per manus Henrici Helyer vadletti Willelmi Wadham pro quadam inquisicione de morte Hugonis Lutrell militis in comitatu Wiltes capiendo, ut per literam dicti Johannis Stourton dicto Johanni Lutrell directam £4 9s. 1d. Et soluto Henrico Helyar pro rewardo suo causa laboris sui precepto Johannis Lutrell 20d. Et soluto Johanni Stone de Wotton mason locato ad faciendum 2 Botreaux juxta portam Castri ad cibum domini per 2 septimanas capiendo per septimanam 18d. 3s., Et soluto Johanni Thresshe de Wotton mason locato ad laborandum cum dicto Johanne Stone circa predictas Botriaux per 2 septimanas capiendo per septimanam 14d., 2s. 4d. Et soluto Johanni Joce locato ad deserviendum Johanni Stone et Johanni Thresshe masons predictis per 2 septimanas capiendo per septimanam 11d., ad cibum domini 22d. Et soluto Johanni Burgh conducto cum caretta sua et 4 equis ad cariandum lapides de la Hangre usque portam Castri pro les Botriaux supradictis faciendis per 1 diem ad cibum domini capiendo per diem 12d., 12d. . . Solutum Thome Couke pro prebenda equorum Walteri Portman existentis apud Dunsterr per 3 vices ad loquendum cum domino in materia sua inter ipsum et Ducissam Eboraci 3s. 6½d. Et solutum prefato Thome Couke pro prebenda equorum domine Elizabeth Courteney existentis apud Dunsterre per 1 diem et noctem 7s. 11d. . . .   Et in 400 de Bukhurnes emptis apud Exon pro Episcopo Bathoniensi et Wellensi per 100 17d., 5s. 8d. Et solutum Roberto Draper pro expensis domino Johanne Lutrell et sororis sue monealis de Shafton equitantis abinde usque Dunster et ibidem 19° die Julii 12s. . . .   Et soluto pro 1 virga et dimidia de fustyan empta pro Jacobo Lutrell precium virge 7d., 10½d. Et soluto pro 1 virga de panno lineo vocato Braban pro dicto Jacobo 7d. . . . .   Et pro permutacione sotularium dicti Jacobi, 2d.

Accounts of Robert Ryvers, Steward of the Household of Sir John Luttrell at Dunster, from Michaelmas 8 Henry VI to Michaelmas 9 Henry VI, 1429-1430.

"In 6 pipes 1 hoggeshed 35 lagenis 3 quartis 1 pynt [vini albi et rubei] emptis pro expensis dicti hospicii per annum . . . £15 7d. . . . Et in 5134 lagenis bone et secunde cervisie emptis . . . £26 23½d.,

[1] Croydon Hill near Dunster.

Et in 7 libris piperis emptis pro expensis dicti hospicii hoc anno 7s. Et in 1 libra 2 unciis croci[1] emptis pro expensis dicti hospicii hoc anno 10s. 4d. Et in dimidia libre saundres empta pro conserva 8d.. Et in 30 libris amigdelarum[2] emptis pro conserva 7s. 6d., Et in 28 libris de ryse emptis pro conserva 3s. 8d., Et in 28 libris de roysons emptis pro conserva 3s. 8d. Et in 2 libris cere pro conserva 12d. . . . Et in 1 barell allec empta ultra 1 barrell recepta de preposito de Mynhed proveniente domino de catallis wayfes ibidem hoc annno 9s. 10d., Et in 100 allec rubeis emptis pro expensis dicti hospicii hoc anno 18d., Et in 1 cade *(sic)* de sprottes empta pro conserva hoc anno 2s. 4d., Et in 70 hakys salsis emptis pro conserva 9s., Et in 600 Schalpens emptis apud Exon cum cariagio eorundem 9s. 8d., Et in 72 stokfyssh emptis pro conserva cum cariagio eorundem hoc anno 12s. 4d., Et in 678 de myllewell et lenges emptis pro conserva ad preceptum domini apud Mynhed hoc anno £8 9s. 6d. Et in 53 congres mersaultz emptis pro conserva ultra 20 de remanentibus 18s. 8d., Et in 1 barell de Storgeon empta pro conserva hoc anno 8s. 6d., Et in 3 lagenis olei emptis pro expensis dicti hospicii hoc anno 5s."

Accounts of Robert Ryvers, Receiver-General of Lady Margaret Luttrell, from Michaelmas 9 Henry VI to Michaelmas 10 Henry VI, 1430-1431.

" Solutum Roberto Drapere pro diversis expensis factis pro anniversario domini Johannis Lutrell militis precepto domine apud Bruton, ut in cera et aliis rebus emptis pro eodem ut patet per billam ostensam coram domina Margareta Lutrell sexto die Septembris anno octavo 14s. 11d. Et solutum pro diversis expensis factis circa anniversarium domini Johannis Lutrell militis tenendum apud Bruton sexto die Augusti anno regis Henrici sexti nono ut patet per billam super auditum hujus compoti ostensam et hinc compoto consutam 33s. 3d. . . . Et in expensis domine Margarete Lutrell et aliorum secum veniencium die dominica primo die Julii existencium apud Dunsterre ad sagittandum cum Thoma Bratton et aliis 2s. 5d. . . . Et in 5 virgis de Fustyan in foro de Dunsterre emptis pro toga domine duplici 2s. 11d., Et in 1 quarterio virge de tarterys empto pro dicta toga 10d. . . . Et in 2 virgis panni lenei vocati Braban pro Jacobo filio domine emptis 14d., Et in 1½ virga panni russeti empta pro dicto Jacobo de Willelmo Stone 9d., Et in 1½ virga albi panni empta pro 1 jupa pro dicto Jacobo 7½d., Et liberatum Johanne Noryce nutrice *(sic)* domine pro stipendio suo a retro existente per manus Willelmi Percare (?) capellani de Wallia et Willelmi Warde-roppe, 6s. 8d., In 6 douseynys panni albi emptis pro liberatura domine ad diversa precia hoc anno 37s., In 10 douseynys panni albi texti pro dicta liberatura hoc anno de Roberto Northam 5s., In dictis 10 douseyns fullandis dando per doseyne 4d., 3s. 4d., In toto predicto panno una cum 1 pecia panni continente 20 virgas tinctando in nigrum colorem per Johannem Dyer per visum Willelmi Warderoppe, dando per doseyne 12d., 17s. 6d., Et solutum Thome Tonker de Clyva pro tonsura totius panni predicti 4s., Et solutum Johanni Dyer pro tinctura cooperture lecti, tapytes, curteynes, costerys, bankerys,[3] et guysshenys[4] tam pro aula domine quam camera et capella apud Karampton 7s."

---

[1] Crocum=saffron.
[2] Amigdalum=an almond.
[3] Banker=the covering of a bench.
[4] Cushions.

"Bruton. Expense facte ibidem per Robertum Draper pro anniversario domini Johannis Lutrell militis tenendo ibidem sexto die Augusti anno Regis Henrici sexto nono. In primis in 6 libris cere emptis pro 5 rotundis cereis inde faciendis precium libre 5d., 2s. 6d. In lichinis emptis pro eisdem 1d. In factura eorundem 1d. In 4 libris cere emptis ut in 4 Torchis locatis de Sacrista ecclesie ibidem dando per libram 5d., 20d. In dono 4 hominibus pauperibus pro dictis Torchis tenendis ad obsequias et ad missam, cuilibet eorum 4d., 16d. In dono oratori pro anniversario pronunciando in villa 1d. In oblacionibus 2d. In pane empto tam pro Priore et conventu quam pro aliis venientibus ad obsequias 15d. In 14 lagenis bone cervisie emptis pro eisdem 2s. 4d. In 1 lagena vini empta pro Priore ibidem 8d. In distribucione facta Priori et conventui ibidem, videlicet Priori 40d., et 15 canonicis, cuilibet illorum 12d., 15s. Item duobus sacerdotibus secularibus 12d. Item 2 clericis 4d. Item 6 pauperibus 3d. Item pro classico[1] pulsando 8d. Item solutum Thome Sartyre nuper Sacriste Prioratus de Bruton pro 5 libri cere ab [eo] emptis cum factura die anniversarii domini precium libre 6d., 2s. 6d. Summa totalis 32s. 3d."

Accounts of Robert Ryvers, Receiver-General of Lady Margaret Luttrell from Michaelmas to Lady Day 10 Henry VI, 1431-1432.

"Soluto Johanni Tresham per visum Walteri Portman ut esset de consilio domine pro quadam die amoris inter Priorem de Bruton et dominam Margaretam Lutrell pro custodia et maritagio Johannis Fitz-james 6s. 8d. . . In expensis Willelmi Bonvyle militis, Edwardi Seyntjon, Thome Bratton, Johannis Laverance, Walteri Portman et certe familie domine Margarete Lutrell existentencium apud Taunton cum 36 equis a die lune 10° die Decembris usque diem Mercurii tunc proxime sequentem post prandium pro quadam die amoris inter dominam Katarinam Lutrell ex parte una et dominam Margaretam Lutrell ex parte altera, una cum rewardis factis coco predicti Willelmi Bonvyle militis et aliis servientibus tunc ibidem existentibus £4 15d. . . . . Soluto Willelmo Wardropere per preceptum domine ad distribuendum sacerdotibus pro anima Johannis Lutrell militis 17° die Januarii 2d. . . Soluto Willelmo Stone de Dunsterr pro 6 lagenis 1 potello 1 pinta vini albi empti de eodem die anniversarii domini Hugonis Lutrell militis precepto domine dando per lagenam 6d., 3s. 4d.

Idem Robertus recepit de eadem Margareta ut in vasis argenteis de ea emptis £20. Et idem recepit de eadem Margareta ut in ciphis argenteis eb eadem Margareta emptis £7 5s. Et idem Robertus recepit de eadem Margareta ut in 1 olla argentea de eadem empta 58s. 9d. Et idem Robertus recepit de eadem Margareta ut in 1 lecto albo de dimidio worstede cum aliis vestibus de eadem emptis et receptis in parte solucionis excessus sui supradicti 33s. 4d. Et sic ad huc excedit £90 6¾d."

---

[1] Classicum=a funeral knell.

APPENDIX I.

CONTRACT FOR BUILDING DUNSTER CHURCH TOWER.

The original of the following contract has unfortunately disappeared from the old chest in Dunster Church, but there is a copy of it in a book of transcripts preserved in the Muniment Room at Dunster Castle :—

"Thys beth the covenants betwyne the paroch of Dunsterr and Jon Marys of Stokgursy in the Schere of Somerset. That is to seyng for the making of a towre in the paroch church of Dunsterr That the sayd Jon Marys schall make suffycyantly the seyde towre with iij french botras[1] and a vice[2] in the fowrth pyler in stede of a botras fynyng[3] at the Alter-tabyll[4] And in the fyrst flore ij wyndowys On yn the Sowth and another yn the North everych of on day with iiij genclas[5] yn the hedd of every wyndow And iiij wyndowys at the bell bedd of ij days with a trawnson and a moynell according to the patron ymade by the avyce of Rychard Pope Fremason Allso the sayde Jon Maryce schall make suffycyantly the batylment of the sayde towre with iiij pynacles the fowrth pynacle stand-ing upon the vice after reson and gode proportion Acordyng to the same worke And the sayde schall be embatyle Allso the sayde Jon Maryce schall make iij gargyllys in thre corners of the sayde towre And the wall to be iiij fote thykk and a halfe yn to the bell bedd And from the bell bedd ynto the batylment iij fote and a halfe suffycyantly to be made undyr the forme forsayde And the sayde paroch schall bryng all suffy-cyant materals withyn the palme crosse[6] of the sayde Church And he to have for the workemanchyppe of every fote of the sayde towre xiij[s] iiij[d] And the sayde worke to be full endyd withyn iij ere nexte folwyng aftyr the date of this present wrytyng And rather yf hit may be by the power of the sayde paroch And the sayde Jon Maryce schall be redy aftyr the stuffe of matyr at all tyme by the warnyng of xiiij days and the crane at all tyme necessary for the same worke with ropys polys wynchchys schall be removyd at the cost of the paroch forsayd with help of Jon Maryce and his mayny Allso the sayd paroch schall fynde all Synternys[7] for the same worke with ropes poleys winchchys and all other thyngys necessary to the sayd work The towre conteynyng yn heyth from the gras tabyll[8] an hundred fote Allso the sayd Jon Marys schall be payd for his labour lyk as he doth his work other ellys at the most xx[s] byfore as hit aperyth yn work Also the sayde paroch schall fynd an howse for the sayde Johon Maryce to sett therein his tole and other necessarys Allso if there be any stone ywroȝte of such quantyte that ij men or iij at most may not kary hym the sayde paroch schall helpe hym Allso the sayde Johon Maryce schall receive of the sayde paroch xx[s] for the pynaclys of the same towre Into the whych wytnys y put thereto my seleez I give and y wrytte at Dunsterr in the fest of Seynt Mychaell the yere of King Herry the vj aftyr the conquest of xxi[ti]."

---

[1] A French buttress must evidently mean an angle buttress.

[2] Vice=winding staircase.

[3] Fynyng=setting back.

[4] Probably a transcriber's error for water-table, the old word for a string-course.

[5] Genlese=cusp. Cf. " Glossary of Architecture."

[6] Palm cross=Churchyard cross. Cf. Nicolas's "Testamenta Vetusta," vol. i, p. 326.

[7] Synternys=centerings.

[8] Grass-table=plinth.

APPENDIX K.

PEDIGREE OF THE LUTTRELL FAMILY.

A very scarce little book entitled "A Geneological (*sic*) Account of the Family of Luttrell, Lotterel, or Lutterell" which was privately printed in 1773 or 1774, proves on examination to be nothing more than a reprint of the very erroneous notice of the family which appears in Lodge's "Peerage of Ireland." The more extended account of the Luttrells of of Dunster contained in Savage's "History of the Hundred of Carhampton" is in several respects less inaccurate.

Far more valuable than either of these printed accounts of the family is a manuscript volume entitled "Historical Account of the Family of the Lutterells from the Conquest, collected from Records, History, Pedigrees, and Registers, by Narcissus Luttrell, Esq." The learned author of the "Brief Historical Relation of State Affairs, from September, 1678 to April, 1714," which was published at Oxford in 1857, by the University Press in six volumes 8vo., spared no pains to make his history of his own family as complete as possible. The chief fault, indeed, lies in its wearisome reiteration of personal names and dates. After the death of the author in 1732, the manuscript presumably passed to his only surviving son, Francis Luttrell, who died Treasurer of the Middle Temple in 1749. At the beginning of the present century it was in the possession of Dr. Luttrell Wynne, a grandson of Dr. Owen Wynne, of Gwynfynnyd, Master of the Mint, who had married a sister of Narcissus Luttrell. From Dr. Luttrell Wynne it seems to have passed to his maternal cousin, Edward William Stackhouse, of Pendarves, whose heir has very gracefully given it to the present owner of Dunster Castle. Several names and dates which had escaped the notice of Narcissus Luttrell have more recently been brought to light by the Rev. Frederick Brown, of Beckenham, who has most kindly communicated them to the compiler of the following tables.

The pedigree of the Luttrells of Irnham is based on authorities cited in the description of the Luttrell Psalter in "Vetusta Monumenta," vol. vi, and in the paper on Holy Trinity, York, in the York volume of the Archæological Institute. Some notes taken from Dodsworth's MSS. at Oxford, by Thomas Hearne, the antiquary, have also been consulted.

The pedigree of the Luttrells of East Quantockshead, Chilton, and Dunster Castle, is based on authorities already cited in these pages, and on wills at Somerset House under the names of Luttrell and Yorke.

The pedigree of the Luttrells of Dunster Castle is similarly based on authorities already cited in these pages, and on wills and administrations at Somerset House under the names of Luttrell, Edgcumb, Malet, Speke, Stukely, Skory, Trevelyan, Francis, Hele, Pym (1672), Tregonwell, Bancks, Rooke, and Ashe; on wills in the Archdeacon's Court at Taunton under the name of Luttrell, on the Heralds' Visitations, and on the registers of the parishes of Dunster, East Quantockshead, Swanage, Buckland Filleigh, Exminster, and St. Anne, Soho.

The pedigree of the Fownes-Luttrells is based on the registers of the parish of Dunster, on entries in the "Gentleman's Magazine," and on private information.

The pedigree of the Luttrells of Kentsbury and Spaxton is based on wills and administrations at Somerset House under the names of Luttrell, Gough, and Ley, on the Heralds' Visitations, and on the registers of the parishes of Dunster, East Quantockshead, Eastdown, Spaxton, and St. Bride, Fleet Street (1606.)

The pedigree of the Luttrells of Rodhuish is based on wills at Somerset House under the name of Luttrell, on the Heralds' Visitations, and on the registers of the parishes of Charlton Mackarell, Carhampton, and Porlock.

The pedigree of the Luttrells of Hartland Abbey is based on wills and administrations at Somerset House under the names of Luttrell, Cheverell, and Gough, on wills and administrations at Barnstaple under the name of Luttrell, on the Heralds' Visitations for Devon and Cornwall, on inquisitions post mortem, and on the registers of the parishes of East Quantockshead, Hartland, and St. Mary Magdalene, Oxford (1642).

The pedigree of the Luttrells of Saunton Court is based on wills and administrations at Somerset House under the names of Luttrell, Hardy, Codrington (1670), Hungerford (1716 and 1754), Wynne, and Lowe, on inquisitions post mortem, on allegations for marriage-licenses in the Vicar-General's Office, on marriage-licenses in the Faculty Office, and on the registers of the parishes of Braunton, Wraxall, Stogursey, Sydling St. Nicholas (1629), Radipole (1613), Chelsea, St. Giles in the Fields, St. Andrew, Holborn, St. Margaret, Westminster (1647), Clerkenwell, and Waltham St. Lawrence, and of the Savoy Chapel, and Lincoln's Inn Chapel.

In the following tables the surname of Luttrell is generally omitted for the sake of brevity. The dates placed before the names of some of the persons are the dates of their marriages.

In the Dining Room. Dunster Castle.

In the Hall. Dunster Castle.

At the Luttrell Arms Hotel.

COATS OF ARMS.
OF THE LUTTRELL FAMILY.

PEDIGREE OF THE LUTTRELLS OF IRNHAM.

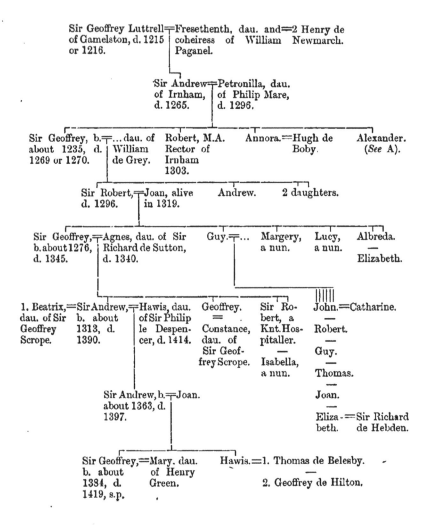

PEDIGREE OF THE LUTTRELLS OF EAST QUANTOCKSHEAD,
CHILTON, AND DUNSTER.

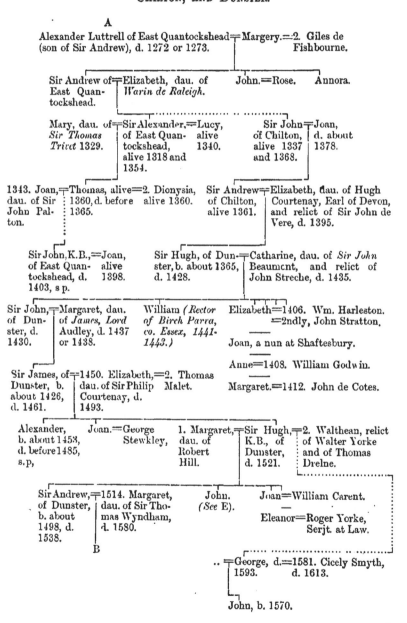

A

Alexander Luttrell of East Quantockshead⊤Margery.=2. Giles de
(son of Sir Andrew), d. 1272 or 1273.   Fishbourne.

Sir Andrew of⊤Elizabeth, dau. of   John.=Rose.   Annora.
East Quan- │ *Warin de Raleigh.*
tockshead.

Mary, dau. of⊤Sir Alexander,=Lucy,   Sir John⊤Joan,
Sir Thomas │ of East Quan- alive   of Chilton, │ d. about
Trivet 1329. │ tockshead,   1340.   alive 1337 │ 1378.
             │ alive 1318 and   and 1368.
             │ 1354.

1343. Joan,⊤Thomas, alive=2. Dionysia,   Sir Andrew⊤Elizabeth, dau. of Hugh
dau. of Sir : 1360, d. before alive 1360. of Chilton, │ Courtenay, Earl of Devon,
John Pal- : 1365.   alive 1361. │ and relict of Sir John de
ton.   │ Vere, d. 1395.

   Sir John, K.B.,=Joan,   Sir Hugh, of Dun-⊤Catharine, dau. of *Sir John*
   of East Quan- alive   ster, b. about 1365, │ Beaumont,   and relict of
   tockshead, d. 1398.   d. 1428.   │ John Streche, d. 1435.
   1403, s p.

Sir John,⊤Margaret, dau.   William (*Rector*   Elizabeth=1406. Wm. Harleston.
of Dun- │ of *James, Lord* *of Birch Parva,*   =2ndly, John Stratton.
ster, d. │ Audley, d. 1437   *co. Essex, 1441-*   ————
1430.   │ or 1438.   *1443.)*   Joan, a nun at Shaftesbury.
                                                  ————
   Sir James, of⊤1450. Elizabeth,=2. Thomas   Anne=1408. William Godwin.
   Dunster, b. │ dau. of Sir Philip Malet.   ————
   about 1426, │ Courtenay, d.   Margaret.=1412. John de Cotes.
   d. 1461.   │ 1493.

Alexander,   Joan.=George   1. Margaret,⊤Sir Hugh,⊤2. Walthean, relict
b. about 1453,   Stewkley, dau. of   │ K.B., of : of Walter Yorke
d. before 1485,   Robert   │ Dunster, : and of Thomas
s. p.   Hill.   │ d. 1521. : Drelne.

   Sir Andrew,⊤1514. Margaret,   John.   Joan=William Carent.
   of Dunster, │ dau. of Sir Tho- (*See* E.)
   b. about   │ mas Wyndham,   Eleanor=Roger Yorke,
   1498, d.   │ d. 1580.   Serjt. at Law.
   1538.
         B

                     .. ⊤George, d.=1581. Cicely Smyth,
                       │ 1593.   d. 1613.

                       John, b. 1570.

PEDIGREE OF THE LUTTRELLS OF DUNSTER CASTLE.

B

Sir John,=Mary, dau. | Margaret. | Honora. | Cecilia, d. | Elizabeth.
of Dun- | of Grif- | = | = | 1566. | =
ster, b. | fith Ryce, | Peter Edg- | 1561. Ed- | = | 1. Sir Richard
about | K.B. She m. | comb, of | wardBar- | Sir Richard | Malet of En-
1519, d. | 2ndly James | Mount Edg- | row. | Rogers of | more, d. 1553.
1551. | Godolphin, | comb. | | Bryanston. | 2. Sir George
| and d. 1588. | | | | Speke, K.B.,
| | | | | of WhiteLack-
| | | | | ington, d.
| | | | | 1584.

Catharine.=Sir Thomas Copley of Gatton.   Thomas,=Margaret, dau.   Nicholas
  —   d. 1571. | and heiress of   of Honi-
Dorothy.=Humphrey White of London.   Christopher   bere.
  —   Hadley. She m.   (See F).
Mary.=Henry Shelley of Mapledurham.   2ndly in 1571   —
                                                      John Strode, and   Andrew.
                                                      3rdly Richard
                                                      Hill.

1580. Joan,=George, of=1622, Silvestra, | John, b.=Ann, | Andrew, b. 1569,
dau. of | Dunster, | dau. of James | 1566, d. | relict of | o. s.p.
Hugh | b. 1560, d. | Capps. She m. | 1620. | Christo- | —
Stewkley, | 1629. | 1630 Sir Ed- | | pherMor- | Ursula, o.s.p.
of Marsh, | | mund Scory, | | gan and | —
d. 1621. | | and 1634 Giles | | sister of | Margaret, o.s.p.
| | Penny. | | Sir Amias | —
| | | | Bamp- | Mary,=Sir Robert
| Sarah.=Alexander   Diana.=1634. | field. | b.   Strode of
| Keynes.   John | | 1567.   Parnham.
| Wogan. | |

Hugh, of | John, b. | John. | George,=Margaret, | Ann.=Thomas
Rodhuish. | 1591. | | Clerk in | alive 1661. | Weston of
(See D) | — | | Orders. | | Callow
  — | Andrew, | | d. 1661, | | Weston,
George, b. | b. & d. | | | | co. Dorset.
1590, d. | 1596. | | John, b. 1637. |
1619. | | | |

Thomas,=1621, Jane, dau. | Margaret,=1607, John Tre- | Susan, b.=1612.John
M.A., of | of Sir Francis | b. 1584.   velyan of Net- | 1594.   Francis of
Dunster | Popham, d. | tlecombe. | Comb
b. 1584, | 1668. | — | Flory.
d. 1644. | | Catherine,=1607, Lewis | —
| | b. 1589.   Pyne of East | Elizabeth,=Thomas
Alexander, | Amy, b. 1630. | Down. | b. 1593.   Arundell.
b. 1622, d. | = | — | —
about 1642. | 1. Thomas Hele. | Elizabeth, b. 1593, d. 1595. | Sarah, b.=1625, Ed-
| 2. George Rey- | | 1600.   mund
| nell, of Kings- | | Bowyer.
| bridge. | | —
a | | | Mary, d. 1609.

a

Elizabeth,=George, of=1652. Hono- | Thomas, | Francis,=1655. Lucy, dau.
dau. of | Dunster, | ra, dau. of | b. & d. | of Dun- | of Thomas Sy-
Nicholas | b. 1625, d. | John Fortes- | 1627. | ster, b. | monds of co.
Prideaux, | 1655. | cue, of Buck- | | 1628, d. | Cambridge, d.
of Soldon, | | land Filleigh. | | 1666. | 1718.
d. 1652.

George, b. | Thomas, | Col. Fran-=1680. Mary, | Col. Alexan-=1702. Doro-
& d. 1650. | of Dun- | cis, of Dun- | dau. and | der, of Dun- | thy, dau. of
— | ster, b. | ster, b. | heiress of | ster, b. 1663, | Edward
George, b. | 1656, d. | 1659, d. | John Tregon- | d. 1711. | Yard, of
& d. 1651. | 1670. | 1690. | well. She m. | | Churston, d.
| | | 1696 Sir Ja- | | 1723.
| | | cob Bancks, | |
| | | and d. 1702. | | Dorothy,
| | | | | b. 1707.

Tregonwell, of Dunster, b. | Alexander,=1724. Mar- | Francis, of=1730. Ann,
1683, d. 1703. | of Dunster, | garet, dau. | Venn b. | dau. and
— | b. 1705, d. | of Sir John | 1709, d. | heiress of
Mary, b. 1681,=Sir George | 1737. | Trevelyan. | 1732. | Charles
d. 1702. | Rooke. | | She m. | | Stucley,
— | | | 2ndly Tho- | | d. 1731.
Frances,=1. 1706. Edward | | mas Dyke, | |
b. 1688. | Harvey. 2. Ed- | | and d. 1764. | |
| ward Ashe. | | | |
— | | | | |
Jane, b. 1684, d. 1688. | | | |

Margaret,=1747 Henry | Ann, b.=1751. Edmund
heiress of | Fownes, of | 1731, d. | Morton Pleydell,
Dunster, | Nethway. | 1820. | of Milborne, St.
b. 1726, | (*See* C). | | Andrew.
d. 1766.

PEDIGREE OF THE FOWNES LUTTRELLS OF DUNSTER CASTLE.

C

1747. Margaret, dau. and ⊤ Henry Fownes, after- = 1771. Frances, dau.
heiress of Alexander Lut- | wards Fownes Lut- of Samuel Bradley
trell of Dunster Castle, | trell, of Dunster and of Dunster, d. 1803.
d. 1766. | Nethway, d. 1780.

Alexander, b. & d. | Henry, R.N. | Col. Thomas, b. 1763, = Catherine, dau. of
1749. | b. 1753. | d. 1811, s.p. ... Cave Browne.
— | d. 1776. |
Ann, b. & d. 1750. | — | Margaret, b. 1747, = 1769. John Henry
— | Ann, b. & | d. 1793. Southcote.
Ann, b. & d. 1751. | d. 1758. |

John, of = 1782. Mary, | Alexander, = 1807. Lucy, | Francis, = 1787. Charlotte,
Dunster, | dau. of | Rector of East | dau. of John | D.C.L., | dau. of Francis
b. 1752, | Francis | Quantockshead | Gatchell, d. | b. 1756. | Drewe of Grange,
d. 1816. | Drewe of | b.1754, d. 1816. | 1844. | | d. 1817.
| Grange. |

Alexander Henry, = 1837. Charlotte | Caroline = 1836. Edward
Vicar of Minehead, | Ann, dau. of Rev. | Lucy, b. Jordan Yeatman,
b. 1808, alive | John Jeremy, | 1811. E.I.C.S.
1881. | alive 1881. |

Alexander John, | Margaret = 1870. John Alexander
b. 1839, d. 1851. | Charlotte. Fownes Luttrell.

John, | Henry, | Henry, B.A. | Thomas, B.A. | Henry, B.A., b. 1789,
M.A., of | b. & d. | of Dunster, | Vicar of Dun- | o.s.p. 1813.
Dunster, | 1789. | b. 1790, | ster, b. 1794, | —
b. 1787, | | d. 1867 s.p. | d. 1871. | Francis, o.s.p. 1796.
d. 1857, | | | | —
s.p. | | | | Francis, o.s.p. 1820.

Mary | Margaret, | Charlotte, | Harriet, | Charlotte. = 1810. Ven. Charles
Ann, | b. 1784, | b. 1786, | b. 1788, | — Abel Moysey, D.D.
b. 1783, | d. 1858. | d. 1791. | d. 1870. | Ann.
d. 1835. | | | | —
| | | | Caroline. = 1823. Henry
| | | | — Fanshawe.
Col. = 1824. | Alexander, = 1824. Jane, | Louisa, d. 1817.
Francis, | Emma | B.C.L., Rector | dau. of | —
of Kilve | Louisa, | of East Quan- | William | Maria, d. 1820.
Court, | dau. of | tockshead, | Leader, | —
b. 1792, | Samuel | b. 1793, | d. 1871. | Mary Frances, d. 1872.
d. 1862. | Drewe, | alive 1881. | | —
| d. 1881. | d | Marcia,

c   *d*

Edward,   Arthur   Florence.＝1851. Richard   Fanny＝1861. John
b. 1831,   John,   Augustus Bethell,   Harriet. Blommart,
d. 1865.   b. 1832,   afterwards Lord   of Willett.
          d. 1847.   Westbury.

Francis,   Reginald,   Henry＝1857. Mary   John＝1870. Margaret
b. 1836.   b. 1839,   Acland, Ann, dau.   Alexander, Charlotte, dau.
＝   d. 1866.   M.A.,   of Joseph   Comman- of the Rev. A.
1880. Anne   b. 1826. Ruscombe   der, R.N., H. Fownes
Helena,   Poole.   b. 1834. Luttrell.
dau. of   Eva.
Stephanus
Maritz.

                    Alexander Collingwood, b. 1870.   Margaret Jane.

Augusta   Charlotte,   John Leader, b. 1871.   Florence Louisa.
Margaret,   b. 1828,
b. 1825,   d. 1842.   Henry Jeremy, b. & d. 1874.
d. 1880.

    Caroline,   Mary＝1861. Henry   George, B.A.＝1852. Anne Elizabeth
    b. 1829,   Anne.   Anstey   of Dunster,   Periam, dau. of Sir
    d. 1856.   Bosanquet.   b. 1828.   Alexander Hood, Bart.

      Alexander, b. 1855.   Edward, b. 1858.   Mary.

    Hugh Courtenay, b. 1857.   Claude Mohun, b. 1867.   Beatrice.

PEDIGREE OF THE LUTTRELLS OF RODHUISH.

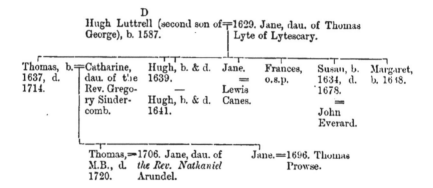

D

Hugh Luttrell (second son of=1629. Jane, dau. of Thomas
George), b. 1587. | Lyte of Lytescary.

Thomas, b.=Catharine,	Hugh, b. & d.	Jane.	Frances,	Susan, b.	Margaret,
1637, d. dau. of the	1639.	=	o.s.p.	1634, d.	b. 1638.
1714. Rev. Grego-	—	Lewis		1678.	
ry Sinder-	Hugh, b. & d.	Canes.		=	
comb.	1641.			John	
				Everard.	

Thomas,=1706. Jane, dau. of   Jane.=1696. Thomas
M.B., d. *the Rev. Nathaniel*   Prowse.
1720. Arundel.

PEDIGREE OF THE LUTTRELLS OF KENTSBURY AND SPAXTON.

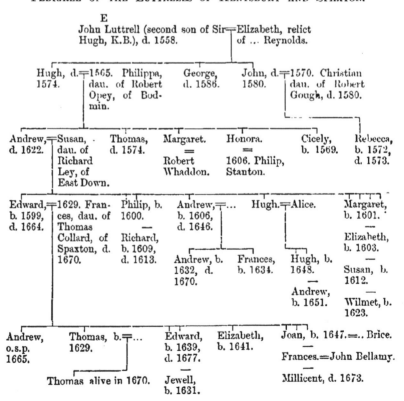

E

John Luttrell (second son of Sir=Elizabeth, relict
Hugh, K.B.), d. 1558. | of ... Reynolds.

Hugh, d.=1565. Philippa,	George,	John, d.=1570. Christian
1574. dau. of Robert	d. 1586.	1580. dau. of Robert
Opey, of Bod-		Gough, d. 1580.
min.		

Andrew,=Susan, .	Thomas,	Margaret.	Honora.	Cicely,	Rebecca,
d. 1622. dau. of	d. 1574.	=	=	b. 1569.	b. 1572,
Richard		Robert	1606. Philip,		d. 1573.
Ley, of		Whaddon.	Stanton.		
East Down.					

Edward,=1629. Fran-	Philip, b.	Andrew,=...	Hugh.=Alice.	Margaret,
b. 1599, ces, dau. of	1600.	b. 1606,		b. 1601.
d. 1664. Thomas	—	d. 1646.		—
Collard, of	Richard,			Elizabeth,
Spaxton, d.	b. 1609,			b. 1603.
1670.	d. 1613.	Andrew, b. Frances,	Hugh, b.	—
		1632, d. b. 1634.	1648.	Susan, b.
		1670.	—	1612.
			Andrew,	—
			b. 1651.	Wilmet, b.
				1623.

Andrew,	Thomas, b.=...	Edward,	Elizabeth,	Joan, b. 1647.=.. Brice.
o.s.p.	1629.	b. 1639,	b. 1641.	
1665.		d. 1677.		Frances.=John Bellamy.
	Thomas alive in 1670. Jewell,			—
	b. 1631.			Millicent, d. 1673.

PEDIGREE OF THE LUTTRELLS OF HARTLAND ABBEY.

F

Nicholas Luttrell of Honibere (son of=Jane, dau. of Christopher Cheverell,
Sir Andrew Luttrell), d. 1592.   of Chantmarel, d. 1627.

Margaret,=1592. Giles   Eleanor.   Elizabeth.   Thomas,
b. 1563.   Dodington.   b. 1562.

Hugh,=Margaret,   Andrew,=Prudence, dau. of William
d. 1612. | d. 1627.   d 1625. | Abbot, of Hartland, d.1639.

Oriana.   Mary.=...Godfrey.   Joan, b. 1584.   Grace,=Robert   Ann,
                                     b. 1590.   Loveys.   b. 1591.

Elizabeth,   Prudence,=1633. Achilles   Ann,   John (see G)
b. 1597.   b. 1601.   Fortescue.   b. 1610.   of Honibere.

Andrew, b.1587.=1609. Mary Punchard.   Charles, b. 1603.   Richard, b. 1604.

William, b.=1631. Rebecca   Nicholas, of Hartland,=1609. Elizabeth, dau. of
1592, d. 1684. | Docton, d. 1671.   b. 1584, d. 1637. | Anthony Monk, of Pow-
                                             dridge, d. 1653.

Prudence, b. 1632.=1680. Hilary Reeve.   Mary, d. 1655.   Eleanor,   Nicholas,
—   —   b. 1617,   d. 1648.
Grace, b. 1633, d. 1666.   Elizabeth, b.   d. 1647.   —
                            1614, d. 1656.   Francis, b.
Elizabeth, b. 1639.=1680. William Gals-   1612, d.1657
           worthy.

Thomas, b. 1616.=1666. Wilmet Docton,   Arthur,   Edward, B.A.,
                  d. 1670.   b. 1618.   b. 1620, d. 1642.

John, b. 1613,=1650. Jane   1636. Mary, dau. of=Anthony, of Hart-=Mary,
d. 1671. | Docton,   the Ven.   Edward | land, d. 1663. | d. 1659.
        d. 1680.   Cotton, d. 1646.

Elizabeth, b. 1651.   Edward,=1663.   William,   Margaret.
—   of Hart- | Mary   d. 1655.   —
Eleanor, b. 1653.   land, d. | Rogers.   —   Elizabeth,
—   1666. | Nicholas.   b. 1643.
Mary, b. & d. 1654.   —   —
—   Anthony,   Mary,
Jane, b.1655, d. 1680.   alive in 1663.   b. 1644.

Nicholas, of Hartland,=Mary, dau. of   Elizabeth,=1698. Thomas
b. 1663, d. 1694. | John Creed.   b. 1664.   Acting.

Mary (heiress of Hartland), o.s.p. 1722.=Paul Orchard.

Andrew, b. & d. 1648.   Christopher,   Arthur,   Jane, b. 1650.—1670. John
—   b. 1654,   b. & d.   —   Mugford.
Thomas, b. 1694.   d. 1655.   1656.   Prudence, b. & d. 1651.
                                              —
                                   Grace, b. 1657.=1678. Peter Caul

PEDIGREE OF THE LUTTRELLS OF SAUNTON COURT.

G

John Luttrell of Honibere╤Frances, dau. of Sir Edward Gorges,
(second son of Andrew and | of Wraxall. She m. 2ndly Sir Edward
Prudence Luttrell), b. 1585, | Southcote, and d. 1651.
d. 1617.

Col. John, of╤1629. Rachel,	Francis,╤1641. Catharine,	Edward, b.═Dorothy, d
Saunton	dau. of Fran-	of Gray's	dau. of Narcissus	1616, d. 1668.	1697.
Court, b.	cis Hardy, d.	Inn,	Mapowder of	—
1610, killed	1653.	b. 1612,	Holsworthy, d.	Dorothy, b.═1631. Jonas
in action		d. 1677.	1686.	1614.	Dennis.
1644.				

Francis,	Francis,	Charles,	Jane, b. 1643, d. 1647.
b. & d.	b. 1655,	b. & d.	
1647.	d. 1656.	1663.	Frances, b. 1648, d. 1657.

Catharine,═1677. George
b. 1653, d.   Lowe.
1684.

—

1682. Sarah,╤Narcissus,╤1725. Mary, dau.
dau. of	of Gray's	of John Bearsley
Daniel Ba-	Inn, b.	of co. Stafford,
ker, d. 1722.	1657, d.	d. 1745.
	1732.	

Dorothy,═1688. Owen
b. 1658   Wynne, LL.D.

Francis, b. 1682,	Narcissus, b. &
d. 1749, s.p.	d. 1727.

Abigail, b. 1661, d. 1669.

1655. Amy═Southcote╤1662. Ann,═1686. Joan,	Arthur,╤...	John,
Pincomb,	of Saunton	dau. of John	dau. of	b. 1638.	d. 1658.
d. 1656.	Court, b.	Codrington	Marcer, relict		—
	1632, d.	of Didmar-	of Wm. Amory,		Rachel.
	1721.	ton, d. 1685.	and of Hugh		—
			Trevelyan.		Frances.

John,	Southcote,	Robert,	Frances,	Ann,	Elizabeth,	Rachael,
b. 1666,	(a lunatic),	b. 1677,	b. 1670,	b. & d.	b. 1680.	b. 1684.
o.s.p.	b. 1672,	d. 1679.	d. 1671.	1679.		
	alive 1742.					

Edward, of Saunton╤Mary, alive
Court, d. 1737. | in 1737.

Captn. Edward,╤Ann, dau. of Sir George	Charlotte,
killed in London	Hungerford, d. 1722.	b. 1695.
1721.	

Southcote Hungerford, alive 1750.╤...

Wilmot,	John.═Hannah, dau. of	Edward.╤...	Elizabeth.
o.s.p.		Wm. Taylor.		

St. John, d.	Hungerford.╤Mary, dau. of	Mary.═Capt. Fleming.
1809, s.p.		Thomas Jervoice.	

Harriet Maria Hungerford.   Matilda Hungerford.

ADDITIONS AND CORRECTIONS.

Page 20, last line.—*For* hundred *read* thousand.

Page 23, line 4.—The inscription is given :—"*Por dieu pries por larme Johane de Borwashs ke feut dame de Mohun.*" *Archæologia Cantiana*, vol. xiii, pp. 532-535.

Page 60, line 12.—*For* transept of the church, *read* churchyard,

Page 64, line 31.—*Add*—Nevertheless he was in 1497 fined £200 for giving shelter or encouragement to the Cornish rebels who marched through Somerset on their way to Blackheath. His neighbour the Abbot of Cleeve escaped with a fine of £20.—"Proceedings of the Somersetshire Archæological and Natural History Society," vol. xxv, p. 71.

Page 84, line 32.—*Add*—She made herself so unpleasant to her second husband that he resolved to take a posthumous revenge on her. In his will dated May 4, 1632, he bequeaths 20s " to Giles Baker my servant who hath lived under the tiranny of my wife to the danger of his life, during the space of two years." He also bequeaths " to Dame Silvestra Skory my wife who I hartely forgive all her wicked attempts against me a Praier book called ' The Practice of Piety,' desiring that she better love and affect the same than hither to she hath done." It was in vain that the widow tried to prove that the testator was of unsound mind. Wills at Somerset House, "Audeley," f. 81.

Page 116, note 4.—*For* Paroulorum *read* Parvulorum.

Page 121, line 20.—*For* currum *read* curruum.

Page 133, line 3.—*Add*—It is worthy of remark that the bend on the shield is cross-barred—an accidental forestalling by two centuries, of the modern system of representing *sable* in heraldry.